Politics, Language, and Thought

The University of Chicago Press
Chicago and London

Politics, Language, and Thought
The Somali Experience

JQ
3585
A38
L34

David D. Laitin

David D. Laitin is assistant professor
in the department of political science,
University of California, San Diego.

The University of Chicago Press, Chicago 60637
The University of Chicago Press, Ltd., London

© 1977 by The University of Chicago.
All rights reserved. Published 1977

Printed in the United States of America
81 80 79 78 77   9 8 7 6 5 4 3 2 1

Library of Congress Cataloging in Publication Data

Laitin, David D
  Politics, language, and thought.

  Bibliography: p.
  Includes index.
  1. Somalia—Languages. 2. Languages—
Political aspects. I. Title.
JQ3585.A38L34   409'.67'73   76-22958
ISBN 0-226-46791-0

*To Delia, who, like Cordelia, loved
"according to her bond, nor more nor less."*

Contents

Acknowledgments   ix
A Note on Transliteration   xi

1   Somalia
The Politics of Language

1. Introduction:
   Political Issues of Language Choice   3
2. The Somali Language and
   the Somali People   20
3. Foreign Influence in Somalia   43
4. Language Politics in Somalia:
   The Politics of Nondecision   84
5. Decision and Political Consequences   115

2   Somali
The Language of Politics

6. Linguistic Relativity:
   A Theoretical Introduction   139
7. Linguistic Relativity:
   An Empirical Formulation   162
8. Linguistic Relativity:
   The Somali Experience   186

Conclusion   221

Notes	225
Selected Bibliography	247
Index	257

Acknowledgments

To do this research, I have received financial aid from the Institute of International Studies at the University of California, Berkeley. And the Institute of African Studies, an adjunct to the University of Nairobi, supported my research by giving me academic affiliation in Kenya. I would especially like to thank Mrs. K. Jerath, administrative assistant at the institute, for providing much-needed counsel.

As for scholarly aid, first and foremost I need to thank a number of highly motivated and intelligent young Somalis who took interest in this study and attempted to help me in all ways they could. Many of them declined recompense, telling me that it was recompense enough that I would be making their language and poetry better known. That kind of enthusiasm provided more encouragement than I could have reasonably expected. I want here to mention Cabdillaahi Maxamuud Jimcaale, Axmad Faarax Cali "Idijaa," Maxamad Yasiin Maxamuud "Cawil," Cabdinaasir Cabdillaahi Xuseen, Billow Xuseen Cabdi, Aardoon Cabdillaahi Diiriye, and Yoonis Maxamad Cabdi.

Much of the work in part 1 of this study builds on the fine scholarly contribution of Xuseen Adam. His thesis "A Nation in Search of a Script," and his kindness in supplying me with important documents, helped me immensely. While Mr. Adam's thesis attempted to solve

Somalia's language problem, my own study focuses more on the social, cultural and political implications of language choice.

Readers of this study, especially part 2, will probably see the influence of Hanna Pitkin on my thinking. Her seminal work *Wittgenstein and Justice* (1972), along with her sage and good-humored advice, led me comfortably through what Wittgenstein might have called the suburbs of political science. Her insistence that I say what I mean, and say no more than I know, made a significant contribution to the clarity of this text. Also noticeable is the influence of professors Percy Tannenbaum, Jyotirindra Das Gupta, and Carol Scotton. Professor Tannenbaum was a fount of usable and useful suggestions, to make the testing go smoothly, and to present the data more clearly, while never losing sight of the general purpose of the study. Professor Das Gupta, who is a pioneer in language politics in the political science community, led me to and guided me through the vast literature in the fields of socio- and psycholinguistics. I met Professor Scotton amid my field research. Although she is a linguist, she was tolerant of my naivety about language. And, having done considerable research herself in sociolinguistics, she helped me avoid a number of pitfalls. Professors I. M. Lewis and B. W. Andrzejewski were both kind enough to read the entire manuscript before it went to press, and both helped in clearing up some inaccuracies.

Ernst Haas and Peter Katzenstein became my audience. Neither of them has any compelling concern for the Somali people; nor does either have any professional competence in sociolinguistics. And I have been unsuccessful at getting either of them to read the later Wittgenstein, either in English or in German. Nonetheless, both of them were sufficiently intrigued by this study to have read and reread this manuscript at various stages, and to offer critical advice. Without their enthusiasm and especially their scepticism, this study would not have been written.

A Note on Transliteration

All Somali names and places are in the new Somali script. In most cases, the reader will be able to correlate the different spellings for the same people and places in the various works available on Somalia. Now that the government recognizes an official script, it is hoped that any confusions will in time be eliminated. Three letters, however, might create problems: c is comparable to the Arabic ع and is the voiced pharyngeal fricative. The former Abdi, Abdulle, and Umar are now Cabdi, Cabdulle, and Cumar; x is comparable to the Arabic ح and is the unvoiced pharyngeal fricative. The former Hassan and Husayn are now Xasan and Xuseen; and q is comparable to the Arabic ق and is the uvular plosive. The former Mogadishu and Isaak are now Muqdisho and Isxaaq. Professor B. W. Andrzejewski provided invaluable assistance in helping me standardize Somali names.

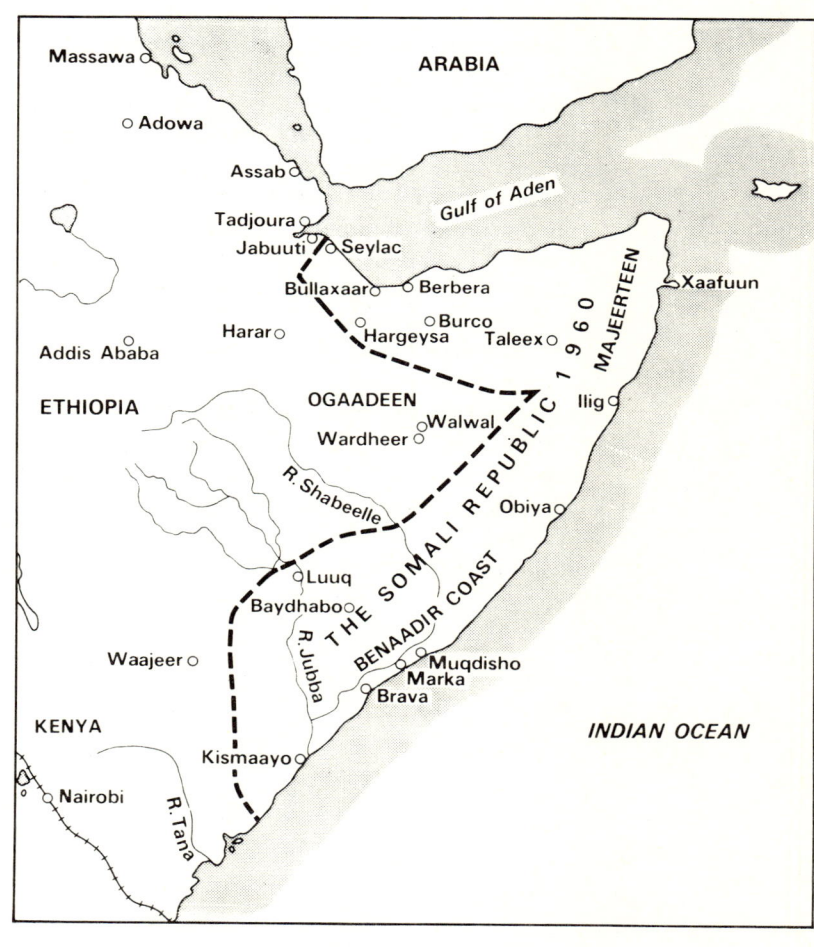

Somalia
The Politics of Language

1

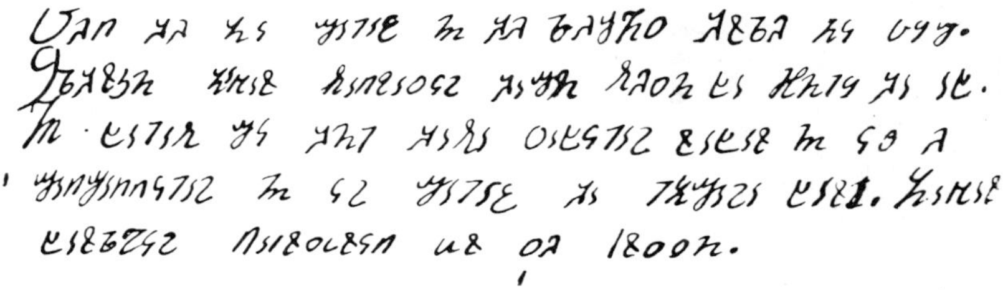

[Cismaaniya script text]

Above: the Cismaaniya script (reproduced from Martino Mario Moreno, *Il Somalo della Somalia*, Rome: Istituto Poligrafico della Stato, 1955, p. 296)

Right: the Arabic script of Sheekh Uways (reproduced from Moreno, p. 365)

Below: the modified Shire Axmad Jamaac script

لَّا الاَهَ الِـهَـكَـلَيْتَوْا مَابَ يَالَوْ
اِلَّا اللَّهُ اِلَّا اَبوكَي وَبْنَ مَابَيْ

اِيمَانْ اَلْوَكَا اِيمَانْ مَلَايِكَا اِيمَانْ كِتَابُكَا
اِيمَانْ رَسُولُكَ اِيمَانْ قِيَامْكَا قُدَرَ لَـهَايَيْ

بُنِي اِسْلامُكَ شَهَادْ اِقْوَارُكَ رَبْ رُمَيْنَيْنْ
فَرْضُ صَلَانُكَ وَاحِبْ لَـهَايَا سَوْ صَلَانَنَيْنْ

Dhaqdhaqaadii Darawiishta ee Sayid Maxamad uu madaxda ka ahaa wuxuu socday muddo ku dhow shan iyo labaatan sannadood.

Wuxuuna dagaalkaasi bilowday 1895 markii Sayid Maxamad ka soo noqday Xajka, wuxuuna joogsaday 1921, markii Sayid Maxamad ku dhintay Imey.

Figure 1   The Three Scripts

1 Introduction

Political Issues of Language Choice

Tocqueville has observed that "the tie of language is perhaps the strongest and the most durable that can unite mankind." And, indeed, patriots have risked life and limb to preserve their language, their orthography, and even their dialect. In many places in Africa, language has even more cultural resonance than in European states, and language is often seen as the most precious national resource. And yet the processes of "nation building" and "modernization" in the new African states very often entail mass education and political administration in a language foreign to most of the citizens of those states. A social situation in which many of the citizens of the state cannot communicate in the official language of the state indeed leads one to ask what the social and political implications of language policy in the new African states are.[1]

Since speaking the language of the state is often the critical condition enabling the citizen to participate in the political arena of that state, language policy should have wide ramifications for the level and degree of political participation. This is often as true for supposedly monolingual states as it would be for multilingual states. For while the multilingual state faces the problem of which indigenous *language* should receive the most support, monolingual states often face the problem of which *dialect* of the shared language should be supported. In Africa, of course, both monolingual and multilingual states face the added problem of whether to choose an indigenous language as the official language of state business, or whether to rely on the language of the former colonial power. Various permutations—an indigenous language as the national language with a European language as the official language, or a set of different regional languages as official languages—are also possible.

Whatever the decision, however, certain citizens and groups will be in a better position to participate in the political arena than others. If in a multilingual state a single indigenous language is chosen as the official language of the state, citizens whose mother tongue is chosen will better be able to procure civil service jobs, and better be able to petition the government when they have demands or grievances. They will be, in a sense, a privileged group in that state. If the language of the former colonial state is chosen as the official language, those groups which had greater contact with the Europeans, or which resisted the colonial presence with the least vigor, will be in a privileged position. In monolingual states, the choice of a European language will again give a privileged position to those who had more social and cultural contact with the Europeans. What I am suggesting is that any decision on the question of national or official language in Africa can have broad resonance for the wider issues of democratic participation and political equality.

Not only might language policy have implications for concerns of democratic participation and political equality, but it might well have consequences, albeit unintended, for political thought and political culture as well. A wide body of literature in socio- and psycholinguistics suggests that language patterns both form and maintain cultural norms.[2] Although very little convincing evidence has yet been brought to bear in support of this notion, the implications for language policy would be great if it were to be confirmed. For if language policy is the attempt to redirect the language acquisition norms of a society, and if language has a bearing on thought patterns, then it might be possible that language change could foster general cultural change. With "political culture" defined as the root beliefs about political arrangements within a political community, one might then be able to demonstrate that to change the language of a political community is to change its political culture.

The case study herein is an attempt to relate questions of language policy to concerns of democratic participation and political equality and to concerns of political thought and political culture as well. The Somali experience is one in which a single nation has been exposed to more than one foreign language. Arabic, Amharic, Swahili, French, Italian, and English have all penetrated the Somali nation, and have all become languages of wider communication. This heterogeneity of foreign linguistic penetration compounded by an inability of the nation to agree upon a script for its language led to a situation where the newly independent state had to rely on three official languages. Any attempt to choose one official language, or a script for the national language, brought unrivaled acrimony. While the level of indigenous linguistic unity of the Somali state is rare in Africa, and while the diversity of the languages of colonial penetration for one nation is equally rare, many of the issues that have emerged from the extended period of language politicking in the Somali nation have considerable resonance both for Africa and for social science.

Democracy

A lively issue in the early literature on political development was whether it was possible for the newly independent states to foster social change through democratic processes. The obvious power of often antidemocratic traditional elites in most of the emerging states impressed outside observers, who wondered whether the power of these elites was consonant with democratic institutions. David Apter, one of the first American scholars to raise the question of democracy in independent Africa, hoped that the democratic institutions introduced by the British into the Gold Coast would remain intact after the Gold Coast became independent. He believed that the "institutional transfer" of democracy from Europe to Africa was a viable strategy:

> So far the British parliamentary model has served as the basis for Gold Coast political development. Therefore a study of its prospects is our major concern. The Gold Coast experiment has important implications for all underdeveloped areas, for it is one test of the processes and prospects of parliamentary government as a means of promoting stability, development, and effective social change. Thus, the Gold Coast is a challenge to political democracy in the West.[3]

Apter was not unmindful of the enormous hurdles which would have to be cleared, but he felt that the people of the Gold Coast had already shown much political ingenuity, and that the British had injected a sense of fair play into the political system, so there was good reason to be sanguine about the prospects for democracy. The hope of these early theorists was that social change could be brought about by democratic institutions; and that this social change would not require a violent or an antidemocratic revolution.[4]

The argument that democratic institutions in the new states could be both representative and authoritative was disputed by another school of theorists. John Kautsky and Barrington Moore, Jr., for example, argued that social change requires a revolutionary movement, and that to create an egalitarian society—which is the social basis for democracy—a revolution would be necessary. Certain traditional elites (Moore concentrated his attention on the land-owning class) would have to be eliminated; and these elites would never voluntarily relinquish their capital. A violent overthrow of these elites was, according to Moore, a necessary precondition for a democratic society. But Moore did not glorify revolution: "The only justification for imposing the costs [of revolution] is that [the poor] would become steadily worse off without it.... It is possible to have the greatest sympathy for those responsible for facing it."[5]

The intellectual debate over the ability of democratic institutions to foster social change soon foundered. A new breed of political analysts, faced by the realities of the first years of independence of the new states, soon began to reject earlier assumptions. While few came around to positions as radical as Moore's, the facts of the one-party state, the no-party state, the military coups, the uncontrolled use of preventive detention, the growth of guerrilla armies, and the high levels of ethnic violence forced many political scientists to rethink the relationship of democracy to political development. A new school soon emerged, one which argued that the question of democracy was not really a relevant one in the third world, and that the important questions involved the furtherance of economic development and the maintenance of political order.[6]

Challenging this new conventional wisdom, or rather despair, over the prospects for democracy in the third world in general and in India in particular, Jyotirindra Das Gupta has argued that the bickering over national, official, and regional languages has had the unintended consequence of fostering pluralist national development and social equality. Reporting in his *Language Conflict and National Development* the deaths caused by the violence and rioting of Indian citizens over the issues of language choice, Das Gupta suggests that in India "the achievements of the national decision-makers in solving the basic national issues have been considerably underestimated."[7] He argues that language politics mobilized people in "organizational modes of participation,"[8] which led to negotiations, bargaining, and compromise. These organizations, founded on the rejection of Congress policy, by their very participation in the decision-making process wound up by lending support to the political system and giving legitimacy to Congress's rule. Arguing their case in Delhi, they were giving their (unintended) consent that it was in Delhi that national decisions should be made. These groups, while "primordial" in origin, became "modern" in their development. The result of their activity was the building of the foundations of institutional pluralism as well as getting the central government to deal moderately well with an issue of public policy. Das Gupta therefore turns the original argument concerning the institutional transfer of democratic institutions on its head. He does not contend that the institutions inherited from the British would, by virtue of their fairness and strength, bring about social change as well as procure popular support; but rather that traditional leaders, by directing their complaints to those democratic institutions with all their vigor, would unwittingly be giving those very institutions their support. And by recognizing the legitimacy of the democratic institutions on language-related issues, they would, Das Gupta implies, be locked into accepting their general legitimacy.[9]

But Das Gupta, like Apter, has concentrated almost completely on democratic forms, giving far less emphasis to democratic substance, that is to say, the social realities which underlie the political institutions. I think it incorrect to take democracy to mean "merely a set of political institutions like universal suffrage, parliamentary government, and decisions by majority procedure," for also important, perhaps more so, are the "set of principles which such institutions tend to realize." These principles involve "impartiality and respect for persons as sources of claims and arguments ... which underlie ... justice, liberty, and equality."[10] So while it may be accepted that the militant disputations concerning language policy in India have enhanced the development of democratic institutions, it is less clear whether they have enhanced, say, social equality or any of the other principles of democratic theory.

A major consideration in my case study is to delineate the relationship of democratic institutions and democratic substance in Somalia. Upon independence, Somalia was graced with a parliamentary system that incorporated institutions from both the British and the Italian democracies. To what extent did these political institutions enhance democratic substance in light of the issues concerning language? In order to answer this question, I have focused on the principle of equality, because, as I have suggested, any political decision in regard to official language inevitably raises questions concerning equality of benefits and equality of participation. I will now discuss two challenges to the principle of equality in light of the problems of language policy: social stratification and regional disparities.

Social Stratification

The Marxist tradition focuses on the notion of economic class, and thereby sees the principal mode of social stratification to be a function of economic structure. Other theories have recognized that societies can also be stratified according to criteria of skin color, religion, and ethnic group. Rarely is society seen to be stratified along lines of language competence. But Pierre Alexandre, a French linguist who has done much research in Africa, has seen the potentiality of the development of an entrenched linguistic elite there: "Herein lies one of the most remarkable sociological aspects of contemporary Africa: that the kind of class structure which seems to be emerging is based on linguistic factors.... This [English- or French-speaking] minority, although socially and ethnically as heterogeneous as the majority, is separated from the latter by that monopoly which gives it its class specificity: the use of a means of universal communication, French or English, whose acquisition represents truly a form of capital accumulation."[11]

The process of European language acquisition has been relatively random in Africa, but certain groups have been systematically excluded from the necessary education. One such group was the African Muslims, who resisted imperialist encroachment by Europe with greater vigor than non-Muslims. This was in part because in most African colonies European education and control were closely associated with Christian evangelism. Consequently, those who had resisted the encroachment of the West most ardently were to find they lacked the language resources needed to curtail the colonial presence. And as the independence movements attained their goals and began to rule, only citizens who could speak the language of the former colonial power could get civil service jobs. The political and social ascendancy of the new linguistic elite was assured.

But self-exclusion is not the only explanation for the differential impact of colonial education. The colonial powers were never prepared to educate a broad base of citizens in a European language. For the British, their colonial language and education policy was set as far back as 1835, when Thomas Macaulay, as president of the Committee of Public Instruction in India, wrote a now famous minute in which he argued that English should play a limited role, only to create a "class of persons, Indians in blood and colour, but English in taste, in opinions, in morals, and in intellect. To that class we may leave it to refine the vernacular dialects of the country, to enrich those dialects with terms of science borrowed from Western nomenclature."[12] This small class, however, in most of the former British Empire, more often sought to maintain itself as a new elite than to help to develop the vernaculars and thereby to maintain the social structure, as it was before British colonial intrusion.[13] That the linguistic elites created by the colonial educational structure soon became entrenched was an especially interesting phenomenon in places in Africa where only those in the lowest status levels would associate with the missions; for they, unbeknownst to the traditional elites, were developing, in Alexandre's metaphor, new capital.

Stratification based on language criteria is more readily apparent in multinational states and empires, where one indigenous language becomes the offical language of the central government. Stalin, for one, was quite explicit on this tendency, and derided Great Russian chauvinism (*smenovekhism*) a number of times. He was quick to see the advantages of administering the Soviet Union as an empire, especially in terms of efficiency of bureaucratic control; but, at least in his earlier writings, he spoke out against its dangers: "From the point of view of the bureaucracy, this is an economical method of ruling, because it is necessary to bother only with one nationality; but from the political point of view it is fatal, for to violate the principle of equality of nations and to grant privileges to any one nationality is to doom one's national policy to certain failure."[14]

In India, when it looked as if Hindi would become the sole official language, some non-Hindi nationalities, which had invested heavily in the English language, were outraged and feared that they would lose their capital. One member of the Commission of Official Languages in 1956 saw the policy as promoting "Hindi imperialism"—a phenomenon parallel to Great Russian chauvinism. And shortly before a fifteen-year deadline for the institution of Hindi as the sole official language of India, riots broke out in non-Hindi-speaking Madras, where the students were educated in English, had a good placement record for the India Administrative Services, and feared their positions would be lost with a Hindiized bureaucracy. Sixty-six people were killed in the demonstrations.[15]

The same tensions concerning language have emerged in nation-states as well, especially when the issue at hand involved the national vernacular competing with an elite language. Those classes in Europe that were able to maintain their bureaucratic monopolies through linguistic skills were severely threatened by the movement to substitute the vernaculars in the civil services. In 1928, the noted French linguist Antoine Meillet, in *Les Langues dans l'Europe nouvelle*, emphasized this point. "The struggle of the languages becomes the struggle for jobs. To impose on the functionaries the knowledge of new common languages based on popular speech is to exclude from their jobs the old bourgeoisie, and substitute for them new men risen from the people."[16] It was in this spirit that in 1930, under a progressive government, Norway required all its civil service employees born after a certain date to be capable of communicating in Landsmaal (country speech). This regulation forced the old elite, literate in Riksmaal (official speech), to learn a language they scorned. But more important, it opened the bureaucracy to a whole new class of people.[17]

In Africa, the new "linguistic elite" is even smaller than are the Great Russians in the Soviet Union, the Hindi speakers in India, or the Riksmaal speakers in Norway. Perhaps Alexandre may have been exaggerating somewhat, but his observation on the size of the new African elite is an arresting one nonetheless: "It is striking to note that independent Africa is presently divided into 'English-speaking Africa' and 'French-speaking Africa.' These two phrases generate particularly dangerous illusions, for I do not believe that the number of Africans able to express themselves effectively in these two languages surpasses ten per cent of the *total* population."[18] The point is that in Africa those who have "benefited" from a colonial education have become an entrenched elite, a social situation that even mass education will not rectify. The meager resources for which educational programs must settle assure that the development of the Western languages will continue to be slow. Social mobility for those groups less exposed to the Western tongue will become increasingly difficult.

Evidence supporting Alexandre's contention that the spread of the colonial languages throughout Africa has been uneven and not reaching all areas is beginning to become available. From a careful analysis of Kampala, Uganda, a capital city where English was believed to have made great inroads, Scotton has found that English is developing at a snail's pace. She foresaw for Kampala "a small and slowly growing elite which values and can speak English, and a large and also growing urban working class which may aspire to English but finds Swahili sufficient for its way of life."[19] Although the leader of Uganda, Idi Amin, has suggested that Swahili be given national stature, the Ugandan bureaucracy has entrenched interests in maintaining English as the official language of the state. The language of the people will remain separate and distinct from that official language.

Scotton's Kampala study also demonstrates the extent to which the status of the "linguistic elite" is maintained and internalized by some urban Africans. Scotton played tapes of four Swahili speakers to a sample of Kampala's population. Her respondents were able to differentiate "good" (Zanzibari dialect) Swahili from "bad" Swahili, and were generally able to place the Swahili speakers geographically. They were generally unwilling, however, even to hazard a guess as to the possible occupation of the speaker. Scotton then performed the same experiment (with a smaller sample of respondents), this time with tapes of Ugandans speaking English. Unlike the situation with the Swahili speakers, the respondents rarely expressed ideas concerning where the speakers were from. But, and this is significant, on questions concerning the speaker's occupation, clear ideas were expressed. The respondents regularly attributed better jobs to those speakers who spoke better English.[20] For Kampala, then, Scotton was able to conclude that linguistic competence in the colonial language was a clear indicator of social status.

That it is jobs which give languages status is amply demonstrated in Kenya today. In Kenya, most political rhetoric favors Swahili, and Swahili has been heralded as the national language. Yet knowledge of English is a prerequisite for most jobs in Kenya's modern sector. Thomas Gorman, a long-time observer of Kenyan education, has commented on the low level of Swahili instruction in the schools. The Swahili teachers, he noted, most often without proper training themselves, complain that since examination in Swahili is not compulsory for a Certificate of Education, most students have no motivation to learn it.[21] And Scotton has noted that, in at least one Kenyan elite school, there has been a "fantastically high failure rate in Kishwahili." That their parents, nearly all members of the Kenyan elite, would permit such unconcern by their children is a good indicator, according to Scotton, of the real status of Swahili in Kenya.[22] In Kenya, as in Uganda, competence in the English language is clearly perceived as the key to both jobs and social status.

The development of entrenched linguistic elites can have vast implications for the maintenance and development of the social basis for democratic society throughout Africa. Democratic theorists usually assume that all citizens are able to participate in governmental affairs, that all citizens have access to relevant information in which to participate in their political society in an informed way, and that all citizens have an equal right to social and political resources. Any structural inequalities, whether of wealth, land, skin color, or of language, can be a challenge to democratic society, because those inequalities consistently give certain groups in the society more social and political resources than other groups. The ramifications of language choice for social stratification and consequently for laying the social foundations for democracy are, then, worthy of consideration.

Regional Disparities

The principle of equality requires not only that social stratification be kept to a minimum, but that regional disparities in wealth, participation, and political influence be minimized as well. Language has a bearing on the issue of regional inequalities because linguistic competence often sets the limits to political participation and, therefore, to access to the government by the citizenry. When there are regions or sections of any state where a significant percentage of the population cannot communicate in the official language of the state, it is likely that those citizens will not only have less influence on matters of state business but will be less often rewarded with the services of the state. These linguistic minorities remain unassimilated and unintegrated into the new putative nationality. While it is true that neither assimilation nor integration is a necessary condition for political participation, it is nonetheless important to point out that inability to speak the language of state business will often inhibit effective political participation.

In his *Nationalism and Social Communication*, Karl Deutsch uses linguistic competence as an indicator of assimilation or cultural similarity. His fundamental concern is to describe the mode in which different segments of a multinational society learn how to communicate, and therefore to become assimilated into a new nationality. Concomitant with the process of assimilation is the process of politicization, or social mobilization. Social mobilization is the process by which citizens, because they have needs or desires which they feel the state can fulfill, begin to participate in political affairs. One of Deutsch's central themes is that, for stability to be maintained, the process of social mobilization cannot outpace the process of assimilation. If it does, according to Deutsch, citizens find themselves needing to communicate before they are capable of communicating. This unbalance, Deutsch suggests, is a primary cause of regional separatist movements.[23]

The official use of, say, English or French, in an African state is clearly one way to slow down the process of assimilation, because it is quite difficult for peoples in outlying areas to develop competence in a European language. Similarly, the official use of the language of one ethnic group in a multilingual African state might keep the rate of assimilation equally low. It may be more difficult for, say, Luos to learn the Kikuyu language than to learn the English language. If one can expect in these cases that the rates of assimilation will be low, one cannot expect the same low rates for social mobilization. The central governments in Africa have been penetrating the outlying areas—

building roads, schools, and hospitals. They have distributed fertilizers and seeds and have made water available to areas suffering from drought. They have also provided jobs to more and more citizens. One should expect many citizens in these outlying areas to attempt to procure their fair share of these resources, whether they are assimilated or not. In other words, in Africa, even if the rate of assimilation is low, the rate of social mobilization has been high. This is precisely the imbalance that Deutsch saw as inimical to stable political development, and it is a situation which ultimately requires that the central government resort to coercive rule. The principle of regional equality also may be challenged in a social situation in which one region acquires the language tools of the state faster than another region and thus more easily acquires and controls the resources of the state.

Closely related to the problem of regional inequalities is the problem of rural-urban inequalities. Wage, income, and standard of living differentials between the rural areas and the urban areas in Africa are substantial. Average wages in the cities are many times the incomes of the people in the rural areas. It is therefore possible that an investment strategy which favors the rural areas enhances equality, and one which favors urban areas exacerbates the already trenchant inequalities. Language policy can be an important factor in facilitating the success of either strategy of allocation.

Rural investment schemes often require effective and continuous communication between the center and the periphery, between the government and the farmers or herdsmen. Rarely have the languages of the former colonial powers pervaded the interiors of African countries; and so administrators who do not speak the language of a particular region face severe limitations in their ability to communicate with the people if their district is in that region. Information can be most easily transmitted to farmers and herdsmen in their own language; and the government, if it wants rural development, should listen to the complaints and advice of its rural citizens. Again, this is most easily done in the indigenous language.

Urban, or industrial, development usually has different requirements. Few African governments have the capital to finance even small industries, and most have had to rely on Western capital and Western technology to bring about urban development. Some African leaders have attempted to court Western business in the hope that it would "settle" in their countries. One positive asset for a country looking for capitalist investment is to have a labor force literate in a European language. This enables managers to communicate effectively with their workers, and facilitates, if it is in the interest of the corporation, the promotion of able indigenous members of the work force to the managerial level. A good strategy for getting Western investment, then, would be to have a European language as the medium of instruction in public education. When that is done, however, that language usually becomes (or remains) the language of the civil service and of elite politics in general.

Language policy, then, can be a crucial ingredient in the formulation and administration of different strategies of resource allocation. Where a government invests a large proportion of its development budget in industrial development designed for an urban society, one may expect a decline in the political importance of the vernaculars. And where a government is committed to investments in the rural areas, one may expect increasing political importance to be given to the indigenous languages. In the latter case, societal equality might be enhanced.

The introduction of European languages in Africa, followed by the creation of new states with a need for a language of wider communication and suitable for administrative needs, led to the general acceptance by most African countries of a European language as the official government language. Those few Africans who had been educated in the European languages had new important skills, new status, and became leaders of a new social structure. Certain regions, in part because of the differential linguistic penetration of Europeans, dominated other regions. The new urban areas, enlarged because of Africa's relations with Europe, began to dominate the rural areas. Whether the newly created elites rule with more or less wisdom than did the traditional African elites is a matter for further investigation, but that they are smaller and more entrenched seems quite possible. For those societies, however, where there had been an egalitarian social structure, with minimal social stratification and with regional equality, the introduction of "linguistic stratification" brought something wholly new. In any event, with language competence seen as political capital, the relationship of language politics to issues of social and regional stratification takes on a new dimension. The major emphasis in the first part of this study is on the issue of language and democratic society.

Political Culture

Sentez-vous cette souffrance
Et ce désespoir à nul autre égal
D'apprivoiser, avec les mots de France
Ce coeur qui m'est venu du Sénégal?[24]

A Haitian poet asked this question. At the Second Congress of Negro

Writers and Artists, Rabemananjara, a Malagasy poet, made the same observation more forcefully:

> Truly our conference is one of language thieves. This crime, at least, we have committed ourselves. We have stolen from our masters this treasure of identity, the vehicle of their thought, the golden key to their soul, the magic *sesame* which opens wide the door of their secrets, the forbidden cave where they have hidden the loot taken from our fathers and for which we must demand a reckoning.[25]

If language is the "golden key" to the "soul" of a people, then to force a change of language on a people is to change its soul, to make it a different people.

Frantz Fanon was another man of letters who recognized the potential importance of language for the perpetuation of the values of the imperial state in the colony. In his *Black Skin, White Masks* he devoted an entire chapter to language issues and claimed: "To speak a language is to take on a world, a culture ... to support the weight of a civilization.... A man who has a language consequently possesses the world expressed and implied by that language."[26] Fanon has been instrumental in focusing people's eyes on the psychological effects of colonial experience. For him, the most debilitating effect of colonialism is a situation where colonized peoples see the world of their colonizers as great and civilized and their own world as primitive and worthless. Could reliance on the languages of the colonial powers help perpetuate this colonial situation even after independence? Even though such reliance is defended for technical reasons or for reasons of inter-national communication within the new states, one of its effects could well be the perpetuation of values consistent with the colonial situation. Use of a particular language can inculcate the thought patterns of the original speakers of that language.

It could be argued that an African state that continues to rely on the language of the former colonial power is not a "nation-state" but really a "client-state." One leader of an emerging "client-state," Jomo Kenyatta, has clearly understood the issues involved. Although Swahili has been called "our national language" and is a dominant force throughout Kenya, most commerce and most political administration are in English. In his first speech to Parliament as president and head of state, Kenyatta concluded his address in Kiswahili, saying:

> Mr. Speaker, I want to say a few words in Swahili because I personally think that the time is not far away when we will be able to speak Kiswahili, which is our own language, in this House....
>
> Now that we have full independence we don't have to be slaves of foreign languages in our affairs, and consequently, brothers, I

wanted to make this point, because everything has to begin somewhere. If I had left this House without uttering a word of Kiswahili, I would have felt somewhat humiliated.[27]

Kenyatta was stressing the point of national pride in having the indigenous language as the language of government, but he also suggested that Kenyans would remain "slaves" of the English-speaking Western world as long as Parliament was conducted in English. Ironically, the recent change to Swahili as the language of Parliament has not liberated the Parliamentarians from the yoke of English, but has rather, because most M.P.'s are unwilling to demonstrate how inadequately they speak Swahili, made for a more acquiescent body—a Parliament of the dumb. Nonetheless there is merit to Kenyatta's suggestion. Continued reliance on the English language in most other domains in Kenya may make the assertion of national autonomy that much more difficult.

Dependency based on language manifests itself most clearly in cultural milieus. V. S. Naipaul, a West Indian novelist who has lived in the United Kingdom most of his adult life, notes that African novelists, to be published, need to amuse, to impress, and to write for the European world.[28] The criteria of successful art throughout most of Africa, Naipaul points out, are set by European tastes, European capital, and European audiences. The reference point for any aspiring artist is therefore external, making emigration a reasonable choice for an artist to reach communion with his audience. In this way, Naipaul contends, Africa will continue to lose much of its intelligentsia. But a return to the vernacular in education, in politics, and in business could also foster a return to the vernacular in art. The audiences for the resulting literature, drama, or song may be smaller (from a world perspective), but African artists would necessarily become less dependent on European values and European publishers. Use of the vernacular in writing can thereby act as a centripetal force on an artistic community, binding the artist to his homeland. A theory of linguistic relativity that suggests that a change in language could entail a change in world view would, if confirmed, support the notion that the acceptance of the language of the colonial states might entail the perpetuation of colonial values.

Students of "political culture" have attempted to understand the various orientations of different national groups in order to find the boundaries of possible political attitudes and actions in different societies. If we were able to determine in one national group the beliefs concerning time, free will, authority or responsibility, perhaps we could better predict, or surely better understand, their more manifest political activity.

An American political scientist, Gabriel Almond, has suggested that this mode of research could be fruitful. He argues that "every political system is embedded in a particular pattern of orientation to political action," and these orientations he proposes to call "political culture."[29] Sidney Verba, who has done considerable research with Almond, has offered this definition of political culture: "The political culture of a society consists of the system of empirical beliefs, expressive symbols, and values which defines the situation in which political action takes place. It provides the subjective orientation to politics."[30] Verba insists on the word "beliefs," distinguishing it from "attitudes" or "opinions" because, he says, he is "interested in patterns of thought more deeply rooted and more general than the latter two terms imply."[31]

Yet in his empirical analysis in the same volume, Verba returns to "attitudes" to analyse the German political culture. He tells us that "in studying German political *attitudes* . . . we shall be studying an interesting part of the history of political analysis as well,"[32] and prepares his reader for the results of a number of "public *opinion*"[33] surveys given in Germany. These surveys were quite intensive and were designed to discover whether, after the fall of Nazism, there had been a "change in the direction of more democratic *attitudes*" in Germany.[34] Verba's conclusions were not sanguine. "When one looks at the attempts to create a political culture more conducive to stable democracy in Germany, one is struck by the difficulty of such an enterprise. The set of *attitudes* to be striven for—the sense of political competence, the willingness to engage in politics, to bargain, to cooperate—are not attitudes that are easily taught."[35]

Verba helped develop a theory of "political culture" which called for the examination of root beliefs. But in practice, he reported attitudes and opinions instead. He is no more guilty than other scholars who have tried to understand a society's political culture. Since attitudes and opinions are very often flexible, and subject to change with changing political circumstances, to attempt to predict the future of a society on the basis of attitudinal data is dangerous. It is here that language and the theory of linguistic relativity may provide an answer. For if language is a key to the perception of the world, if it shapes a people's *Weltanschauung* as linguistic relativists suggest, then a study of language may yield insights into the root beliefs of a culture.

But more than methodology is involved. What I am further suggesting is that language choice in Africa may have an ideological (political cultural) dimension that has heretofore been neglected, or left to the poets. If language policy has in it elements of political-cultural control, decisions on national and official language will take on a greater importance for people interested in the course of events in Africa.

The African Situation

Language politics in Africa has captured few headlines. Rarely has the issue of national language or official language in African states aroused the ire it ignited in India, Pakistan, Canada, Belgium, Ceylon, or even peaceful Norway. Yet the politics of language choice in Africa may not remain submerged. Africa is language-rich, and the new states have needed to weld together diverse nationalities. With a conservative estimate of some 730 languages in Africa,[36] and with an estimated continental population of 280 million, there are surely more languages per capita in Africa than in any other continent. The requirements of "nation building," the process of creating nations to coincide with state boundaries, have necessitated continued reliance on the colonial language. Furthermore, the goal of "modernization" has led to the belief that economic development and administrative efficiency would be enhanced through continued reliance on the languages of the "modern" states.

The newly independent African states' use of European languages for political administration and for education does not mean, however, that the African vernaculars are on the wane. Nor does it mean that acceptance of an indigenous language as the official language is not possible. Already Tanzania, Ethiopia, and Somalia have experimented with the use of indigenous languages as the language of the state. Uganda has recently given added political status to Swahili, and it has been suggested that it may one day supplant English. In western Nigeria, more schools are beginning to give added status to the Yoruba language. And in Senegal, support for the development of the Wolof language goes beyond academic circles.

There are reasons to believe that indigenous languages will gain acceptance for official use. For one, the second generation of African leaders has been far less exposed to education in Europe and America than has the first generation and may well be less committed to the European languages. Second, it is becoming increasingly apparent that African countries, since they have limited economic resources and are less able to procure foreign aid in an era of détente between the United States and the Soviet Union, do not have the resources to effect large-scale social or economic change. Their opportunities for political initiative are very narrow. It is therefore reasonable to project that language issues will be placed on the political agenda, if only because policies changing the official language are relatively easy to implement and could generate support from the countryside. That the Somali

Republic relied on the languages of foreign societies in its early years of independence, and that it eventually accepted Somali as the official language of the state some twelve years after independence, makes it a fruitful case study.

2 The Somali Language and the Somali People

> Our misfortunes do not stem from the unproductiveness of our soil nor from a lack of mineral wealth. These limitations on our material well-being were accepted and compensated for by our forefathers from whom we inherited, among other things, a spiritual and cultural prosperity of inestimable value: the teaching of Islam on the one hand and lyric poetry on the other.
>
> Cabdurashiid Cali Sharma'arke, 1962[1]

The Somali people inhabit a vast arid desert; and economically their republic is one of the poorest in Africa. Yet they have baffled Western armies, resisted Western religion, made a mockery of Western administration, and intrigued Western scholars. A short discussion of Somali ecology is a necessary introduction to Somali language politics. In describing the interrelationship of the Somali language and Somali culture, I hope to make evident why the Somalis have made such lasting impressions on most non-Africans with whom they have come in contact.[2]

Somalis are tall, range in color from reddish brown to black, have aquiline features, and appear to most Westerners to be handsome. Nearly all Somalis are of the Islamic faith, and some of their religious leaders claim descent from 'Aqil Abī Tālib, cousin to the prophet, and of the Quraysh (the Prophet's) lineage. They number anywhere from three to five million, and they dominate what is often called the "Horn" of

Africa, made up of the present Somali Republic, the French Territory of Afars and Issas, the Ethiopian Hawd and Ogaadeen and the Northeastern Province of Kenya.

The basic and most noble Somali calling is camel herding, and the most significant sign of wealth consists in the number of camels a Somali owns. For a Somali nomad, to drink camel's milk is to be truly happy, and many nomads live almost exclusively on camel's milk. Indeed, it is said that the origin of the word "Somali" comes from *soo* (toward self) and *maal* (milk). Over the four seasons, the nomadic groups travel considerably, looking for water and for grazing land. Since good grazing is often many days of walking from the wells, the nomadic communities need to be highly skilled in managing their stock. In less arid areas, Somalis rear goats, sheep, and cows, but these animals carry considerably less status and value. In the south, semi-nomads and agriculturalists plant some sorghum and maize, but nearly all Somalis keep close ties with the nomadic cycle.

The Somalis have found little promise in their land. On the northern, or the Red Sea coast, the plain is scorched and gets little more than four inches of rainfall a year. It is called the *guban* (*gub* means "to burn") and few have settled in this coastal area. South of the *guban* are the *oogo* highlands, which climb up to six thousand feet above sea level. In some areas of the highlands, up to twenty inches of rain fall each year. South of the *oogo* is the *hawd* which is about three thousand feet above sea level; here there are natural water basins and good grazing land. In the south, going west from the Indian Ocean, there is more vegetation. Two permanent rivers, the Jubba and the Shabeelle, flow from the Ethiopian highlands. In the area between the rivers there is some agricultural promise, but the countryside is nonetheless arid semidesert, and rainfall is scarce. Cali Madoobe, once a popular restauranteur and amateur politician in Muqdisho, attained local fame when he suggested on the British Broadcasting Corporation's Somali Service that the moon be ceded to the Somalis so that he could open a restaurant there. After all, he mused, the moon is a place of plenty compared with Somalia.

The prospects for substantial economic development of this region are therefore slim, barring discovering of oil or more extensive finding of what seem to be limited amounts of uranium. The Somalis live today very much as they lived centuries ago. Any discussion of Somali political life should therefore be based on an assumption of only limited possibilities for economic growth. The nature of the poverty throughout the Somali lands does not emerge from general economic statistics, although per capita income is low. William Travis, a British entrepreneur and author who attempted to develop a viable turtle canning business in Somalia in the 1960s, encountered poverty at its most extreme. He found infants abandoned in the Somali bush and brought them to the police inspector in Marka, who eventually had to tell Travis to leave the babies to die. When he asked the commandant how the nomads could abandon their children like that when the Somalis call their children their "drops of blood," he was told, "Yes, they love them and they weep blood within their hearts when they do this thing. But have you not heard of the 'seventh'?" Travis reports:

> The police chief went on to tell me more of the great drought and how it affected the nomads. As the vegetation wilted and died so the herdsmen were forced to drive their cattle further each day. It was no good staying near water holes and wells, it was the grazing that mattered. In times like the "seventh" the beasts must be moved some twenty miles daily, so that they might gather sufficient nourishment to be strong enough to walk perhaps twenty-five miles on the morrow, should the scarcity of vegetation require it. This continual extension of the normal range had to be kept up according to the dictates of the drought. Once the animals were no longer able to cope with these long daily marches then the whole unit of men and stock was doomed, for the nomads would never leave their flocks but would die with them out in the burning *guban*. To deal with these grim migrations the nomads had stripped their way of life down to the hard kernal of necessity. Nothing superfluous did they carry, no unnecessary labour did they indulge in. But the "seventh," for all their care, could prove their undoing unless they pruned still further down into their stark lives. On continual daily treks of thirty miles they could still just survive, but once this limit was exceeded there was something which held them back and endangered the whole unit: the young women, nursing babies of up to two years of age....
>
> A fertile woman was of more value than her baby and their beliefs could not countenance the blood-guilt of child murder. But for all to live the extra load must be shed, and so when the 'seventh' made its terrible demand the two-and-unders were discarded and left behind, whilst the others struggled on across the wasteland, perchance to die as well, perchance to live, but having wrung from their harsh land a brief respite through their bitter sacrifice.[3]

In a desert context of this nature, it is not easy for someone from a temperate climate to understand what economic development might mean. "Do not be like those Americans we see here," a Somali official told Travis, "who rush around here thinking they will solve all our problems with a new tractor and a bottle of Coca Cola."[4] The physical environment of the Somali desert offers little hope for economic prosperity.

Although, as we shall see, Somalis consider themselves a single nation, deeply felt primordial cleavages have divided the Somali people. The primary cleavage in the Somali nationality lies between the two genealogical groups, the Sab and the Samaale. The former are the southern agriculturalists and are considered to be mixtures of Somali with the indigenous Bantu and Galla populations in the interriverine area. The Digil and the Rahanwiin are the two major Sab clan families. The Samaale consist nowadays in four major clan families: the Isxaaq, the Hawiya, Dir, and the Daarood. The Isxaaq and the Dir are situated mainly in the north (former British Somaliland); the Hawiya in the south (former Italian Somalia); and the Daarood span both north and south.

Each clan family is further broken up into agnatic groups which form the bases of each Somali's identity. The Daarood clan family is today broken down into five clans—Marreexaan, Ogaadeen, Warsangeli, Dhulbahante, and Majeerteen, the latter three considered to be natural allies as part of the Harti group. Each of these clans is further broken down into primary lineage and *diya*-paying (from the Arabic *diya*, bloodwit) groups, numbering from a few hundred to a few thousand men. A diya-paying group is a group which is directly responsible for payment of blood compensation for the infractions of any of its members. It provides, as it were, liability insurance. Taking one primary lineage, the Majeerteen, one can detect important but intricate cleavages between the Cismaan Maxamuud, Cumar Maxamuud, and Ismaaciil Samatar, to name just three subgroups of an even wider network of divisions. In discussions of Somali politics, I shall often make reference to some actor's identity in this way: Cumar Maxamuud (Majeerteen, Daarood), reflecting primary lineage or diya-paying group (clan, clan family). Before clans were outlawed, the question most Somalis asked when they encountered a stranger was *Tol ma tahay?* ("What is your agnatic line?") because it was always assumed that his genealogy would greatly influence the ensuing relationship. Figure 2 is a useful reference for the discussions in later chapters concerning Somali politics, but it should not be used as an authoritative reference for anthropologists, as it is highly condensed, and it neither accurately portrays genealogical distance nor does it show the great fluidity and instability of groupings. I feel that I need to pay the cost of this inaccuracy to assure a modicum of coherence to the non-Somalist. I refer the reader who wants a more accurate picture to I. M. Lewis's *Peoples of the Horn of Africa.*[5]

Despite these cleavages, Somalis share a common culture. In terms of language, for instance, an overwhelming majority, at least 95 percent, of the people who inhabit the Horn can understand the Somali language. Dialect differences do inhibit communication, as the lan-

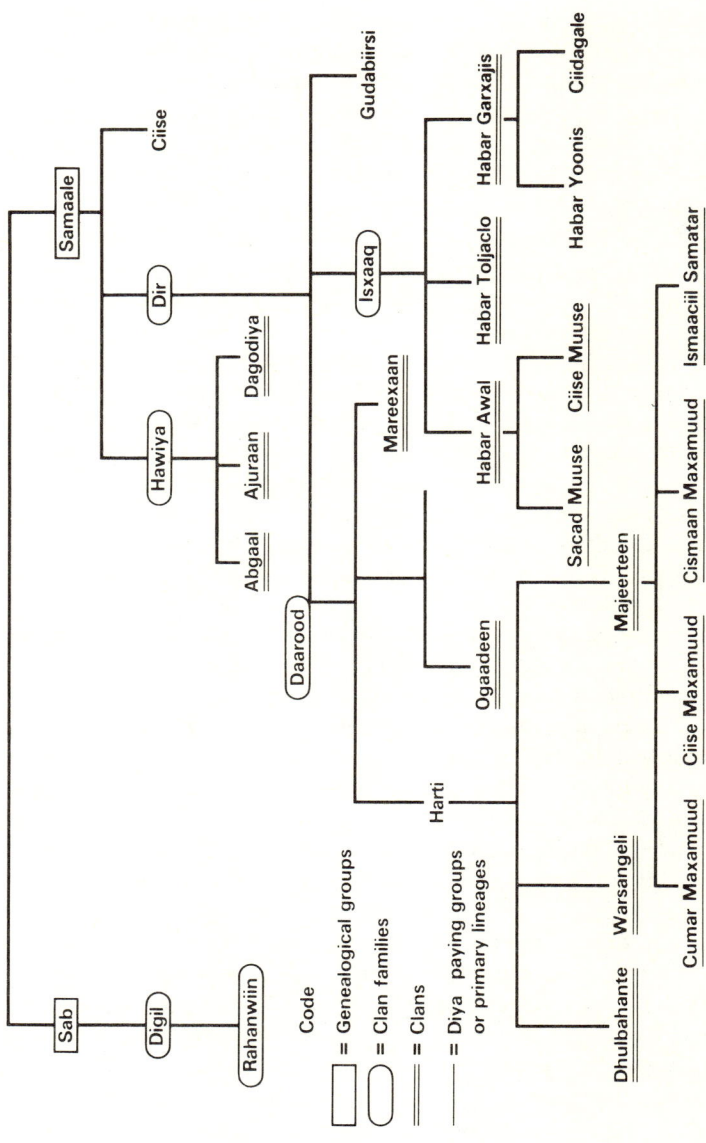

Figure 2 Schematic Outline of Somali Clans

guage in the north is different from the language on the Indian Ocean coast and still different from the language of the Sab clans. Many northern Somalis cannot understand the language of these clans, often referred to as af-Rahanwiin, and it has been considered as different from Northern Somali as Italian is from Latin. In the coastal town of Brava, the people speak a dialect of Swahili, called Ci-Miini, which bears no resemblance to Somali. But the Bravenese men speak af-Rahanwiin to the merchants in the market. Even with these dialectical differences, nearly all Somalis, Samaale and Sab, Bravenese, coastal and inland, can more or less understand the (northern) dialect of Radio Muqdisho.[6]

The Somali language has been classified as part of the Afroasiatic branch of languages and the Eastern Cushitic subbranch. Somali is therefore related to such languages as Saho-Afar (spoken in Eritrea and Southern Massawa and in French Somaliland), Galla (probably the predominant language in Ethiopia), Sidamo (in southwestern Ethiopia), and a number of others.[7] Although there are a large number of Arabic words in the Somali vocabulary, estimated to be about 20 percent, the structural relationship between the two languages is tenuous.

The Somali language, in a country with little economic potential and sorely lacking in material culture, is perhaps their most outstanding cultural achievement. Richard Burton (British explorer, scientist, geographer, artist, and linguist) wrote in the nineteenth century that "the country teems with poets, poetasters, poetitos, poetaccios,"[8] and Andrzejewski and Lewis contend, "It is perhaps not too much to claim that the Somali are a nation of bards."[9] Poetry, song, and proverb in Somalia are rich in metaphor and explosive in content. A classical poem, *gabay*, often has more than one hundred lines, each line having two sections. The stringent rules of alliteration demand that each section have at least one word which begins with the poem's alliterative letter. This poetic rule requires of the poet considerable skill and imagination. As we shall see later, Somali poetry is of great importance in Somali cultural and political life.

Somali political structure, again despite the fragmentation of clans, is, like the language, fairly uniform throughout the Horn. A Somali owes political allegiance to his *reer*, that is to say, his extended family. *Reer* can refer to any level of agnatic membership—clan family, clan, primary lineage, or diya-paying group, depending on the political context. Reer membership, as with all levels of agnatic membership, is fluid, and reers are often in the process of being redefined, split up, or merged. Political units are more clearly defined by explicit contrasts, called *xeer*, and these contracts are worked out inter- and intraclan.

Although many clans are guided by al-Nawawii's Shafi'ite legal text, *Minhāj al-Tālibīn* or by other Shafi'ite authorities, the xeer determines such questions as how much compensation should be paid for homocide, wounding, or insult. Xeer agreements are generally among groups of between 250 and 3,000 men, are capable of incorporating men related by uterine ties and foreign traders, and, like the *reer*, are subject to change.[10]

All male members of the xeer are eligible to participate in the deliberative council, the *shir*. The shir has the right to declare war and to make peace. It arranges for settlement of collective debts, discusses xeer dealings with central authorities, maintains the group wells, and protects grazing areas. Status in the shir is based on wealth, skill in public oratory and poetry, religious knowledge, and bravery, but high status confers no special rights or privileges. As Lewis has pointed out, in the shir "all men are councillors, and all men politicians."[11] Some of the *shir*s do elect a sultan, (*suldaan,* or alternatively *boqor*, or *garaad*), but this role confers almost no additional authority. Men of religion, *wadaad*s, are oftentimes objects of deference in the shir, but neither do they carry special power nor authority. They are sometimes asked to add sanction to agreements already made, and to open war meeting with prayers, but their advice can be overruled by the warriors (*waranle*).

Oftentimes when disputes arise between xeers, informal courts, *guddi*, are created for arbitration purposes. They have no powers to enforce their rulings, but since both parties have agreed to accept arbitration, there is a strong push to accept the ruling. These proceedings generally have large audiences, and the weight of the audience's moral suasion after the decision is made further supports its acceptance. Occasionally a man's entire herd is killed as punishment for not complying with the judgment of the guddi.[12]

Even in the agricultural south, political institutions are fluid, with no clearly defined authority roles. In modern Afgoy, four or five recognized wise men, *akhyaar*, lead town meetings, *googul*, but these meetings are rarely held, and policy for town activity is usually the result of informal, unofficial conversations. The authority of the sultan, too, is based on current performance, and involves no political perquisites. The Geledi people of Afgoy (Rahanwiin clan family) are quite proud of the fact that one of their leading sultans, Yuusuf Maxamuud, although he was able to lead an army of up to 25,000 men, had no private body of followers, owned no land of his own, and exerted "power through rather than over his people."[13]

"What is generally characteristic of the northern Somali political system," according to I. M. Lewis, "is its striking lack of formal political offices. Even the office of clan-head is generally little more than a nominal title corresponding to the degree of social and territorial exclusiveness which the clan more than other orders of grouping possesses.... Within [the diya-paying groups] and at every level of association policy is determined by the majority decisions of all the adult men of the group concerned meeting in *ad hoc* councils. This lack of stable and formally defined political offices thus seems consistent with the extreme fluidity of political groupings."[14] And Virginia Luling, a student and colleague of Lewis's, makes a similar observation from her study of a Sab clan in the south. "The loose form of political organization found here and elsewhere in southern Somalia," she concludes, "though it allows a higher degree of authority to clan elders than in the north, does not generally give permanent power to any fixed hereditary office."[15] The lack of any clearly defined authority roles in political institutions is firmly embedded in Somali conventional wisdom. Two well-known proverbs, *Nin ani yiri dad iska sooc* ("The man who dictates separates himself from others"), and *Suldaanka ba wax baa la sii baraa* ("Even the sultan needs to be taught"), suggest the Somali aversion to people who claim to rule over (rather than through) them.

Somali political history has been guided primarily by the need of growing Somali clans for more water and more grazing land. From the origins of the Somali clans, around the tenth century, there has been a general migration southward in search of more grazing land, which continued until this century when Britain stopped the migrations at the River Tana, in the Kenya colony. This set severe limits on population growth, and led to greater pressures on existent resources. Inter- and intraclan fighting over wells and grazing lands was therefore not uncommon. Never did the idea of a wider Somali identity, based on common language and similar political institutions, serve to limit warfare among and between clans. National consciousness developed gradually.

The first Somali "nationalist," Axmad Gran, led Somali troops in a jihad, or holy war, against the Christian Abyssinians, but it is doubtful whether Axmad Gran the Somali was the same historical Axmad Gran who led the jihad. Nonetheless, the Somalis' Axmad was furthering an Islamic identity and not necessarily a Somali identity, in part because in the fifteenth century the Somalis were only a congeries of warring clans. And from 1899 through 1920, the man most often considered the father of Somali nationalism, Maxamad Cabdille Xasan, fought another jihad, this one against the British and their attempt to bring Christian values to the Horn of Africa. But even the Sayid, as Maxamad Cabdille was often called, considered himself a "Dervish," a fighter for Islamic values, before a Somali. In a number of messages to the British, the Sayid demonstrated his willingness to separate himself from his own secular identity: "An essential condition is that you must not listen to the words of the Somalis for they will not be helpful to you. They only think of eating, and do not consider the future, and they are mischief makers."[16] And elsewhere: "It is quite clear that the Englishman can have heard nothing except from the mouth of the Somali.... Now were it otherwise, that he did not listen to the words of the Somali, but worked from out of his own judgment, then had the result been better." And in his poetry, he has railed against Somali values: "Musuqmaasuq [corruption] is a Somali habit / Each time they come over to you with a fresh color."[17] But in his twenty-one-year jihad against the British, he formed alliances which went well beyond his Ogaadeen, Daarood membership, and wide coalitions of clans formed against him. By railing against the Somalis and their values, and by forcing them to build cross-clan coalitions, he was unwittingly giving substance to an emerging notion of a (secular) Somali identity.

The Sayid's efforts were compounded by the British, the French, the Italians, the Arabs, and the Abyssinians in the early twentieth century. The scramble for Africa and the realities of European hegemony divided up Somali clans arbitrarily, with no consideration for clan boundaries or the fact that nomadic people are not tied to certain places. The very fact that the Somali peoples were divided up arbitrarily also promoted cross-clan unity among the Somalis.[18] Somali nationalism has therefore been growing steadily in the past century. Although it had strong roots in commonalities of language, political institutions, and religion, its political expression arose in part out of foreign contacts.

The Somali Republic emerged independent in 1960 with a fervent nationalist spirit. The five-pointed star of the republic symbolizes the five different regions of the Somali nation. Somalia had been an Italian colony since the early part of the century. It was under British military administration for a decade in the 1940s, returned for a decade of Italian trusteeship in the 1950s, and was granted independence in 1960. British Somaliland was then under British rule, first under the administration of the colony of India, and subsequently as a British protectorate. It received its independence in 1960, a few days before the Italian trust territory, and the two regions merged on 1 July of that year to become the Somali Republic. Central to the aims of the Somali Republic (now called the Somali Democratic Republic) is the eventual incorporation of the other three Somali areas, including the French Territory of Afars and Issas, the Ethiopian Ogaadeen region, and the Northeastern Province of Kenya. The ardent desire to incorporate these lands felt by most politically aware Somalis has enhanced the fervor of Somali nationalism.

The People

Perhaps the most startling aspect of Somali culture for the newcomer is its fundamental egalitarianism. This manifests itself in a number of different ways. When I was teaching at the National Teacher Education Center in 1969, I attended daily meetings of my departmental staff to talk over issues concerning curriculum and individual student and teacher problems. It took me a long time to accept the fact that the school's bus driver and cook could come into our meetings, sit down, and actually participate. To the Somalis this did not seem strange, and I watched once, incredulously, as the bus driver discussed an educational issue. To the Somalis, our meeting was not unlike the shir, where all adult males of the political community (the xeer) are legitimate participants. His participation demonstrated as well the lack of any authority roles in Somali society; in no realm are certain people more legitimate spokesmen than others. This is reflected in the Somali language, where there are few honorific titles and no words for "Mr.," "Mrs.," or "Sir." Everyone from the nomadic child to the president of the Republic is called by his first name, often by a childhood nickname, and a person's name is almost never preceded by a title.

Certain groups, however, are left out of this egalitarian system, for certain caste groups have, in traditional Somali politics, been considered social inferiors. First of all, the *midgaan*s, *yibir*s, and *tumaal*s are Somali half-castes who hunt and do leather work and metal work. These people are generally associated with xeers but have not, until very recently, shared in the political life. Somali myth has it that they are unclean (their ancestors ate forbidden meat), and intermarriage between Somalis in the regular agnatic lines and a migdaan or tumaal has been, in traditional circles, forbidden, In the south, among the Sab clans, there is a noble-*xabash* distinction which is also a caste relationship. Although the xabash are part and parcel of the Sab clan structure, they are clearly distinguishable from the nobles by their dark skin, flat noses, and "hard" hair. There is no intermarriage, only limited social contact, and nobles cannot eat at a xabash house. Amongst the Sab, there are perhaps some elements remaining of slavery as well, which the Italians were compelled to abolish early in this century. Mostly the nobles, but some xabash as well, bought slaves from Arabs on the coastal markets and used them for farm labor. A number of Bantu people are believed to still live in southern Somalia, legally free, but in de facto bondage to certain families. Finally, the Samaale-Sab distinction which I discussed earlier has some caste overtones, as the Samaale genealogical group tends to look down on the agricultural Sab, and in the politics of independent Somalia, the Sab have felt discriminated against.[19]

Egalitarianism does not preclude nobility, either. For the Somalis in the egalitarian system, every man is noble. Baronness Blixen of Denmark, an early twentieth-century resident of the Kenyan highlands, who managed a coffee plantation, gave prominent place on her personal staff to Somalis. While she was friends with the Kikuyus, she spoke of her Somali staff with awe. Under the pen name of Isak Dinesen, she immortalized her Somali friends and compared them favorably with the ancient Icelanders of the Nordic sagas. "In my day," she recollected in the early 1960s, "there were a large number of Somalis in Kenya. They were greatly superior to the native population in intelligence and culture."[20] She felt that she could get along with her Somali staff only because she had been brought up as a European noblewoman, and was therefore considered to be an equal with the Somalis. In Kenya during Blixen's stay, the Isxaaq Somalis petitioned to the British to be classified as Asians, even though it meant paying higher taxes. One historian suggested that this showed their "deep-rooted sense of ... superiority."[21] R. E. Drake-Brockman first met Somalis when he was with an East African escort, and the Baganda in charge told him who they were: "Somalis, Bwana, they no good; each man his own Sultan."[22] Somalis consider themselves all equal at a high level of nobility.

Their almost universal sense of nobility is closely related to their unbounded pride in their Somali-ness. Richard Burton in 1854, while planning an expedition through Somaliland, then considered to be "the most dangerous [country] in Africa," was the first Westerner to remark on this aspect of Somali character. Burton himself was not without pride, and claimed to be taking the *First Footsteps in East Africa*. He was nonetheless quick to note Somali pride when he first organized his Somali staff. He remarked on their "accepting almost any job without feeling a sense of inferiority, perhaps because they believe that they are superior to everyone else."[23]

What was true in Burton's time is true today. Margaret Laurence, a Canadian and the wife of a British engineer sent to Somalia in the 1950s to work on a water basin project, was impressed with Somali self-assurance. Anxious to avoid being a neocolonialist herself, she was concerned that her houseboy, Maxamad, was showing too much deference. But she soon realized, "I need not have worried, for he was not humble in that detestable way, nor was any Somali I ever met."[24] Also in the 60s, Yuusuf Dhuxul, a Somali journalist, participated in training group sessions with Ethiopians and Kenyans and other Somalis, organized by American academics, to see if new solutions could be worked out for the problem of "unredeemed" Somalia. The Kenyans feared that there was American Central Intelligence Agency involvement, and let their fears be known to Yuusuf. Yuusuf nonetheless participated, having reached his separate peace on the issue: "Now, I do not believe that the CIA are above doing that sort of thing, in fact, it is known that they often masquerade in academic gowns.... But I am not bothered in the least, because I really cannot believe that I could be more stupid than the CIA; or is it a case of Somali arrogance again."[25] A similar arrogance manifests itself in the songs played on Radio Muqdisho:

> The best dance is the dance of the eastern clans,
> The best people are ourselves,
> Of this I have always been sure.[26]

Somali pride asserts itself especially in questions of language. A Somali proverb has it that *af Somaaliga wa mergi*, "the Somali language is sinuous," because words can take on new and different shapes all the time, allowing for rich metaphor and poetic allusions. In order to demonstrate Somali pride in their language, I replicated in my field research an experiment first done by Wallace Lambert. Lambert did his work in the bilingual area of Quebec, playing tape recordings of voices to groups of French-English bilinguals. Unbeknownst to the subjects, a single speaker would be recorded twice, once in English and once in French. The subjects were asked to evaluate these voices in terms of general character and intelligence. Lambert found that the subjects, whether originally French or English speakers, consistently rated the same person higher on nearly all the categories when he was reading in English than when he was reading in French. The clear suggestion is that the language of the ruling societal elite gives speakers of that language greater prestige than the language of the "oppressed" gives to its speakers.[27]

One would assume, then, that in Africa, those who can speak the language of the elite—the language of the civil service—are considered more intelligent, ambitious, and dependable (three of Lambert's categories) than those who cannot. Waajeer is in Kenya's Northeastern Province, and the Somali students in Waajeer know that only by learning English can they get jobs in the modern sector. Many are intent on getting those jobs. I had 139 bilingual students in Waajeer listen to four voices, two in English, two in Somali, each reading the same news story.[28] First they heard speaker A read it in Somali, then speaker B in English. After this they heard speaker A read it in English and then speaker B in Somali. The listeners, or "judges" as Lambert called them, were asked to evaluate each of these speakers on a set of nine categories. For each of the judges I compared responses between each of the speakers in each of his guises. I gave a "plus" rating to each speaker for each judge that rated him higher in his Somali guise than in his English guise, and a "minus" rating to each speaker for each judge that rated him higher in his English guise. Each speaker was scored for each of the nine categories. The findings, along with a composite score for each speaker and a composite for both speakers together are presented in table 1.

Table 1	Judgment of Speakers in Somali and in English by Somali Students			
	Speaker A		Speaker B	
Category:	+	-	+	-
Tall	32	34	41	26
Thin	26	46*	27	40
Intelligent	33	29	33	28
Dependable	42*	24	27	43
Kind	38	31	41*	21
Having character	38	31	33	31
Ambitious	46	33	26	36
Religious	47*	27	42	29
Sincere	34	31	36	34
Composite	55	48	49	54
Composite A and B		+ 63		- 51

+   Somali guise rated higher
-    English guise rated higher; no score given if rating was the same
*   Significantly higher score (sign test, $p < .05$) than same person in other guise

The sample, mode of translation, and administration are discussed in chapter 7.

The data suggest that there is no statistical difference in the responses of "naive" judges when the speakers were speaking English and when they were speaking Somali. Although there were a few differences that were significant (sign test; $p < .05$), on no category were the two speakers rated higher, in a statistically significant way, in one language. In the "religious" category, speaker A was rated significantly higher when he was speaking Somali, and speaker B was also rated higher when he spoke Somali, but not significantly so. Simliarly with "kind": speaker B was rated significantly higher when he was speaking Somali, and speaker A was also rated higher in Somali, but again not significantly so. On both "kind" and "religious" the judges were therefore more inclined to favor the Somali speakers.

In the category of "thin" (Somalis who aren't thin are usually held under some suspicion by their peers), however, speaker A was rated better when he was speaking English (a surprise), and speaker B was also rated rated better in English, but that was not significant to the $p < .05$ level. This was the only category in which there was a general preference for the English speakers. For "dependable," speaker A was rated significantly higher when he was speaking Somali; but the ratings were nearly reversed (not to the level of statistical significance) for speaker B. In the composite figures, it is apparent that the differences between the ratings for the Somali guises and the English guises were small, but if anything, the judges were predisposed to rate the Somali speakers higher.

This small study suggests that the language of the colonial society has not taken on the prestige in this Somali environment that it seems to have done in other colonial settings. Obviously, further tests of this sort ought to be done in other language areas of Africa; but given the findings in Canada and elsewhere by Lambert's associates, and what we know about the "colonial situation" in much of Africa, these null findings do suggest an unexpected level of supprt for speakers of the vernacular among bilingual Waajeer Somalis.

The converse of pride in oneself is scorn for others, and Somalis are egregiously xenophobic. Again Richard Burton, an astute if harsh judge of character, was quite explicit on this. "In mind the Somal are peculiar as in body," he noted. "They are a people of most susceptible character, and withal uncommonly hard to please. They dislike the Arabs, fear and abhor the Turks, have a horror of Franks, and despise all other Asiatics."[29] The Sayid Maxamad Cabdille Xasan, harsh enough on his fellow Somalis, exemplified the Somali feeling toward foreigners in a communication to the British Commissioner at Berbera in March, 1917, shortly after Turko-German troops handed Britain some severe setbacks.

> And you know, and I know, what the Turks have done to you and what the Germans have done to you, you of the British government. The suggestion is that I was weak and had to look outside for friends; and if, indeed, this were true and I had to look for assistance, it is only because of the British, and the trouble you have given me. It is you who have joined with all the peoples of the world, with harlots, with wastrels, and with slaves, because you are so weak. But if you were strong you would have stood by yourself as we do,

independent and free. It is a sign of your weakness, this alliance of yours with Somalis, Muqdisho menials and Arabs, and Sudanese, and Kaffirs, and Perverts, and Yemenis, and Nubians, and Indians, and Baluchis, and French and Russians, and Americans and Italians and Serbians, and Portuguese, and Japanese, and Greeks and cannibals and Sikhs and Banyans, and Moors, and Afghans, and Egyptians. They are strong, and it is because of your weakness that you have to solicit as does a prostitute.[30]

Margaret Laurence again confirms a Burton judgment. She tells us that when her husband's project was successfully completed, and he was happily watching the nomads watering their camels at one of the new waterholes, the nomads immediately asked what he was doing at *their* watering hole. They did not want a foreigner interfering with their precious resource. Yet while Laurence had been developing the holes, the Somalis had persistently accused him of being a spy and tricking their people into the use of poisonous water.

Somalis have learned to tolerate foreigners when they are of some use to them. Thus, although Americans would have stones thrown at them in some areas of the republic, and today Russian aid functionaries get taunted as their busses pass by, aid groups get treated with due respect on the official level. But the Somalis want foreigners to know their place. In 1970 President Maxamad Siyaad Barre made this quite clear to the Mennonite missionaries who were providing much needed education to many Somalis. Acknowledging that there were Somalis who had converted to Christianity, Siyaad contended that "if they had associated themselves with expatriate Christians in order to get material gain, the government did not object, but if they took their faith seriously, they would be shot."[31] The Somalis say, *ninkii faralahaa Ferenji baa loo helay.* "The weak man is protected by the European,"[32] and that epitomizes the Somali view of foreigners. When you need them, use them, but intrinsically they have little to offer the Somali.

Somali pride and xenophobia were natural allies in what turned out to be a century of Western colonial resistance. From the European point of view, the Somalis were ungovernable. Colonel James Outram, the British political agent in Aden in the mid-nineteenth century, strongly advocated that the British not try to control the economic or political activity on Africa's Horn. He wrote that the Somali were "of such a wild and inhospitable nature that no stranger could possibly live amongst them."[33] A few years later the British consul of Zanzibar, J. W. C. Kirk, noted the same thing, but evaluated it somewhat differently. "It is wonderful," he wrote, "how little we have yet managed to impress the Somalis ... with respect for our superior power."[34] How prophetic these lines were will become more apparent in chapter 3, where I discuss the level of colonial penetration into the Somali lands. A. M. Brockett has probably summed the matter up best when he said that the Somalis have been self-governing for most of their history except for a brief interlude over the past century, "during which other powers have claimed to rule them."[35]

When some Somalis did begin to copy the ways of the West, they faced enormous counterpressures from their own community. Maxamad Cabdille Xasan, who was not only a great military leader but is also the most revered poet in Somalia's cultural history, composed these lines to point out the path of righteousness:

> He who knows God and follows the Divine law...
> And who does not fight as an askari for the uncircumcised infidel
> And who does not turn up his nose at the origins and ways of the Somali
> And who does not perform menial services for the wages of the unbelievers
> Or accept without complaint their niggardly wage;
> He who devotes himself to the holy war and is garlanded with flowers
> He who turns against the English dogs ... [36]

A well-known Somali folktale (*sheeko*) also makes the point that the Somalis should not abandon their ways because of the foreigner. The tale is about a hyena who is able to convince a young maiden's father to let him marry his daughter. After the marriage ceremony, the hyena moves into the maiden's house but refuses to lie on the bed or sit on the chair or eat human food. Instead he sits on mud and eats raw meat and ash. The maiden runs to her father and cries for help, and so the father asks the hyena either to abandon his wife or his hyena ways. And the hyena answers: "My dear father-in-law, the most disgraceful thing that one can do is to abandon one's own traditions, customs, and doctrines, and in my case, rather than ape the human habits and their ways of life, and thus bring forth disgrace to all the hyena mankind, I give up my bride."[37] And the hyena runs away.

The theme of cultural contamination through foreign influence recurred when the Somali Republic adopted a policy of promoting the English language in Somalia at the expense of Somali. To be ruled by the ways of the foreigner goes against the very grain of the Somali character.

Although in some sense Somali pride is group pride, and traditions are group traditions, Somalis have an unbounded love for individual freedom. When the Baganda policeman declared that, for the Somalis, each man is his own sultan, his insult reflected a point of pride among the Somalis. Burton again saw this as he dissected the Somali character. In his official report to the British government he mentioned that the Somalis "evince a gentleness of disposition and a docility which offer fair hopes to civilization in this region of barbarism. [They are] people who, in my humble opinion, are capable of being raised high in the scale of humanity.... Every free-born man holds himself equal to his ruler, and allows no royalties or prerogatives to abridge his birthright of liberty."[38] And in his journal he emphasized that, among the Somali, "You must abandon your prejudices, and for a time cast off all European prepossessions in favour of Indian politeness, Persian polish, Arab courtesy, or Turkish dignity. 'They are as free as Nature e'er made man'; and he who objects to having his head shaved in public, to seeing his friends combing their locks in his sitting room, to having his property unceremoniously handled, or being addressed familiarly by a perfect stranger, had better avoid Somaliland."[39]

Life in independent Somalia is not wholly different from what it was in Burton's time in regard to the assertion of freedom by individuals. In 1968, eight years after independence, the Ministry of Planning and Coordination was doing a "Multipurpose Survey of Baidoa District," and the Somali officials, trying to get basic information from Somali farmers, themselves encountered typical Somali resistance to any governing authority: "There was a young man at 'Bonka' [they reported] who, shaking his dagger, threatened to cut into two anyone who volunteered information. Such attitude could, however, be expected from a young man trying to assert his individuality, with his hair done the traditional way, a dagger by his waist, a spear in his hand and above all with some water in the 'Var' and the season's harvest in the pit."[40] In the nomadic areas, Somalis have been crossing the borders into Kenya and Ethiopia for twelve years now to avoid taxation. The Somalis seem intent on resisting any centralized government, whether foreign or indigenous.

The love of freedom is also sanctified in Somali folklore. In one story about a gazelle and a sheep, the sheep asks the gazelle why he runs away from man, especially since he is always near starvation. If he did follow man, the sheep argues, the best pasturage would be made available to him. The gazelle responds: "A sheep cannot understand. My family and yours are not alike. We are the children of liberty and of open space. As for me, I prefer to die on my own feet while running away before being gorged with food by a master who would kill me when I became fat or who would kill my children. My heart is not the heart of a sheep."[41] Nor, it should be added, is the Somali's.

Nobility, pride, egalitarianism, xenophobia, and love for individual freedom represent the secular side of the Somali character. But Somali religious values are equally significant and often at odds with secular values. Islam preaches subservience to God and acceptance of one's own fate. It is a religion which makes great personal demands on the individual and urges him to become part of a religious community. While the Islamic faith cannot explain the long and bitter Somali resistance to the British, it may give many Somalis comfort in facing their harsh physical environment.

While Somali folktales preach the values of tradition and freedom, they also preach the value of submission to fate. In one tale, a sultan is said to have heard about a soothsayer with a great reputation. The sultan summons the soothsayer, telling him to predict events for the year, and offering to make him rich if he is correct. The penalty for error will be decapitation. The soothsayer, baffled, wanders through the bush, whereupon he meets a serpent, who gives him good advice but is treated in a dastardly manner by the soothsayer in return. The sultan, overjoyed with the advice, sends the soothsayer on another mission, with the same result. Both times the sultan is able to avoid disaster by following the soothsayer's advice. A third time, however, when the prediction has been for a good year, the soothsayer makes good his promise to the serpent and apologizes for his earlier behavior. The serpent responds: "Every time, you did what the circumstances forced you to. Now finally I shall tell you about myself. I am not a serpent. I am Fate. You will not see me after this day—farewell!" The Somalis have a keen sense of the limits to personal freedom, but these limits derive from God and not from other men.[42]

Language and Society

Good speech is an important political resource in the shir, the traditional legislative council. As linguist B. W. Andrzejewski and long-time shir participant and now trained linguist Muuse X. I. Galaal have put it: "The extensive and conscious cultivation of the art of speaking is one of the most striking features of Somali culture.... Quotations from poems and alliterative proverbs, characterized by their pithiness and condensed imagery, adorn the prose style of sermons and speeches at assemblies, arbitration tribunals and political meetings."[43] Political power in the shir can rarely be garnered or maintained without oratorical or even poetic skill.

And so poets in Somalia have political power in their own society far beyond their colleagues in other cultures. As I noted earlier, the political and religious leader, Sayid Maxamad Cabdille Xasan, spread his messages throughout the Somali lands, to both friends and enemies, through poetry. In his general history of Somaliland Lewis noted that "poetry ... plays a vital part in Somali culture, and the extensive use of radio broadcasting has enhanced rather than diminished its significance. Often a poem is not merely the private voice of the author, but frequently the collective tongue of a clan or other group, and propaganda either for peace or for war is more effectively spread through poetry than by other means."[44] Before the advent of the radio, poetic messages "spread ... so quickly across vast distances that some people in the nomadic interior believe[d] it to be transported by jinns or even by God Himself."[45] Today many nomadic groups have access to a radio, and important messages with rich allegory are sent by Somali poets over the air. In Somalia, not only the poem but the poet as well gains political stature. "Somalis often say that a good poet can sow peace and also hatred," Andrzejewski reports; "he can win friendship by praise and appreciation, deepen an existing feud, or lead to a new one.... It is not unusual for a poet to rise to the rank of a clan leader."[46]

In long poems that do have a political message, it is not uncommon for the poet to sing praises to his own poetic and political prowess. In one poem written by a Dhulbahante poet with the intent of getting the Ogaadeen (both Daarood) peoples to fight off encroachment by the non-Daarood Isxaaq, Cali Dhuux, the poet, attempted to cap his political argument this way: "Have I not put these four (points) one after the other, like the [marked sticks in the] Deleb game? / Have I lost the alliteration in the letter D with which I began? / Have I not set it out clearly? Errors and prevarication spoil a poem!"[47] Salaan Carrabey, the leading Isxaaq poet (who was about ninety when he died in the early 1940s), felt impelled to answer his young Dhulbahante colleague. He told the Dhulbahante people that the Isxaaq had a right to the land, and that the Dhulbahante should not meddle in business concerning the Ogaadeen and the Isxaaq. But he too had to adorn his poetic output with self-praise:

> I find that composing verse is as natural to me as milking:
> No one can vie with me in the coining of new words, which come like dust
> In reciting poetry I excel others by (my) distinctive style and chant....
> Some people think that I have become a senile old man or simpleton
> Have I not made my point with vigour? (Others) let (their) poems stray.
> Have I not laid the keel for it and provided it with a melody?
> Every poem has its aim: have I made it lose its way in any place?

> Have I not put the (right) road these four points,
> which I have taken care to alliterate in the letter
> H?[48]

He does have to concede, however, that young Cali Dhuux has poetic promise, but has an answer to Cali's braggadocio:

> Although he may know the art of alliterating,
> when I appear
> It is very likely that a (simple nomadic pastorialist like Cali) who ventures into bush country will get lost.
> Some things ought to be kept hidden, and covered up with clothes;
> And this topic was not appropriate, but he goes on babbling![49]

The point here is that excellence in poetry enhances a political cause. Salaan makes that point more explicitly in another of his poems, where, when destitute and abandoned by his relatives, he lists his political accomplishments: "In both wisdom and oratory I am fully accomplished; / I am a man whose words judges quote, and excellent in every respect."[50] Poets, because of their unique ability to remold the language, to neologize, to say things in a memorable and convincing way, have attained positions of considerable power in Somali society. In an otherwise classless society, they form something of a meritocratic class.

If poetry is a means for garnering political power in Somali society, it is also the principal means of diplomatic exchange. In an illiterate society, long and complicated diplomatic messages have to be remembered by the messengers, with no crucial ingredients lost. Complex themes are more easily memorized when in alliterative verse, and leaders can be sure that their message is being transmitted accurately if it is enclosed in a memorizable medium. Further, the alliterative poem generally has a long introduction, *arar*. The arar speaks about anything but the issue at hand, which is couched in allegory, or allusive diction, *guudmar*. A poetic message can be deliberately misinterpreted by the receiver, without his appearing to be stupid. Therefore, the person for whom the message was intended is never put in a position where he has to answer yes or no, or where he has to make a quick decision. He is able to go into further allegory, circling around the issue in other ways, to prevent direct confrontation. Because poetry meanders into an issue, it is well suited to extended bargaining without any loss of face, inasmuch as the actual point of disagreement is rarely singled out.

Salaan Carrabey was a master of *guudmar*. Once he tried to intervene as head of a clan between two other clans, both closely related to his own, when the two clans were about to go to war against each other. He composed a beautiful seventy-three-line poem, artfully explaining that war based on pride would bring famine and disaster. "Oh, clansmen, stop the war!" was the way he began his plea. Throughout the poem he spoke about the evils of all wars and the beauties of peace. His "real" message, however, was slipped in between lines 36 and 41:

> And now if you start to devour each other
> I will not stand aloof
> But adding my strength to one side
> I shall join in the attack on the other."[51]

Salaan was making quite clear that if his two relatives (i.e. from related clans) were to fight, he would upset the balance of power, but on whose side he would not say.

In the diplomatic colloquy between Cali Dhuux and Salaan Carrabey which I already cited, the art of diplomacy reached poetic heights. Qumaan Bulxan, a member of the Ogaadeen clan, joined in. Cali urged the Ogaadeen people to ward off the Isxaaq:

> If you are not weaklings, your chance for revenge has come
> I want you to fight, in an issue which should concern you
> Arise, you fools, from the place where you (idly) sit, your lips drooping![52]

The Ogaadeen people felt beaten after years of war and had no intention of fighting. But their pride was hurt by Cali's lines. And so Qumaan felt impelled to answer:

> You always kindle fires by which you are not burnt yourself,
> And setting ablaze a heavy log, you know how to incite people against one another;
> But maybe the encampment, all in smoke (and flames), will burn the homestead in which you yourself dwell.
> If in this matter you are sincere and honest, if no sin can be imputed to you,
> And if your heart is not seeking the flames of Hell,
> Cousin why are you rejoicing in our grief?[53]

The "poetic combat" went on for years, with other poets taking part as time went on. No fresh fighting took place after the beginning of the diplomatic exchanges, lending some truth to the Somali saying that "allegory cools down speech" (*guudmar hadalka wuu qaboojiyaa*).[54] Andrzejewski and Galaal, the chroniclers of the combat, have suggested that, through the use of poetry, clans that were being humiliated by loss of grazing land were able to regain if not their prestige then at least their self-esteem. And thus they felt it unnecessary to fight to regain their honor.

The use of guudmar has another important function in Somali society. Since written communications, until recently, have not been possible, anyone wanting to send secret personal or political messages faced a serious problem. To write messages in Arabic often means that the sender has to pay a wadaad to write it, and the receiver would have to pay another wadaad to read it. That could be prohibitively expensive. An important Somali skill was thereby developed: to hide verbal messages from the messengers. An example of this skill in operation is in a story about a young sufi, or Islamic mystic, Raage Ugaas, who, although he came from a wealthy family, renounced worldly goods and joined an itinerant band living an ascetic existence. Since this group attempted to teach the nomads the joys of restraint, they felt that they could not beg or even complain when they themselves suffered from thirst or hunger. One day Raage met a man who was going to his father's country, and gave him the following message: "I am safe and I am learning things well and I am at such and such a stage in my studies. The members of the college are in good health, we are all right and are learning things well. I shall just say to you that for the evening prayers I use the ablutions which I performed for the early morning prayers." The messenger, who did not understand the intent of the message, duly delivered it to Raage's father. Raage's father, after some thought, did understand. Since one must perform ablutions before each prayer if one passes water, feces or wind since the last prayer, that must mean that Raage is suffering from starvation. So when the messenger was preparing to return to where Raage was, Raage's father gave him the vessel of thirty pieces of dried meat and some ghee, with the following message: "Your father said that today the month has reached its thirtieth day and the water pond is full for us." When Raage received the container and the message, he saw the vessel level was down two handspans and that there were twenty-three pieces of meat, and so he asked the messenger for the remainder. The messenger was startled, but Raage explained to him the thirtieth day referred to the number of pieces of meat and that the full pond referred to the full vessel.[55]

A common error that Westerners make in attempting to understand Somali society is to dichotomize speech and action. For Somalis, speech and action are not dichotomous and are in fact complementary. One important Somali proverb, *Rag waa raggii horey; hadalna waa waxay yireen*, "The real men are the men of old, and speech is what they said," exemplifies this point. Hannah Arendt claims that the notion that speech was one important kind of action was prevalent in ancient Greek thought. She wrote that for the Greeks, "Finding the right words at the right moment, quite apart from the information or communication they may convey, is action," and that this connection is "puzzling to the modern understanding."[56] The poetic exchange between Cali Dhuux, Salaan Carrabey, and Qumaan Bulxan, and the shared message between Raage Ugaas and his father, are, from the Somali point of view, examples of great action.

Not unlike other nations, the Somalis often consider speaking their language a sufficient condition for nationality. The first citizenship law in the northern region defined a Somali as "any person whose mother tongue is the Somali language and who follows Somali customs." And the first citizenship law of the merged republic defined a Somali as any person who "by origin, language or tradition—belongs to the Somali nation."[57] Where the relationship of language and nationality perhaps differs from that of some other nations is that the Somali language is the most powerful symbol of their nationality. One of the poems played on Radio Muqdisho during the height of the Somali political campaign to get control of the Somali-populated areas in Ethiopia and Kenya listed a number of towns in unredeemed Somalia, alliterating on the letter W:

> Wani, Wandid, Walwal, Wel Zuber, Wasow,
> Wirkow, Wabiyarow
> Wadale, Wanta, Wajir Weine, Walkama,
> Walwal and Warder
> All men capable of carrying arms whose call is
> "Waryaa"
> Have made an agreement and are your brothers.
> The clarion is sounding and it is time
> And the alarm signal for everyone is Waajeer.[58]

The symbol of brotherhood, at least in this song, is those people whose call is "waryaa." *Waryaa* is a Somali word used to call a (male) person's attention, and used numerous times throughout the day. Indeed, when the government in Muqdisho attempted to find symbols that would be equally meaningful to all the five points of the Somali star, it was language, more so than any other social institution, that was able to provide those symbols.

3
Foreign Influence in Somalia

> The British, the Ethiopians, and the Italians are squabbling,
> The country is snatched and divided by whosoever is stronger,
> The country is sold piece by piece without our knowledge,
> As for me, all this is the teeth of the last days of the world.
>
> Faarax Nuur[1]

Since 1506, when the Portuguese ransacked the coastal town of Brava with an army of six thousand spearmen, the Somali desert has been the scene of an unusual amount of foreign contact. The Arabs, the French, the British, the Italians, the Ethiopians, and the Kenyans have all, at one time or another, attempted to rule the Somali people. Numerous treaties were made dividing the Somali lands without any consultation with the Somali people. Yet throughout the centuries, the Somali people never submitted to any foreign rulers. They maintained their dignity, their freedom, and their social institutions. While the Somali lands were being "sold piece by piece without our knowledge," the political and cultural implications of those sales did not, for the Somalis, necessarily signal the "last days of the world."

As I have already suggested, the continued stability of Somali social structure during centuries of colonial contact may be attributed in part to its resiliency. Also important was the limited economic potential of the Somali desert, and the concomitant unwillingness of any foreign power to expend resources in conquering the Somalis. But part of the explanation lies in the objectives of the different foreign powers, and the way the powers pursued those objectives. In an attempt to put into focus the colonial impact on Somali society, I have limited myself to three of Somalia's foreign legacies—the Arab, the Italian, and the British. Arabic, Italian, and English were the three competing official languages of the Somali Republic in its initial years of independence.

The nature of the colonial experience in Somalia was such as not to bring about any major social transformation. While at different times the Arabs, the Italians, and the British may have thought they were ruling the Somalis, in fact the Somalis were generally able to ignore or repel attempts of foreign peoples to exert authority. The colonial powers, with only the most limited authority, were unable to establish with the Somalis the kind of master-servant relationship they had achieved in other colonial territories. If there had been major social transformation in Somalia, then language would not have provided such a methodologically convenient measure of change.

To attribute value change to language change is to reassess the nature of the colonial impact on Africa in general. For if language change can induce value change, the most significant implications of the colonial experience may not be manifest for generations. In a sense, the long postindependence period of (European) language acquisition by a substantial percentage of the African populations may have a greater impact on African society than the fact of European rule. Having resisted the effects of colonialism for centuries, the Somalis may, by submitting to English as their de facto official language, have begun traveling the road to colonial submission after they attained political independence. Where conquering armies failed, a conquering foreign language could succeed. Since for many years the debate on national language in Somalia centered on questions of how many people knew each language, and how well, it is important to have not only a general statement of the low level of foreign cultural penetration in the colonial period, but also an appreciation of the differential scope, distribution, and breadth of understanding of each of the foreign languages.

Arab Influence

> *The first to lay the foundations of Egypt's foreign policy toward Africa were the Egyptian Pharaohs. . . . Their aim was to extend Egyptian influence over the Sudan and some regions that are today called Somalia and Ethiopia. They succeeded at times and failed at others.*
>
> From Ghali and Isa,
> *Mabadi al-'ulum al-siyasiya*
> (*Introduction to Political Science*)[2]

Because the Arabs are the (mythical) progenitors of the Somali race, were a part of the nineteenth-century imperialist scramble for Africa, and now form a significant unassimilated minority within modern Somalia, their influence on Somali social structure is complex and hard to determine. Before the nineteenth century, religious, economic, and cultural contacts between Somalia and the Arab world were profound; yet the Somalis maintained their separate identity. Between the mid-nineteenth century and mid-twentieth, modern Egypt twice attempted to create a wider Arab nation, of which the Somalis would be a part. But Egypt lacked the resources to overcome her European rivals in their attempt to exert authority throughout Africa. The forms of Arab religion, culture and language have penetrated deeply into the Somali culture, but their substance has not necessarily done so. Somali cultural, political, linguistic, and perhaps even religious values seem to have maintained their integrity despite the geographical proximity of and the centuries (even millennia) of close contact with the Arab world.

The earliest dealings between Egypt and what is today Somalia were perhaps during the reign of Mentuhotep III (2019-2007 B.C.), when the kingdom of Punt, what is today the Somali Red Sea coast, was raided a number of times. By the time of the Egyptian eighteenth dynasty (1570-1365 B.C.), this relationship had changed. Because Punt was the land of incense, it was considered a holy land or a land of God, and so the men of Punt (who were physically similar to modern Somalis) were depicted by the Egyptians with the inverted beards traditionally worn by Egyptian gods. After a long period of decline, Egypt seems to have restored contact with the Red Sea coast in the fourth century A.D. as she traded for slaves in what is today Ras Xaafuun. Existing records demonstrate that from the fourth through the tenth centuries, Seylac and Muqdisho were entrepôts for trade between Egypt, Arabia and India.[3]

From the seventh century, the era of the Prophet Muhammad, the Middle East was in turmoil, and the Red Sea and Benaadir coasts became havens for refugees of the endless internecine wars. The first arrivals may have been those early followers of Muhammad who were scorned and reviled by their Meccan compatriots. Muhammad had compassion for their plight and advised them to settle in Abyssinia, a land of righteousness. After an initial group of eighty-three pilgrims, Arab immigration to Africa's Horn continued for centuries. In the eighth century, Sunni refugees from the struggle of the Abbasid Caliphate migrated to the Benaadir Coast and are reported to have founded Muqdisho, Marka, and Brava. According to the Chronicle of Kilwa, the supporters of the Prophet's grandson Zaid ibn 'Alī ibn al-Husain (d. 740) established themselves on the South Benaadir coast, and then went inland to escape the rule of the Muqdisho Arabs. Absorbed by the native population, they were the precursors of today's Bajuni peoples in southernmost Somalia.[4] By the early tenth century both Arab and Persian colonizers were well established on the Benaadir coast.[5]

In the thirteenth century, the Benaadir coast became a sultanate ruled by the Fakhr al-Dīn dynasty. Ibn Sa'īd, an Arab explorer, tells us that the inhabitants of Marka—"the capital of the country of the Hawiya which contains more than fifty villages"—were Muslim. In the same period, Ibn Battuta visited Muqdisho, and found a sheekh of Hamitic origin who, while speaking the local dialect (which he called Muqdishii), also knew Arabic.[6]

The period from the late fifteenth to the middle of the seventeenth century was one in which the Portuguese overcame Arab dominance on the Somali coasts, but in certain areas Arab-Islamic rule was maintained. For a short period in the sixteenth century, the Muzaffar Sultans were able to overcome Portuguese dominance on the Benadir coast. And in the late seventeenth century Seif I of Oman briefly occupied Muqdisho. The importance of the Benaadir coast was greatly reduced in these centuries, allowing the Somalis from the interior to exert more and more control over the coastal cities.[7] On the Red Sea coast in this period, the Turks, in a series of wars with the Portuguese, were able to establish Islamic hegemony,[8] but here too, as with the Benaadir coast, there was only coastal control with no organized penetration inland. Up to this time the Somali coast had served merely as a link in the large chain of trade throughout the Middle East, and as a place of refuge for those Arabs who were banished from their home areas. The rather long period of Arab decline was matched by the growth and development of the Somali culture inland.

In the nineteenth century, Egypt emerged as a modern state under Muhammad 'Alī, who brought new life into the decaying Arab empire. But he was never able to contend adequately with the concurrent emergence of European colonial designs, partly because of his own internal problems. In 1840 he was involved in an operation to crush the power of the Wahhabis, a traditionalist Islamic movement in Arabia, and was therefore forced to withdraw from the Gulf of Aden when Britain decided to occupy it. The Egyptians leased the Somali Coast from Turkey in 1866 and maintained de jure control at the pleasure of Britain, since Britain preferred to see Egyptians there than French or Germans. Besides, it saved Britain the trouble of putting down the Somali clan warfare, a job that had to be done if Somaliland was to continue supplying Aden with provisions. Britain therefore signed a treaty with Egypt's Khedive Ismā'īl in September 1877 acknowledging the Khedive's jurisdiction over the Somali coast to Ras Xaafuun, with Berbera and Bullaxaar as free ports.[9] When Egyptian activity challenged British interests more directly, of course, Britain was quite willing to demonstrate Egypt's weakness. An Egyptian attempt to extend Egypt's control to Kismaayo on the Benaadir coast was stifled by the strong British protest.

Despite these limitations to their control, the Egyptians attempted to administer their small and precarious holdings. In Bullaxaar, Berbera, and Tadjoura on the Red Sea coast, the local sheekhs were paid regular salaries, and the Egyptian dream of a united Egypt, Sudan, and Somalia was being articulated.[10] Under the governor Radwan Pasha, the Egyptians levied dock and transit dues, import taxes on goods from the interior, a health tax, light dues, grazing charges, and passport fees. They had to finance their colony this way because the British were unwilling to pay duties on their exports to Aden, and the 1877 treaty exempted the British from duties at the free ports. The Egyptians also felt bound to give aid to their protected peoples. In Berbera, when an ancient fresh-water aqueduct was restored by Egyptian engineers, the Egyptian authorities wrote home of the celebrations and festivities of the Somali people in thankfulness for Egyptian aid. They also gave orders to start building stores, a custom building, a mosque, a hospital, a police station, and a house for the governor.[11] The hospital, which could take fifty patients when it was completed, was reported a great success compared with British medical efforts, for many Somalis would not go to non-Muslim doctors.

The Egyptians also modernized the market at Bullaxaar, standardized weights and measures, appointed a sheekh who led prayers at the mosque, and taught the people "to help them understand their religion." They attempted to build roads as well, and encouraged commerce in goats in their pacified territory. Both in Berbera and Seylac, the Egyptians built quays to improve the ports, and they established regular mail service from Berbera, Seylac, and Aden to Suez. In Seylac they also built schools, housing, a hospital, and offices. They sent a team from the Agricultural Ministry to assess the potential of salt and nitrate deposits as well.[12]

The emerging Egyptian African empire did not last long, however. In 1882 the new khedive, Tawfiqi, who owed his position to Britain's intervention, was forced again to rely on British protection from his own army. Egypt became a virtual British protectorate, with Lord Cromer its virtual ruler. And when the khedive's armies were unsuccessfully facing the Mahdi rebellion in the Sudan, the British arranged for Egyptian evacuation of Somaliland, for fear that either Ethiopia, France, or Italy would fill the developing vacuum.[13] The Egyptian governor, describing this evacuation, wrote of "the sorrow of the people, the fear in them; and they come in groups to say their farewells; and they walked from one to three days to do it."[14] Those getting their salaries from the Egyptians probably did mourn, as did others who preferred the Egyptians to the British. But Radwan Pasha did represent foreign control, and it was not Somalia's chosen leaders that Britain was evacuating. Egypt's imperialist design was abandoned even before an adequate foundation could be built. Egypt in the nineteenth century had neither the internal unity nor the power to overcome the expanding European nation-states in the attempt to establish her hegemony over the Somalis.

It was not until after World War II that modern Egypt reappeared on the world stage, and again looked to the potentialities of African expansion. With Gamal Abdul Nasser's 1952 revolution, Muhammad 'Ali's theme of "unity of the Nile valley" again began to be heard. At the 1955 conference in Bandung, Indonesia, substance was added to that ideology, as Nasser emerged as the new leader of the third world in its attempt to overcome European imperialism. His prestige, already great, was enhanced when he established Egyptian control over the Suez Canal in 1956. In 1957, Nasser made an unsuccessful attempt to form a military alliance with Ethiopia and the Sudan, which was seen as a nucleus for a "Greater State of the Nile Valley," encompassing the Sudan, Somalia, Ethiopia, Egypt, and Uganda.[15]

Nasser was still experimenting, however, and was unsure himself of the nature of this Nile Valley State. Certainly he had a vision of empire:

Surely the people of Africa will continue to look at us—*we* who are the guardians of the Continent's northern gate—*we* who constitute the connecting link between the Continent and the outer-world.

We certainly cannot, under any conditions, relinquish our responsibility to help spread the light of knowledge and civilization up to the very depth of the virgin jungles of the Continent.[16]

But these elements of imperial superiority were tempered by a recognition of the great cultural, religious, geographical, and racial similarities between Egypt and the other Nilotic peoples. At least in conference with fellow Africans, Nasser's followers had been more circumspect. In 1959, for instance, Husain Zalficar Sabri, deputy Egyptian prime minister and Chairman of the Conference of Independent African States, said in Monrovia that "the Egyptian region of the United Arab Republic was freely intermixed with peoples all along the River Nile, up to the innermost heart of Africa.... We have mixed blood in our veins."[17]

The official ideology straddled the fence between national and imperial development. Appeals were made to "restore" Egypt's "ancient boundaries" and to the historical necessity of a nation of Nilotic peoples. Also stated was the necessity of Egyptian hegemony to assure the continuity of African freedom. Finally, elaborate studies were published demonstrating the historic, religious, and linguistic ties of all Nilotic peoples.

The objectives of this policy were manifold. Nasser wanted to establish successful policies in Africa to counterbalance a weakening Egyptian economy and the increasing failure of his Middle Eastern policies. Further, he recognized that overpopulation was one of Egypt's greatest problems, and saw an African empire, as did his European imperial precursors a century earlier, as a way of relieving overpopulation. Official Egyptian publications advocated subsidies for emigrants, and Abdul Ghany Abdallah Khalaf Allah, in his *The Political Future of Africa*, advocated increased technical assistance as a way of inducing Egyptians to emigrate.

In August 1965 it was even argued in the *Rose el-Youssief*, a highly regarded pro-government journal, that Mali and Somalia should be used to grow wheat for the United Arab Republic. Finally, the African empire was seen as the place to sell Egyptian manufactured goods. It was well recognized that Egyptian goods could be produced more cheaply than European, but that the European colonialists controlled the trade routes. Egypt also attempted to block Japanese and Israeli entrance into these markets. As one measure of Egypt's success, the value of its exports to Somalia was 96,000 Egyptian pounds in 1960; and 2,191,000 in 1964.[18] Throughout the preindependence period for Africa, Egypt used its national radio station to further its aims on the continent. Since Egyptian ideology wavered between a United Islam and a United Africa, its messages were often contradictory. Egyptian radio broadcast Somali liberation songs and urged independent Somalia to invade the Hawd, occupied by the Ethiopians.[19] But they broadcast pan-Somali propaganda in Arabic and Somali in regard to Kenya's

Northern Frontier District, while advocating Kenyan sovereignty over the area in their Swahili service.[20]

One of the founders and early presidents of the Somali Youth League, Xaaji Maxamad Xuseen, was awarded a scholarship by the Egyptians. He regularly appeared on Radio Cario in the early independence years to attack Somali President Cabdillaahi Ciise's moderate policies toward Ethiopia, and continued to preach a pan-Islamic policy for Somalia. Propaganda pamphlets were also distributed throughout Somalia, with arguments purporting to demonstrate the affinity between Egypt and Somalia.[21] The Egyptian government sponsored a number of cultural drives in Somalia, relying on public address vans, mobile cinemas, and posters to spread ideas of pan-Islam.[22] But this second attempt by Egypt to establish her hegemony on Africa's Horn was also to fail. As had happened a century earlier, Egyptian preoccupation with the Middle East and her inability to control the Arab world made it impossible for her to expand successfully in Africa. Moreover, the twentieth century is the century of self-determination. The spirit of Bandung was one in which all African peoples were to demand independence, and not one in which they would want to subject themselves to another foreign power, however sympathetic they were to Nasser's visions.

The Arabs have had a long but disjointed relationship with the Somali people. While the Somalis probably came from Arab stock, they do not consider themselves Arabs; though sharing a geographical region, the Somalis have developed a way of life separate from that of the Arabs. Modern Egypt has twice attempted to establish its political hegemony over Africa's Horn but has rarely exerted any political control.

The nature of the perceived genealogical ties between Somali and Arab, at least on the part of the Somalis, reflects the Arab legacy on Africa's Horn. The origin of the Somali people has never been clearly established. Sir Richard Burton states rather unequivocally, but with little evidence, that "the Somali ... are nothing but a slice of the great Galla nation Islamized and Semiticized by repeated immigrations from Arabia."[23] Professor Lewis believes it more likely that the Somalis are a Hamitic group, separate from the Galla, who were subject to considerable Arab influence.[24] The Somali clans have foundation myths which specify noble Arab progenitors. The Darood clan family traces its beginnings to Daarood Jabarti bin Isma'il, son of a well-known Arabian saint, and of the Quraysh, the Prophet's lineage. It is said that he was shipwrecked off of the Somali coast and, upon reaching land, married a Hawiya girl. Their children were the first of a new Somali race, so the myth goes. Daarood's arrival has been placed anywhere from the late seventh century A.D. to the late fourteenth century, and controversy still abounds whether it was he or his father that was shipwrecked, and even as to the identity of his father.

Sheekh Isxaaq bin Axmed, the progenitor of the Isxaaq clan family, is said to have migrated from Hadramaut in Arabia in the twelfth or thirteenth century and to have landed at Maydh on the Somali coast. He is considered one of the founders of Somali Islam. Members of the Isxaaq clan still make the pilgrimage to the Sheekh's shrine at Maydh and sing praise to his noble Quraysh heritage: "Oh pure of soul, oh rightly guided one, oh Lord of the Prophet's descendants, grant me favour."[25]

Despite the fact that numerous Somalis attempt to trace their genealogies to the Prophet, or to his lineage, this aspect of their genealogy has little practical or political importance. In traditional Somali culture it is important for each child to learn his genealogy up to the level of clan family; but after that, no real significance emerges. J. Spencer Trimingham has noted that the Somalis "are extremely proud of being Somali and though they may delight in the fiction that they are descendants of the Prophet or his companions and have constructed elaborate genealogies, they do not consider themselves Arabs."[26] Somalis attach little political significance to their supposed Arab descent and go out of their way to distinguish themselves culturally from Arabs. The pride in the Arab descent coupled with the political irrelevance of the myth sets a pattern in Somali-Arab relations. While the Somalis are happy and even proud to pay deference to their Arab heritage (the form), they are not willing to pay deference to Arabs (the substance).

This point is underscored when one attempts to assess the general level of Somali-Arab cultural assimilation. As observers have gone inland from the coast, for instance, they have seen that the influence of Arabic culture weakens. In her study of Geledi (Afgoy) in the 1960s, only about twenty-five kilometers from the coastal city of Muqdisho, Virginia Luling remarks that the people, though aware of the Arabs, have only limited experience of them. "There were certainly Arabs to be found in the coastal cities, but they did not settle further inland, so they may have been familiar as political or business contacts, but not as neighbors."[27]

Muuse Galaal (Somali poet, historian, sheekh, teacher, UNESCO representative for the Ministry of Education, and presently a member of the Somali Language Commission) has suggested a number of reasons why the level of cultural contact is so low. Arab men eat the head, stomach, hoof, and neck of animals—the parts which are "reserved" for Somali women. Arabs even eat the skin, brains, and lungs, which no Somali (not even a woman) could eat. Arabs also eat fish, which, while not against any Somali custom, is detested by most Somalis. What man, Galaal asks, could risk having an Arab wife in his kitchen? Most Arabs in Somalia, Galaal claims, are Shī'ites, and not Sunnis, and are therefore at religious odds with the Somalis as well. Finally, Galaal notes, where Arabs do miscegenate, it is with peoples they have enslaved. The Somalis, being warlike, and close racially to the Arabs, have never been enslaved by them.[28] So although the Arab peninsula was the foundation of the religion of the Somali people, the degree of Arab cultural influence has been rather small.

And not only has assimilation been rare, but "in many ways Somalis despise Arabs."[29] The Arabs who came to Somalia were often merchants, and most Somalis disdain trading and feel that the Arabs were neither noble nor honest. Arab proprietors keep to themselves, an expatriate community, rarely learning the Somali language. They have often been accused of exploiting the Somali nomads by charging outrageous rates. "To be a trader's agent and a flunkey is business fit for Arabs,"[30] says a Somali poet. When war broke out in the Northern Frontier District in Kenya, Somali nationalists delighted in the opportunity to loot Arab shops. Not that the feelings aren't mutual. The Arab expatriate community fears and mistrusts the Somalis. Sir Richard Burton found this to be a prevalent attitude in the nineteenth century; he quotes an Arab maxim: "Show not the Somali thy door; and if he find it, block it up!"[31] Despite millennia of trade and close contact, then, there has been very little cultural assimilation of either Somalis into an Arab culture or of Arabs in the Somali culture.

Politically and administratively too, as we have seen, the extent of Arab penetration has been small. While Arab sultanates exacted tribute on the Benaadir coast for centuries, no attempt was made to control the lives of the Somalis outside of the coastal towns. The only goal of the sultans was facilitation of trade, which did not require political rule. A genuinely close relationship between the Sudan and Somalia, based on Islamic ties, has been cultivated since independence, and Somalia did join the Arab league in 1973. These contacts, however, have been of marginal significance in Somali politics.

Economically the Arab world has been far more successful. A healthy trade between the Arab world and the Horn of Africa has existed, off and on, for over three thousand years. Even today, nearly all of Somali exports in animals and their products go to Arabia, Aden, and the UAR. In 1965 this volume earned 103 million Somali shillings representing 41 percent of the total export income for that year.[32] In 1961 Somalia received a loan of four million pounds sterling from Egypt for establishing several industries, such as cement, textiles, meat processing, sugar, and building; and in 1962 a loan of five million Egyptian pounds for industrial cooperation and cultural agreements. Various technical assistance teams were sent to Somalia to evaluate development schemes. But the relationship was still based on trade and not on economic transformation. The trade in livestock enables Somali nomads to buy cloth, tea, sugar, and other provisions, but does not change their way of life.

Religion seems to be a better example of Arabic influence. Yet it is extremely difficult to assess just what behavior constitutes changed life patterns or world view due to Islamic conversion. The nature of the real Islamic message is itself ambiguous. A well-known passage from the jurisconsult Ahmad Ibn Hanibal suggests that deep understanding of the Qur'anic message is not essential for Muslims: "I saw the Almighty in a dream and asked, 'O Lord, what is the best way to manage to be near you.' He replied, 'My Word, oh Ahmad.' I inquired, 'With or without understanding?' He said, 'With or without understanding.'"[33] In the Islamic tradition, once the basic rituals are observed, not much else is required of the believer.

The Somalis do pay unusual deference to the Islamic religion. The Arabic word *hijrah* entails the notion of both migration and conversion, manifested by the early Arab migrants to the Somali shores, who brought with them the Islamic religion. The Somalis are all Sunnis, the orthodox Muslim sect, and follow the Shafi'ite school of law, a school that relies largely on oral transmission of the tradition and tends to reject the *'Ijma*, the scholarly writing of Eastern Islamic jurists. Many Somalis are devout in upholding the five pillars of Islam, and statements attesting to Islamic identity are almost ritual in modern Somalia. Maxamad Abshir, former commander of the Somali police force, in a public discussion, demonstrated this pervasive feeling. "How can you differentiate between the Muslim identity and the Somali identity?" he asked. "To me, being Somali and being Islamic are one and the same thing. The terms 'Somali' and 'Islam' are synonymous in my mind."[34] The two most revered Somali nationalist figures were devout Muslims, and both defined themselves as Muslims first and Somalis second. Axmad Gran, not a Somali himself but the leader of Somali troops, was in virtual holy war against the Abyssinians in the fifteenth century; and Maxamad Cabdille Xasan, a committed mystic of the Saalixiya order, was clearly more disturbed about the religious than about the political consequences of British imperialism in his twenty-one-year battle to rid the Somali lands of the British and other heathen.

But in her study of the Geledi people, Luling found that only the most devout, few in number, said their daily prayers with regularity. She found that most boys did attend the Qur'anic schools, the *dugsi*, but most completed the course without going through the whole Qur'an. Luling noticed further that what is learned in these schools is the shape and sound of the sacred words, not their meaning. The Qur'an is "a supremely sacred object.... It is supremely holy because of its divine origin ... but once the element of meaning is removed, it is equally so whether read, heard, sprinkled or swallowed." Even the sheekhs can only "intone a few passages or write out amulets."[35]

Furthermore, the Somalis retain many pre-Islamic practices and beliefs, going back to devotion to *waq*, the sky god. Not only is the *is tun* (annual stick fight) still practiced—I watched boys in Qur'anic school chanting the songs for this event—but in many Somali areas the *roobdoon* or rain-making ritual, and the *dubshid* or fire-kindling ritual, can still be observed. Noting these rituals, Trimingham argues that "the true Somali has tended to accept the exterior forms of Islam whilst remaining comparatively unchanged in his inner life. Islam satisfied him most because it does not attempt to revolutionize his inner life."[36] That Islam is a universal religion with a clear impact on all peoples who have accepted it is surely a myth. To a large extent the Somalis have taken the forms of the religion and molded it to suit their purposes and institutions.

Educationally the Arab world has had some impact on Somalia. Although the schools built in Berbera and Seylac in the mid-nineteenth century were short-lived, the twentieth century saw more effective penetration. A modern school system, which until 1971 was under the Arabic medium of instruction and was taught by Egyptian instructors was perhaps the best in Somalia, for both technical courses and the humanities. From the *dugsi*, students went to an Arabic intermediate and secondary school where they developed a firm grasp of the language of instruction. Scholarships for excellent secondary school graduates were available for study in Cairo, and in 1960, 160 of the 1,000 Egyptian scholarships earmarked for Africans went to Somalis.[37]

According to the Somali Ministry of Education's annual report of 1967 (the last year they supplied such data) sixty-seven expatriate teachers from the UAR were working in Somalia, a greater number than in any other country. In the Southern Region that year (no data available for the north), there were 124 adult education classes in the Arabic language, elementary level, with an enrollment of 4,276 students. On the intermediate level, there were ten classes with an enrollment of 344.[38]

The UAR, unlike Britian and Italy, offered no scholarships for higher education for Somalis in 1966-67 (they emphasized scholarships for study and vocational training in agriculture, university teaching, and Islamic studies, but this aid was not reported by the Somali Ministry of Education).[39] Saudi Arabia, however, offered ten, and the Sudan eight. Both of these offerings chose from the Arabic-trained students.[40] In the 1968 Ministry of Education report, the UAR is recorded as offering two scholarships, Saudi Arabia seventeen, Algeria and Jordan two each, and the Lebanon three. Students from the Arabic secondary school competed for these scholarships.[41] Donald Scott, an American aid functionary, reports that in 1959 there were nine Arabic schools in the Southern Region, with 1,500 Somali students.[42] These figures are low in view of the size of Somalia, but significant in view of the relatively high academic standards upheld in Arab-aided schools.

The ambivalent relationship between the Arab world and Somalis is brought into bold relief when we look at the role of the Arabic language in Somali culture. Scholars have had considerable difficulty in assessing the diffusion of Arabic in Somalia, as have had the numerous language commissions. Professor I. M. Lewis, for example, in his *Modern History of Somaliland*, claims that in Somalia "Arabic itself is sufficiently widely known to be regarded as a second language."[43] And Lewis again, this time with Andrzejewski, reports that the educated elite are "fully literate in Arabic," and they cite many hymns and poems in Arabic composed by bilingual Somali artists.[44] Elsewhere, however, Lewis notes that there is little work in history, Qur'anic commentary, and grammar among the Somalis; and that in Arabic, only hagiologies are prevalent. "This apparent dearth of any strong corpus of locally written literature," he concludes, "reflects the fact that only a small proportion of religious men are in fact fully literate in Arabic."[45]

The contradiction cannot be resolved by looking at the educational data. In the Northern Region, where there is some data on the *dugsis* (because the British government attempted to subsidize them) there were 1,200 students enrolled in aided schools in 1951, 2,750 in 1957, and 2,930 in 1961. The UNESCO Educational Planning Report, which cited these figures, implies that nearly as many were enrolled in nonsubsidized Qur'anic schools. According to the 1969 Ministry of Education annual report, 23,748 students were enrolled in the four grades of elementary school throughout the republic, and in those four years Arabic was stipulated as the language of education. But to assume, because education in the Qur'an is widespread or because elementary education in Somalia was in Arabic, that there is general knowledge of Arabic is unwarranted. Most observers have noted that there is little to no comprehension of the Qur'an in the *dugsis*, and even the Ministry of Education has castigated many of its elementary teachers for having "no command of the language of instruction in elementary schools."[46]

Other data are equally unconvincing. The 1971 Ministry of Education annual report gives results of the General Certificate of Education (GCE) examinations administered in Great Britain to secondary school students. One hundred seventy-eight Somali students sat for the classical Arabic examination that year, and 106 students passed, making for a 59.9 percent pass ratio. One hundred eighty-eight students sat for the compulsory English language exam with only eighteen passes, or 9.5 percent. But here too the figures are misleading, since these examinations, from Cambridge, were written for native speakers of English who never saw a word of Arabic until they reached the upper grades of school. For Somali students, the English language examination was unjustly difficult and the Arabic examination relatively easy.[47]

The Arabic language—through the spread of Islam, extensive trade with the Arab world, and the Arabic educational system—has indeed permeated modern Somalia. The history of Arabic spoken on the Benaadir coast by non-Arabs goes back, as we have seen, to the thirteenth century. Nearly all Somalis know some Arabic, and a few know it well; but since Somali has remained a dynamic means of communication itself, Arabic, despite Egyptian efforts, has remained a foreign language to nearly all Somalis. Though all Somalis pray in Arabic, though most greet their friends and clansmen in Arabic some of the time, and though more Arabic words have been adopted into Somali than words from any non-Cushitic language, rarely if ever do Somalis converse in Arabic among themselves. The Somali relationship with the Arabic language is typical of all Somali dealings with Arab institutions.

Because Somalis share with the Arab world common ancestors, common physical features, a common geographical region, a common nomadic heritage, and a common religion, all developed and built up over millennia of close contact, it might be concluded that Arab influence in Somalia has been toward the development of a "nation" rather then an "empire." Yet this is not the case. The Somalis were able to maintain their cultural uniqueness, their institutions, and their national identity and, in fact, to play a mediating role between Arabs and Black Africa in the postindependence era. It is most clearly language which has separated the Somalis from the Arab world. Despite the prevalence of the Arabic language throughout Somalia, the Somali language remains vital and has been able to preserve the separateness and integrity of the Somali culture.

Italian Influence

> *Africa is only the whetstone on which we Italians shall sharpen our sword for a supreme conquest in the unknown future.*
>
> Gabriele d'Annunzio,
> Italian poet and politician, 1911.[48]

The history of Italian colonialism in Africa is filled with irony. Italians never became imperial Prosperos, nor were Italy's subjects colonial Calabans. The history of Italy's African empire was not one of the forcible imposition of Western values and institutions on docile or defiant subjects; but rather of a confused and nondirected stance toward an unneeded desert and a rebellious desert people. It is not surprising that the legacy of more than a half a century of Italian rule in Somalia is hardly greater than the Somali addiction to *pasta* and Italian "westerns" and the development of a small corps of Somalis literate in Italian.

In the middle of the nineteenth century, with Britain and France making territorial inroads in Africa, Italy, having just completed her *risorgimento*, felt that she too should enjoy the symbolic perquisites of a modern European state, however undesirable from an economic point of view, especially so because some members of the ruling elite sensed that Italy had low status in Europe. Italy therefore entered in the politics of European expansion with little preparation or foresight. The story of Italy's first African acquisition demonstrated this well. With the opening of the Suez canal, other European states were securing coaling stations on the Red Sea. Although in 1870 Italy would have only 1.3 percent of the tonnage going through the canal, and in 1913 only 101 Italian ships would be using the canal route as compared with nearly 3,000 British vessels,[49] the Italian navy was sent to the Red Sea to lay claim to a station for Italy. The navy recommended the Bay of Assab, and so in 1870 the government induced a private entrepreneur, Raffaele Rubattino, to purchase land there, as Italy did not want the diplomatic difficulties of foreign government ownership.

Public opinion was either indifferent or hostile to the settlement at Assab. Most Italian parliamentarians were still inward-looking, believing, like Garibaldi, that the Italian marshlands should be colonized before Africa. It was not until the 1880s that notions of Italian expansion again began to be articulated. Phrases like "imprisonment in the Mediterranean," or "the key to the Mediterranean is in the Red Sea" began to be heard. Pasquale Mancini, foreign minister under Agostino Depretis, had visions of an East African empire. He articulated the goal of eventual Ethiopian conquest to the Chamber of Deputies in May 1885, a few months after Assab was bought from Rubattino, and Massawa was annexed, both forming a new protectorate of "Eritrea." Meanwhile, Italian explorers were getting their bearings. George Révoil explored the Majeerteen, but during his first trip inland he met sufficient hostility to force him to return to the coast. Antonio Cecci, however, went on a mission to explore the Jubba river, and he was much impressed. "It will become the most natural artery for the exportation of the abundant coffee harvest of Kaffa," he wrote, passionately extolling the "rich commercial resources" of Somalia.[50] At the time of Depretis's death in 1887, however, Eritrea was still Italy's only African possession.

Francesco Crispi, the Sicilian radical who succeeded Depretis, brought new vigor to Italy's colonial image. Before he became prime minister, Crispi had never considered the advantages of acquiring an empire. Yet by 1887 Italy was on the verge of industrialism and was facing social upheaval. With the rapid erosion of its agricultural land and the rapid growth of its population, the national unity of the *risorgimento* was beginning to wane. Crispi sensed this, yet recognized that Italy could not afford a social welfare state, which might have alleviated much of the suffering. With the emergence of wider suffrage and the need to consolidate Italian unity, Crispi adopted a pose of imperialist megalomania. While most of his parliamentary colleagues attributed this stance to insanity, Sicilian birth, and/or Albanian ancestry, it was to guide Italian energies through 1896, when Italy suffered a disastrous defeat at Adowa, at the hands of Menelik II.[51]

Through this policy of expansionism, Crispi was able to recruit three sets of allies—strange bedfellows, to be sure, especially considering Crispi's Sicilian, populist, anticlerical background. First he was able to capture the support of a corps of chauvinist intellectuals. Eduardo Scarfoglio, editor of *Il Matino*, a popular southern Italian daily, went himself to Harar in Ethiopia and saw it as easily conquerable, perfect for Italian emigration, and a key to Italian greatness. This image of an Italian Ethiopia was regularly propagandized in his journal. Leopoldo Franchetti, deputy and sociologist, also advocated Italian emigration to the Ethiopian highlands, and Italian "Australia." Pasquale Turiello, Neapolitan journalist and political theorist, was yet another supporter of Crispi's new views. He was writing books like *National Virility and the Colonies*, demanding that Italy play the role of great power.

A second new ally was the church. Crispi had broken with the Vatican in 1867, but by the 1890s they began seeing eye to eye. As early as the 1830s, Italian missionaries such as the Lazarist Sapeto had been established at Massawa on the Red Sea coast. Padre Guglielmo

Massaia, apostolic vicar of Gallaland, had tried in the 1860s to interest Cavour in penetrating Brava as an outlet for Ethiopia's wealth, but Cavour was then occupied with Italian unification. The sharp distinction between church and state in unified Italy left the church virtually ignored by the Italian state in Africa, so that Crispi's sudden interest in Africa brought him into an unholy alliance with the Vatican.

A final source of support, quite unexpectedly, was the reactionary nobility. Given the unsettled conditions in Italy, the old nobility remained a threat to Crispi's parliamentary control. Crispi wisely saw in the colonial experience the opportunity to export the nobility in adventurous activities, reducing their potential influence at home. His radical imperialism was therefore by no means mad. But in Italian policy, nowhere was any concern for a civilizing mission demonstrated. Imperialism for Crispi was a rationally calculated strategy to maintain power in economically distraught and unstable Italy.

Crispi's attempt to unite Italy through enhancing its prestige began with diplomatic failure in attempts to secure Tunisia, Libya, and Kismaayo on the Benaadir coast. It was not until 1889 that Italy was able to achieve its first diplomatic coup; a treaty of protection with Abyssinian Emperor Menelik II, which Italy got as a reward for supporting Menelik in his battle of succession. In this, the Treaty of Ucciali, Italy believed that Menelik was submitting to an Italian protectorate (the Amharic version, however, did not grant this) in exchange for Italian weapons. Progress was soon made on the Indian Ocean coast as well. In late 1888, Yuusuf Cali, the sultan of Obiya, asked Italy to give protection against Zanzibari influence. Although the coastal region at Obiya was desolate and with no economic promise, Crispi siezed the opportunity and ordered a naval mission "for the purpose of declaring the Italian protectorate, and, according to the circumstances, to proceed to the effective occupation of territory."[52] Soon afterward, Filonardi signed a similar agreement with Cismaan Maxamuud, Yuusuf's son-in-law and sultan of the Majeerteen.

Italy then began negotiations with Great Britain for a clear definition of the southern or Benaadir coast. Great Britain began to see the advantages of having a relatively docile buffer between the Red Sea Somali coast and Kenya, over both of which areas it exercised control, and much preferred the Italians there to the French or Germans. The British therefore worked out an agreement on the Benaadir ports. The Imperial British East Africa Company sublet these ports to the Italians well before the Italians were ready to occupy them. In fact, when Robert T. Simons, British administrator in Kismaayo, was signing treaties of protection with Somali chiefs south of the river Jubba in the agreed-upon British sphere of influence, a number of chiefs from the northern bank appeared. Simons, not wanting to disappoint the chiefs, was in the ironic position of signing these agreement on British stationery, crossing out "Imperial British East Africa Company" and replacing it with "Royal Italian East Africa Company." He signed treaties in the name of the Italian government with more than a dozen chiefs. A long time passed before Italian ships arrived to make the treaties into realities.[53]

Amidst depression in Italy in 1892, Giovanni Giolitti came to power, but his concern with bureaucratic efficiency left little room for colonial exploits. Furthermore, "Giolitti's personal disregard for foreign affairs was proverbial,"[54] and, to the embarrassment of the British, he failed to organize payments to the sultan of Zanzibar for the Italian protectorate of Benaadir. Somehow British pressure—backed by the then Italian consul at Aden, Antonio Cecchi—on Giolitti's foreign minister, Benedetto Brin, brought results, and Filonardi was given the Italian concession in Benaadir and the Majeerteen. In an attempt to avoid any and all Italian government responsibility, however, Filonardi was given the duty to pay the concessions to Yuusuf Cali, Cismaan Maxamuud, and the sultan of Zanzibar.

Giolitti faced ever greater economic chaos, and in 1893 Crispi returned to power. Quickly declaring martial law, he attempted to maintain an image of peril within Italy to remain in power. He then began preparing for war in Eritrea; the strategic importance of Somalia, articulated years earlier by Mancini, was again discussed. In 1895 Baron Alberto Blank, Crispi's new foreign minister, contracted Vittorio Bòttego to explore the upper Jubba for the Italian Geographic Society, but the explorer was also entrusted with a number of strategic questions. Crispi's impatience for colonial glory would not wait for Bòttego's conclusions, however, as Bòttego was still out in the field and saw none of the Italian defeat at Adowa in March 1896, the first major defeat of an European army by Africans. Italy maintained control of Eritrea, and her Somali territory was secure, but the highlands were lost. Crispi's political career was over, for he was not even permitted to speak again in parliament. The special coining of Umberto with his imperial crown had to be melted. Mack Smith provides a suitable epitaph for Crispi's foreign policy: "Italy," he says, "had wanted an empire, and had acquired at great expense a desert."[55]

Much to the chagrin of Antonio di Rudini and Luigi Pelloux, Crispi's successors, Italy still had her desert. The ambitious plans advocated by Antonio Cecchi for an expanded, well-capitalized Benaadir Company were supposed to have coincided with a glorious victory over the Ethiopians. Instead it took the Chamber of Deputies three years to ratify a new agreement with the Benaadir Company. The vote of 173 to

151 in the chamber reflected the feeling that a company was preferable to a colony, rather than any support for the Milanese industrialists behind the company.

This attitude signalled a change in Italy's imperial stance from irresponsible expansionism to irresponsible administration. The Italian government did not want to suffer the ignominy of withdrawal, and instead gave the administration of her territories to a company responsible to no one. The parliamentary debate over the issue of the Benaadir Company led to the collapse of its stock on the Italian market, and the company was never to overcome problems of undercapitalization, mismanagement, and stagnancy. Even though it managed to stay in the black, very little capital was risked, and no effort was made to transform the indigenous economy.

The Italian government received its just reward for neglect when a mission by an Italian philanthropic society found clear evidence of slavery in the Benaadir protectorate, and company awareness of it. This was expressly against the provisions of the 1885 Treaty of Berlin and a great embarrassment to a country with liberal pretensions. When a government commission confirmed that the heads of the company knew of the slavery, Italy was forced to accept the political responsibilities entailed in commercial control. Foreign Minister Tittoni, still quite reluctant, asked in the Chamber of Deputies, "At a time when very serious economic problems call for our attention in Italy, why should we waste money elsewhere?"[56] Nonetheless, against her will and better judgment, Italy assumed direct administration of southern Somalia in 1905.

Although Italy faced considerable internal dissent at the turn of the century, her economy was entering an era of sustained industrial growth. Concurrent with this upswing, the voices of imperialism again arose. Gabriele d'Annunzio, Italian poet laureate, began to articulate ideas of racial superiority. Mazinetti, the playwright, also began to express ideas of Latin supremacy. The young journalist Benito Mussolini was inspired by these notions and began to popularize them in his writings. The major political manifestation of this new ideology was a long, frustrating war in Libya, in which Italy, while winning, was able to garner neither money nor glory.

This period of Italian chauvinism brought somewhat more successful results in Somalia under governors Carletti and de Martino, who were finally able to get some funds for expeditions into the interior. By 1907, Tittoni began to accept some of the responsibilities of empire: "It is necessary for the government to assert itself materially and morally over the populations surrounding the Benaadir stations ... and ... gradually undertake the peaceful penetration of the interior and extend our direct administration to the line of the Webi Shabeelle."[57] This new policy enabled the administration in Somalia to finance a war against the Biimaal people in Marka, who were getting arms from Maxamad Cabdille Xasan, the Dervish leader who was centering his efforts on expelling the British from their protectorate in the north. But it should be noted that the Italians acted within Somali clan politics to attain these victories. Cismaan Axmed Yuusuf, sultan of the Geledi, initiated contact with the Italians to get them as allies to defeat their enemy, the Biimaal, who were allied with the "predatory lawless northerners" under the leadership of the Sayid Maxamad Cabdille Xasan. Somalis saw the defeat of the Biimaal as a Geledi rather than an Italian victory.[58]

By 1914 Governor de Martino could claim Italian sovereignty up to Bulo Burti on the Shabeelle River, to Baydhabo in the interriverine plain, and to Luuq on the Jubba. An indirect rule system was efficiently set up, replete with 577 warrant chiefs and 72 *qadis* (judges). All of these men, and one Dervish, were on the government payroll.[59] Rather than fight Maxamad Cabdille Xasan directly, as did the British, they gave him full rights to roam in a specified area between the spheres of influence of Yuusuf Cali and Cismaan Maxamuud, thereby allowing him both a place to escape from the numerous British attempts to capture him, and time to regroup. By the outbreak of World War I, Somalia was, for Italian purposes, pacified. But there were no attempts nor any plans to bring about social, economic, or cultural transformation.

The Fascist era brought the final attempt at a glorious Italian East African empire. Mussolini, whose radical nationalism favored political expansion, also had to weigh the implications of the new American immigration policies for Italy. Expecting that Italian emigration to America would be virtually cut off, he believed that Italy would have to go it alone as a great power and would have to establish for herself an outlet for population and investment. And so colonial expenditure began to expand—from 107 million lire in 1921 to 530 million in 1930. Although most of this money had "been dissipated on the profitless desert of Libya,"[60] it was an open secret that Mussolini had his eyes on the Abyssinian empire. In 1935 he provoked an incident at Walwal, where, for some reason, Italy claimed rights of usage to the wells, although it was clearly marked as Abyssinian territory even on Italian maps. Mussolini is said to have told his subordinates that he wouldn't have taken Walwal as a gift; he wanted to use a colonial war to harden Italian forces for future wars. Italy eventually conquered Abyssinia, and had grandiose ideas for her African empire.

The Fascists began to call their desert in Somalia *la Grande Somalia*. They established a zone of agricultural plantations along the Shabeelle River, and bananas, cotton, and sugar did reach Italian markets but at much higher than competitive prices. In 1926, 400 tons of bananas were produced in these plantations, with no exports to Italy. Over the Fascist era the production grew steadily until 1937, when 49,000 tons of bananas were produced, with 24,900 tons going to Italy. The Fascists set up the *Regia Azienda Monopolio Banana*, which assured that all Somali bananas would go exclusively to Italy, in Italian ships.

Mussolini's final conquest, that of British Somaliland at the beginning of World War II, was marked by lack of foresight and planning, a failing which seemed to typify Italy's whole African experience. Mussolini had not fully recognized the proportions of the imminent world war. While he could well have attacked Britain's vital interests in the Nile, he chose instead Somaliland, possibly because he wanted the largest expanse of territory he could get before Britain sued for peace, or because of the propaganda possibilities of laying claim to the first British colony to be conquered for a hundred years. The Italians easily took the British protectorate, but the ten ill-equipped Italian divisions were, in a matter of months, overrun by two British divisions, even when Britain itself was being deluged by German bombs. The Duke of Aosta had to surrender with nearly a quarter of a million men.[61]

At war's end, Italy was able to regain some of her lost prestige when the Four Powers, unable to agree on a trustee for Somalia and rejecting the Bevin plan for a united Somaliland under British tutelage, left the issue to the United Nations General Assembly. Despite demonstrations led by the emerging Somali Youth League in Muqdisho against the return of the Italians, Italy received a ten-year trusteeship over Somalia, with a independent UN-sanctioned board to set social, educational, and political standards for the development of the trusteeship and to see that they were met. In December 1950 the Italians returned to Muqdisho in order to preside over the ten-year devolution of one part of her former empire. In July 1960, true to her international agreements, Italy transferred power in southern Somalia to the Somalis.

According to Robert Hess (in *Italian Colonialism in Somalia*), Italian colonialism had no real motive or ideology, so that Italian activity from the beginning "was characterized by confusion, uncertainty, hesitancy, and inner contradictions."[62] Hess concludes that "the uniqueness of Italian colonialism in Somalia lies ... in its unusual dependence in its early stages on the good offices of another European power, its unhappy experiments in minimal colonial involvement and continuing aversion in the pre-Fascist period to large-scale colonial activity, and its sorry history of failures."[63] Indeed, the fact that Italy's commitment was minimal meant that her impact was equally unimpressive.

Economically, almost nothing was done before the Fascist era. The members of the Filonardi Company and the Benaadir Company were traders; they replaced the Arabs rather than bringing about any kind of economic change. Even the Fascist-inspired plantations have had little economic consequence for Somalis. The labor used was usually forced; and in the Genale irrigation project for banana production, many Somalis claim that the Fascists used slaves. This forced labor came from the Bantu populations along the Shabeelle river, and not from the nomadic Somalis. The plantations, while they have led to Somalia's second largest export item, have had little impact on the pastoral or subsistence agricultural economies.[64] In 1939, Italy's trade with all her colonies was only 2 percent of her total trade, and the Italian population of New York City was still ten times that of the entire empire. So there is little evidence of any economic transformation in Somalia or of real significance of empire to Italy.

The story is similar in regard to land. Because the Shabeelle did not become Italy's Nile, Hess notes, "the Somali were spared the hardship of being deprived of large areas of their land.... Consequently, throughout the colonial period the Somali did not suffer alienation of their lands, and the traditional way of life was little affected by the activities of the Italian concessions along the rivers."[65] Virginia Luling observed no Geledi distress or bitterness about the land. The paucity of settlers, the unproductiveness of the land, and the problem of labor (the Geledi people themselves would not have considered doing farm work) meant that "the taking up of land did not have the profound effect on South Somali society which someone familiar with other colonial territories might anticipate." No Geledi became landless, and only a few became plantation laborers. As of 1969, only about thirty Italians were living in Afgoy, the town in which Luling worked; not enough, from Luling's point of view, to have caused a serious land alienation movement.[66]

Politically, the effects of Italian rule seem to have been equally limited. In Geledi (I am again relying on Luling's analysis) the nomadic peoples had a titular head attached to their shir—an important modification of their political structure—but this seemed to have been more a de jure than a de facto change. With the more sedentary Geledi, the sultan became qadi or warrant chief, and class sturcture was left unaltered. Perhaps the major political change due to Italian rule was pacification. The Geledi, who were warriors, had to stop their policy of expansion and conquest and thus lost their supreme status on this part of the Benaadir coast. The Geledi were also forced to emancipate their slaves; but this was done only on the statute books. The Geledi people had traditionally engaged in service trades and managed the work of the xabash and the slaves, and they continued to do so. "The traditional political structure was preserved intact in its outline, but with its functions restricted."[67] Modern political institutions were transferred to Somalia at a very late date. In the early years of the trusteeship, a Territorial Council, led by the Italians, was initiated. It was not until 1956 that a Somali National Assembly began to operate. This was but four years before independence.

Few Somalis were trained in administration until the period of trusteeship. But during the Fascist years, a police corps called the *Corpo Zaptié* was formed, with Somali, Arab, and Eritrean recruits housed in barracks, taught Italian, and trained in tactics. This force numbered around 800 men.[68] The Italians also trained soldiers to fight against the Ethiopians, recruiting especially among the more settled populations. The nomads were less willing to fight for the Italians.

The Italian educational input, in Hess's words, was one of "virtually complete neglect." In 1907, the Dante Alighieri Society established a school at Muqdisho to teach Italian to Somali children. Its one teacher received a salary of sixty lire monthly. The school soon closed, and no attempts to open new schools were made until 1922. Some of the schools for Italian children accepted some mulattoes, Arabs, and Somalis, but this was a mere token. The Fascist era brought some change but, again, very little. Up to 1929, the Italian government provided some three hundred thousand lire per annum for education, but in 1929, under the Fascists, the figure jumped to three million. By 1934, 1,265 Somalis were in Italian schools, with elementary schools in Muqdisho, Marka, Afgoy, Jowhar, Brava, Baydhabo, Jilib, and Kismaayo. However, there were no Somalis in Middle Form (grades 8-10) or higher. "Of all the Italian colonies, Somalia received the least aid for schools."[69]

Education developed far more rapidly under the trusteeship agreement. The Italian government, as administering authority, made a number of solid commitments in article 4 of that agreement:

> The Administering Authority, recognizing the fact that education in its broadest sense is the only sure foundation on which any moral, social, political and economic advancement of the inhabitants of the Territory can be based, and believing that national independence with due respect for freedom and democracy can only be established on this basis, undertakes to establish a sound and effective system of education, with due regard for Islamic culture and religion.
>
> The Administering Authority therefore undertakes to establish as

rapidly as possible a system of public education which shall include elementary, secondary, vocational (including institutions for the training of teachers) and technical schools, to provide free of charge at least elementary education, and to facilitate higher and professional education and cultural advancement in every possible way.

In particular, the Administering Authority shall take all appropriate steps: (a) to provide that an adequate number of qualified students ... receive university or professional education outside the Territory ...; (b) to combat illiteracy by all possible means. . . .[70]

While the postwar Italian government did not live up to the letter of this agreement, it did improve on its earlier performance. In the 1957-58 school year, out of an estimated total elementary school population in the Italian trusteeship of 212,000 pupils, 14,000 Somalis were enrolled. In Muqdisho, with an estimated 10,000 eligible pupils, 4,000 were enrolled in Italian subsidized schools.[71] In 1961-62, there were 17,938 Somalis enrolled in pre-preparatory, nursery, and primary schools. In lower secondary schools, 556 students were enrolled; in upper secondary school, 159; and in the Teacher Training Institute, 102 (see table 2).[72]

Table 2 Somali Education: 1961-62

Level	South: Italian System	North: British System
Preprimary, preparatory and primary	17,938	4,305
Intermediate	556	1,766
Secondary	159	159
Teacher training	102	54
Totals	18,755	6,248
Estimated total population	1,290,000	640,000

Sources: Enrollment figures cited in text. On population, see A. A. Castagno, "The Political Party System in the Somali Republic," in James S. Colemen and Carl G. Rosberg, Jr., eds., *Political Parties and National Integration in Tropical Africa* (Berkeley: University of California Press, 1964), p. 515.

Furthermore, Italy set up a University Institute in Muqdisho and trained students in public administration. Some graduates, including Cabdurashiid Cali Sharma'arke, former prime minister and president of the Somali Republic, went on to achieve higher degrees in Italy. In 1967, seven years after independence, twelve Italian teachers were in Somalia teaching at the secondary school and the institute. Thirty scholarships were made available to Somalis directly from Italy; and

Italy contributed to the hundred scholarships made available from the European Economic Community.[73] In 1970, Italy contributed an Italian-language faculty in the American-sponsored teacher college.

These figures can be somewhat deceptive, however. Although the educational system, moribund in Somalia for a half-century, did grow under Italian trusteeship, and, although a number of Somali students learned considerably from their schools, for the average student the educational system was quite ineffective. No clear curricula were developed, and no attempt was made to develop materials that would be useful for teaching in Somalia. The schools were remarkably haphazard in their administration and had none of the "character-building" routines to develop ideals of Western promptness and responsibility so prevalent in British colonial education.

In contrast to the political, social, religious, and administrative impact of the period of Italian rule, the influence of the Italian language was significant. I. M. Lewis was impressed by the level of Italian in Somalia, and claimed it was "fairly widespread"—partly because Italian is relatively easy to learn. But, perhaps more important, "it was the policy in Somalia to regard Somali as a barbaric tongue which must give place to the civilized language of the rulers."[74]

In the 1920s, when Cismaan Cali Yuusuf developed a script for Somali, the Italian administration attempted to suppress it, but not only because it was perceived as a barbaric tongue. Rather, the colonizers saw the connection between language and nationalism and wanted to suppress any further manifestations of national consciousness, especially after the death of Maxamad Cabdille Xasan, who died after a twenty-one-year nationalist battle with the British. Refusal to understand the potentialities of Somali carried over to the trusteeship years. Although the Italians consistently said that they would teach in the schools whatever language the Somalis themselves wanted, they always added, "in adjunct to Italian." Even in the final years of the trusteeship and among the more enlightened administrators, there was a subtle, if unintended, discrimination against the Somali language in Somali education.

"Perhaps even more important than Italian films, food, schools," writes Luling, "is the impression which the years of Italian occupation have left on the people's view of the world. The clearest sign of this is the use of the Italian language. All public officials trained in southern Somalia to date were educated in it. Up to 1967 it was the third official language of the Republic and taught in all the schools of the South. Even among the majority who never had any kind of secular education, many have picked up a working knowledge of Italian, or at any rate know a few words of it and it has left its mark in the common language of the area."[75] Indeed, a number of Italian loan words have permeated the southern dialect. *Safaleti* is the word for girl's handkerchief, coming from the Italian *fazzoletto*. *Matabale* comes from the Italian *notabile*; and *baramila* means waterproof, from the Italian *impermeabile*.

In 1952, the Somali editor of *Corriere della Somalia* remarked with some approval how well the Italian language had spread already through the Somalized civil service. Nonetheless, he argued that it would always remain a foreign language to the Somalis and therefore advocated that the Somali language become the administrative tongue, "with maximum and most reverent respect for the Italian culture and to its contribution to Somalia's progress."[76] This was part of a remarkable ten-year debate among Somali intellectuals and Italian intellectuals and administrators in the *Corriere* (to which I shall return in chapter 4). The debate demonstrated, among other things, that the Somali intelligentsia in the south was perfectly capable of entering historical, political, and cultural debate in the Italian language.

In the north, of course, no Italian was spoken. After political integration, when northerners became more active in the south, "some indeed had even found it sufficiently useful, despite their Anglophone contempt for the language, to pick up Italian, although it was becoming increasingly obvious that in the long run English would be the main foreign language."[77] The linguistic division between the north and the south was to be the source of considerable political friction in the independence era (see chapters 4 and 5).

The Italians never succeeded in their attempted role of colonial masters. They were sometimes perceived as allies (by the Geledi in their fight with the Biimaal) and sometimes as enemies (by Maxamad Cabdille Xasan and his Dervishes), but rarely were they seen as masters. The love-hate relationship, so often present between colonized and colonizer, seemed not to occur in the Somali case—in part because of the incompetence of the colonizers and in part because of the vitality and resiliency of the colonized society.

The Italians were again and again ridiculed by the Somalis. The Geledi elders still remember the Italians escaping from the British mines in 1941, not to return. The year is still called *ka-la-roor*, runaway. The Somalis have been heard to call the Italians the Xabash of Europe.[78] The Somalis are keen observers of their foreign contacts, and have an excellent taste for quality, in nearly any field. They were able to discern, quite easily, the ironies of Italian colonialism. In one of his poems to the British, Maxamad Cabdille Xasan vented his anger as well as his understanding of European politics, especially of the low status of the Italians.

> I had no issue with the Italians until you
>   summoned them to your aid.
> It was you who intrigued and plotted with them;
> It was you who said, "Join us in the war against
>   the Dervishes";
> And they did not say, "Leave us, and stop
>   conspiring with us";
> Did you never tire of these evil machinations?
> Was it not through these schemes that the
>   landings at Obiya took place?
> Did they not greatly aid you with their arms and
>   supplies?
> You fools, those who attacked yesterday on your
>   side,
> Will they not strike at me from the back if we
>   fight tomorrow?
> Will they be prevented from attacking me, by
>   disclaiming their bond with you?
> *It is you who lead to pasture these weaker infidels:*
> *Can I distinguish between you and your*
> *livestock?*[79]

Even in the postindependence era the Somalis often looked down upon the Italians. William Travis, British businessman in Somalia, recollects that "the majority of these [Italian] expatriates were from the lower sections of their own society and we found them crass, uneducated and unbelievably gauche as compared with the dignified Somalis, compared with whom the Europeans made a poor and perhaps ridiculous spectacle."[80]

The Italian presence in Somalia can therefore be characterized as one of inconsistent goals and low levels of penetration. There was little attempt to institutionalize stratification among Somalis or to induce a colonial mentality among the subject peoples. The Italian language was transferred to some extent, but without the cultural values or political institutions from which it derived.

British Influence

> *In my eyes [Somalia] seems to be a coast without harbours, trade, produce, or strategic advantage. But as everybody else is fighting for it, I suppose we are bound to think it valuable.*
>
> Salisbury, Secretary of State
> for Foreign Affairs.[81]

If the notion of the British Empire united those who saw a need for

British glory with those who felt a need to help the downtrodden peoples of the world, Somalia missed its thrust. Britain did not seek a Somali colony was never able to accept the responsibilities that came with political control of that territory. That the Somali people were never subjugated by the British is only partly explained by the strength of the Somali character; it was also due to British penny pinching and negligence.

Early nineteenth-century Red Sea politics for Britain involved protecting her trade routes with the East, especially India, and especially against French competition. Britain paid little or no attention to the Somali coast, had no imperial plans there, and was happy to see the area under the control of the Ottoman Empire, a non-European rival. In 1825, a British brig from Mauritius had been plundered near Berbera, and two of its Lascars murdered; so the Indian navy (under Britain's control) blockaded Berbera until February 1827, when the Habar Awal signed a treaty agreeing to pay 15,000 Spanish dollars in compensation. The treaty also has some articles to promote friendship and commerce.[82] But no commerce was planned at that time.

In January 1839, with the opening of steamer service from India to Suez, Britain needed a coaling station on the Red Sea. The British therefore captured Aden, a fairly useless rock but with a good harbor, from the sultan of Lahj. Not only would Aden be a good station for trade between Britain and India, but it would also be a way for the British to keep an eye on Muhammed 'Alī, who, they feared, had grandiose imperial designs. An awakened modern Egypt could cause problems for the Indian empire. Further, the Aden station seemed a good place to station ships for piracy control, and a way to secure the coffee trade of the Yemen.[83]

The main problem with the Aden station was that it could not provide food for either the ships or the expatriate community there; so Britain considered establishing trade with Berbera, across the Red Sea and a little over a hundred miles away. In 1840 the East India Company sent Captain Moresby of the Indian navy to the Gulf of Aden, where he concluded a number of treaties with the Somalis. In Berbera he relied mostly on Xaaji Sharma'arke, an elder of the Habar Yoonis clan, to get land, commercial rights, and a promise that the Somalis would enter no treaty that would endanger British interests. Similar treaties were signed in Seylac and Tadjoura, none making reference to the fact that these cities were on lease to Egypt from Turkey. The British were therefore unwilling to exert any kind of control, for fear of stepping into a quagmire. In 1843, when their ally Xaaji Sharma'arke attempted to seize Seylac, he lost it to the Turks, and Britain refused him aid.

A few years later, the Royal Geographical Society in England began to put pressure on the East India Company to release some officers to explore "the productive resources of the unknown Somali country in East Africa."[84] An expedition was approved, over Colonel James Outram's objections, with Burton and Speke as its leaders. During this trip, Burton was the first European to enter the walled city of Harar; but later on, at Berbera, his camp was attacked, he and Speke were injured, and Lieutenant Stroyan was killed by Somali raiders. The British then blockaded Berbera, and another treaty was signed with the Habar Awal in November 1856, which abolished the slave trade and gave Britain the right to send a resident to Berbera.

Officials at Aden, now fully reliant on the goats coming in from the Somali coast, began requesting more British control of Berbera, especially since the Turks were sending ships there to exact tribute. In 1869 the Turkish flag went up in Berbera but the government of India refused to take action, reckoning that any agent it sent to Berbera would get killed and that the Turks, despite their flag, were too weak to challenge Britain's interests. That decision, from Britain's viewpoint, was a good one. The Turks and then the Egyptians kept control of the Red Sea Coast for fourteen more years, thereby keeping the Germans, French, and Russians out.

Occasionally the British were forced to deal with the Somalis in this period, but they tried to keep themselves out of any entangling alliances. They wanted the Khedive to build a lighthouse at Cape Guardafui, for instance, on the Majeerteen coast, but no action was taken. A number of shipwrecks had occurred on this treacherous turn, to the enrichment of the plundering Majeerteen peoples. The British therefore dealt directly with the sultan of the Majeerteen, paying him an annual sum to protect shipwrecked persons and to guard wrecks from plunder. But the British government was unwilling to ratify this treaty, which they kept on a *de facto* level, not wanting to "give other powers a precedent for making agreements with the Somalis, who seemed ready to enter into relations with all comers."[85]

When the British maneuvered the Khedive to evacuate the Sudan, the situation in Berbera became uncertain again. Rumors abounded that the Somalis were ready to declare for the Mahdi. The Italians and French, dissatisfied with their Red Sea holdings, were rumored to be considering annexing Berbera. The Aden establishment was quite nervous. In 1879-80, 2,017 out of 2,063 cattle and 92,790 out of 93,441 sheep imported by Aden came from the Somali Coast and Tadjoura.[86] The British consul for the African coast from Tadjoura to Ras Xaafuun, F. M. Hunter, was sent to Berbera immediately. A fortnight before leaving he had said that he would avoid money compensation since "the very sight of a dollar seems to upset the balance of the not naturally stable Somali mind"; yet with two warships behind him he did pay twenty-nine elders of the Habar Awal a small sum to get them to agree to make no treaties with any other power.[87] Despite Gladstone's liberal policies in England and his government's statement in 1884 that we "do not wish to establish anything in the nature of a Protectorate over the inland tribes,"[88] Hunter well understood that the Treaty of Berlin did not recognize spheres of influence. He therefore took the opportunity to sign treaties with the Habar Toljaclo, the Habar Garxajis, and the Warsangeli, so that by 1885 Britain was able to declare the whole Somali coast a protectorate. Hunter was deterred by the Gladstone policy only from making treaties with the Somali clans around Harar, for the orders were clear not to go beyond the coast.

The new protectorate was in an anomalous position. There was no legal basis to any exercise of internal sovereignty or jurisdiction. The British were reluctant to make it a colony because that would entail a moral obligation to administer it properly. The Indian government, which really wanted control of the Somali coast, had no desire to pay for it. It was administered as a dependency of Aden, which came under the jurisdiction of Bombay, and all matters of importance were decided in Calcutta. In 1885, the India Office summed up the policy objective toward the Somali coast: "The primary objects of Government are to secure for Aden a supply market, to check the traffic in slaves, and to exclude the interference of the foreign powers. It is consistent with these objects, and with the protectorate which the Indian Government has assumed to interfere as little as possible with the customs of the people, and to leave them to administer their own internal affairs."[90] Only rarely did the administering authority interfere. In 1886 Britain did enter in an intra-clan fight amongst the Habar Awal that was threatening the market at Bullaxaar. Hunter sided with the Awal Yoonis clan over the Jibriil Abokor, but he did not employ any physical coercion. He captured the livestock of the Jibriil Abokor, holding the animals until the clan leaders came to recover them and had paid retribution, including costs for the British troops. This precedent-setting way of dealing with warring nomadic clans is still used today. In 1892, with Stace, a Tory, as administrator of the Somali Coast, a camel corps was established to stop the raiding of goods on the trade routes.

But the true nature of British "protection" was revealed in 1896, when Menelik was fighting the Italians. As Menelik marched eastward, the Ogaadeen Somalis and other clans were being plundered and murdered. The Somali clans asked Britain for aid but were refused. From this episode, A. M. Brockett, diplomatic historian, concludes that "the only protection involved in this protectorate was the protection of the British and Indian interests."[91] After the Italian defeat at Adowa, Britain realized that the Somali protectorate was in jeopardy but denied the Indian government's request that the British government inherit it. The Foreign Office argued that India wanted Aden, that Aden required Somali provisions, and that therefore India would have to pay the costs of the international politics involved in administering the coast. But all recognized that something had to be done.

In 1897 the British sent J. R. Rodd to negotiate with Menelik. His instructions were to assure that the French would not make inroads where the Italians had lost. Nowhere in his instructions was there any concern for the rights of the Somalis. In the treaty he signed in 1897, Rodd gave Menelik rights to the Hawd, an important Somali grazing area and a region that was presumably "protected" by British treaties with the Somalis in 1884 and 1886. This treaty, Brockett argues, again demonstrated that the British "were ready to abandon people with whom they had treaty relations if they could thereby avoid trouble with a neighboring power."[92]

Rodd returned to Britain and suggested that the Somali coast become a British protectorate. What with the failures in the Sudan and Uganda, he argued, the Somali coast could provide a crucial link in the new Nile protection policy. The Indian government was only too glad to relinquish Somalia, and the transfer took place on 1 October 1898. For the British, this new protectorate would be nothing but a nightmare. For the next twenty-one years they were forced to contend with the Sayid Maxamad Cabdille Xasan, religious mystic, brilliant warrior, and committed nationalist. As one popular journalist put it, the English people should be aware that, "an English Government made itself responsible, by breaking its sacred pledges, for the flaying and burning alive of men, women and children, and mutilations too fiendish to be mentioned, until a third of the entire male population of a British 'Protectorate' had been done to death."[93]

The Sayid, in 1884, when he was about thirty, made the pilgrimage to Mecca and became a disciple of Muhammad ibn Salih. Salih, a disciple of the Sudanese mystic Ibrahim al Rashidi, branched off from the Ahmadiyah Sufi order and founded his own "Saalixiya" order. Educated in the most conservative Islamic tradition, Inan Cabdille Xasan (as the Somalis call the Sayid, literally "the son of Cabdille Xasan") came into contact with Somalis who were, in his eyes, Westernized and influenced by the British and the Catholic mission. He vowed to rid his homeland of the European infidels. It was unclear to the British then, as it is unclear to scholars today, whether the Sayid wanted British recognition of his control of the Somaliland interior or whether he wanted full scale war against the British. Whatever his desires, he got the latter. During this transition period, which lasted until 1905, the British sent four expeditions to capture the man they called the "Mad Mullah." They perceived that his attempts to control the interior were leading to bloodshed and would eventually put in jeopardy the free flow of cattle and sheep to Berbera. The coastal clans, who had put their prestige on the line by supporting the British, were afraid of the Sayid and encouraged the British to advance against him. When the fourth expedition was completed in 1905, costing about one and a half million pounds (not including sea support), the country was thought to be pacified, even though the Sayid was still free. In fact, he was acquiring arms through the ports of Bosaso and Ilig, and by 1905 the level of livestock trade to Aden had been cut in half from the 1899 level, so that the success of the four expeditions was dubious. The British indeed wanted a pacified interior but were unwilling to pay for it, and for seven years they let their authority deteriorate. A small camel corps was eventually organized in 1912 in an attempt to put reins on the Sayid's activities. But after a few initial successes, the leader, Richard Corfield, began to disregard a fifty mile patrol limit. Corfield's team of eighty-five men challenged an estimated Dervish force of 2,750 at Dul Madoobe, and Corfield was shot dead. He will long be remembered in Somali country, though, for one of the Sayid's most striking poems describes (quite inaccurately) how Corfield died and the glory of the battle of Dul Madoobe.[94]

The First World War distracted the British from their embarrassments in Somaliland. But shortly after the war a new army was organized to destroy the Sayid. A major air battle was planned to level his fortress at Taleex. That expedition in 1920 did succeed in putting to rest the Dervish movement. But the Sayid escaped with his close family and maintained his personal freedom until he died, a year later, probably of malaria. During that last year, and many times previously, the British attempted to buy Inan Cabdille Xasan off, by offering him a "salary" to rule over a specified area and to accept some geographical limits to his control. While he engaged in correspondence with the British and met with their agents, the Sayid only used these sessions to vent his vitriolic irony. Perhaps he is most admired today for his refusal to compromise with the British, for refusing to negotiate on their terms, and for confronting directly rather than compromising with the implications of British colonial rule.[95]

The political situation remained static after the death of the Sayid until the Second World War, when Italy attacked British holdings in the North. In a matter of months, Britain repulsed the Italian forces and soon "liberated" the southern region and Ethiopia. During the war, the Kenyan Northern Frontier District, the Ethiopian Hawd and the Ogaadeen, the north and south of Somalia—that is to say all Somali populated territories except for the French holding at Jabuuti— were in British hands. The British, with Ernest Bevin as their advocate, attempted to create a united Somaliland and therefore requested that the UN grant them a trusteeship over the conquered Somali territory. The Russian government, however, objected to any enhancement of British influence in Africa; so the Bevin plan was rejected. But lack of British concern for the needs and desires of the Somali people was the hallmark of Britain's whole colonial policy in the Somalilands. Their disposition of their empire brought this into bold relief. They "returned" the Hawd and the Ogaadeen to the Ethiopian government, based on their treaty of 1884 in which they ceded Somali territory to Menelik in exchange for his help against the plunderings of the Ciise clans. They attempted to buy the Hawd back from Haile Selassie in 1956, but this was a mere gesture. And in 1963 they allowed the Kenyan government to assume administrative control over the Northern Frontier District, despite an informal plebiscite which demonstrated overwhelming desire of the people to join the Somali Republic.[96] Britain did, though, advance the date of independence of the north to 26 June 1960, to allow Somaliland to merge with the Italian trust territory of Somalia on July first.

In assessing the nature and extent of English influence in Somaliland, it is important to distinguish between the makers of British policy and the colonial officers sent out to the field. The Somalis never came into contact with the former, yet suffered from their heavy-handed and short-sighted policies. Their contact with the latter, however, is of some interest here. Many of the British administrators had an awesome respect for the Somali land and the Somali people, and some even defied and tried to subvert British policy to demonstrate support for the Somalis. Ironic as it may seem, Richard Corfield's death has been so interpreted; according to his biographer, Corfield felt that he had to defy his orders in order to show his loyalty to the Somali clans that showed such loyalty to him.[97]

In 1921 Margery Perham (sister-in-law to Major H. Rayne, logistics advisor for the final British campaign against the Dervishes) visited Somaliland, her first trip to Africa. Upon her return, she wrote a novel about her experience that contained some important insights into the personal feelings of the colonial officers of the time. She portrays the outgoing governor of Somaliland, "Sir John Chard," whose views are eventually vindicated in the novel, as arguing that a large British force would be counterproductive: "It's because the Somal is a warrior and troops rouse him; they don't cow him. He reckons he's as good a man as we are and so far we haven't been able to destroy that belief."⁹⁸ His parting words to the new governor are these:

> And with all his faults, I like the Somal. He's like no other native on earth. There's no formula for handling him.... He's treacherous, hysterical, truculent, vain, avaricious. But he's a warrior and a stoic, and he's the cleanest native I ever struck. Call his hysteria temperament, his truculence courage, and his vanity a proper pride, and you see him in a new light. He's got dignity, he's got intelligence. He's good to look upon. But, best of all, he's an eternal surprise. This race can produce individuals fit to rank with any, and examples of faithfulness and—yes—love, that would go into history textbooks in Europe.⁹⁹

Reports of real officers bear out Miss Perham's judgment. Alys Reece, discussing her husband's illustrious career in the Northern Frontier District, confides that "many British officers felt a sneaking sympathy with the Somali case, in spite of the trouble they made."¹⁰⁰ In a similar vein, Douglas Collins, a major in the British occupying force in Italian Somalia, intimates that all the British officers were shocked when they heard the Ogaadeen was to be ceded to the Ethiopians. Most of them, and especially Collins—had become Somalophiles.¹⁰¹ John Drysdale, British political officer in the Somali Republic at the time of Kenyan independence, was another supporter of the Somali cause, who wanted Britain to cede the Northern Frontier District to Somilia. After leaving the British service, he was impelled to write two long explanations in the Somali independent journal *Dalka*, dissociating himself from British policy. He subsequently became political adviser to the Somali prime minister. Although the British officers had Somali servants, rarely did any kind of traditional master-servant relationship develop; in many instances, long and intimate friendships were formed.

Despite warm feelings between the administrators and the Somalis, and despite the millions of pounds spent to put down the Dervish movement, the extent of British penetration into Somaliland was remarkably small. During the protectorate years, as we have seen, the Indian government wanted no administrative responsibilities in Somalia. By 1897 there were only three European officers on the coast, employing four clerks. Since the Indian government refused grants-in-aid, the administration was run on the duties levied: 1886-7, £8,961; and 1896-97, £21,263. Expenditures in those years were £6,986 and £13,055, which meant that the administration was underspending its budget.¹⁰² By 1947, the whole protectorate budget was only £213,139.¹⁰³ These were budgets aimed not at transforming life in the Somali desert but merely keeping order in a few outposts.

In the Somali-populated Kenyan Northern Frontier District, the extent of political and administrative control was no different from that in Somaliland. Gerald Reece, for example, in the 1930s was the only British officer in the whole Marsabit District, which was then a full two-day trip (in the dry season) from Isiolo, the nearest British post. His only duties were to attempt to stop clan fighting and to prevent the Somalis from migrating southward. With only one other European, a policeman, at the Marsabit post, there was almost nothing he could enforce.[104] Similarly, when a government official was murdered by a Somali in 1902, Sir Charles Eliot, commissioner of the East Africa Protectorate, claimed that it should be considered a criminal rather than a political act. "Its only political importance," he argued, "was that it showed the audacity of the Somalis and their small respect for our government."[105] A rather large British contingent stationed at Waajeer, in the heart of the Somali desert, seemed to be consumed by the land. They spent their time building an enormous limestone ship, replete with mast and cannon, two hundred miles from the sea. They drank profusely and contentedly in this "Royal Waajeer Yacht Club."

In the brief, ten-year sojourn of the British in the Italian colony of Somalia little was done to set up an administration. Here, at least, the British had law to back up their lack of concern. The Hague Convention Rules of 1907 stipulated that after military conquest a country should have an administration that maintains the status quo, and so "the British authorities were bound to prevent all attempts to change existing conditions within the territory."[106] Some twenty years after Britain left, British anthropologist Luling wrote: "The British occupation, though it was to have political consequences of fundamental importance, by beginning the end of the colonial system, seems to have left little mark culturally on the area. The only introduction I can definitely assign to it is the game of hopscotch which is played to this day by the children of Afgoy."[107] The political consequences to which Luling refers were the result of the British willingness to tolerate, and even to give their encouragement to, the activities of the Somali Youth League, the first modern political party in Somalia and the one which would rule in Somalia in its first decade as an independent republic. Indeed, many of the leaders in the postindependence period, including General Siyaad himself, were trained by the British military administration. But Luling's point is that very little of that impact was felt by the nomadic majority. Although it is true that the Somali Republic did inherit from the British a party system and a legislature, it should be pointed out that the establishment of a legislative body in British Somaliland only occurred in 1957, just three years before independence. It would be folly to suggest that institutionalized parliamentary procedures were transferred to the Somali political structure in that period. What did happen is that traditional Somali lineage politics began to be played in a new forum.

The British were able to profit economically from the Somali protectorate without transforming the traditional economy. Despite the fact that the Indian administration kept on reporting deficits, the Somali protectorate was economically beneficial to India. The Indian government insisted on charging the protectorate for army garrisons and for the Royal Indian Marine ship stationed at Aden (one-half of cost). The accounts were thus manipulated by the Indian government, Brockett has pointed out, only to "show" Egypt that the coast was a losing proposition, and to absolve India from having to pay Turkey the 15,000 Turkish pounds tribute that Egypt was paying when it had occupied the coast. In 1898, when India turned over responsibility for the protectorate to the British government, the Somali coast had contributed more than £36,774 to Indian revenues, but the books recorded it as a loss of £71,667.[108]

The Indian government put almost no money into development, and the Egyptian public works and buildings were allowed to deteriorate. A few buildings were put up to enhance trade, but repeated fires destroyed them. The Indian government gave limited encouragement to a fiber manufacturer who wanted to set up a concession in Habar Awal country, but the entrepreneur had to make arrangements with the Somalis himself. While the British, until they engaged in their attempt to crush the Dervish movement, did profit from the Somali protectorate, they did not attempt to transform the Somali economy. Upon independence in 1960, the economy of British Somaliland was virtually unchanged from the early nineteenth century.

At least until the Second World War, formal secular education barely existed in British Somaliland. In 1887 the Indian government built a small school, but it was destroyed the following year in a fire. It was rebuilt, and in 1897 it provided instruction in the Qur'an, arithmetic, and Arabic to roughly 240 boys, half of them Arabs and half Somalis. When the British government took over the protectorate from the Indian government, Lieutenant-Colonel J. H. Sadler was made first consul general. He attempted to create something during his rule, perhaps reacting to the visit of a British Member of Parliament who, after visiting Seylac, wrote that "it is difficult to understand how such ramshackle, dirty hole as the town is can be in such a condition after seventeen years of our rule."[109] Sadler opened up elementary schools at Bullaxaar and Seylac in 1905. The schools had a total of about 150 students, mostly the children of Arab and Indian merchants; but with the retreat of the British shortly thereafter, these schools were closed.[110]

The Dervish war over, the British made another attempt in 1930 to do something constructive in their protectorate. They subsidized the Qur'anic schools, but that policy met with little success. The Somalis, it needs to be mentioned, were at least as reluctant to subject themselves to British education as the British were to supply it. During the Second World War, however, Somali attitudes began to change. Educated East Africans were being brought up from Kenya to administer their country. The Somalis wanted those jobs and began to open themselves up to education in English. In 1942 three elementary schools were opened at Hargeysa, Berbera, and Burco. By 1945, seven schools with an enrollment of over 400 boys were operating.[111] In 1949-50, the Colonial Development and Welfare Act helped establish a number of schools, including two intermediate schools. By 1950, the government no longer had to use persuasion to fill up the rolls; competition for the limited spaces in elementary school was keen.[112] Most Somali students were able to see the schools merely as places where important skills could be learned. They tolerated British control only because those skills were being transferred.

Although education expanded in the next decade, Great Britain was under little international pressure—since the northern region was not a trust—to increase the scope of Somali education. In 1951 there were 639 Somali students in elementary school, 274 in intermediate school, and none in secondary school. A decade later, elementary enrollment had gone up to 4,305, intermediate places to 1,766, and secondary school enrollment was 159.[113] A comparison of the extent of the British educational system and the Italian just after independence shows that the British school system reached fewer Somalis per capita than the Italian (see table 2). But if the Italian school system did expand faster than the British, better curricular development, better discipline, and better education in general marked the British system. The British system therefore may have had a greater impact than the Italian on those students it reached.

Britain did establish schools in the southern region. In 1944 some 190 Somalis were attending schools where English was being taught. In 1947, the Four Power Commission, investigating the scene in Southern Somalia in order to make recommendations to the Trusteeship Council, found seventeen elementary schools for some 500 Somalis, and a teachers' training school with 50 Somali students. Of the 52 teachers in these schools, only 5 had taken the "War Course" for teachers in Nairobi. The commission reported that "of the remainder few have any recognized qualifications."[114] In the Somali province of the old Northern Frontier District, education was almost completely neglected. In 1964 there were some 900 Somalis in the Northeastern Province in primary school, making up 2.1 percent of the population aged 7-13. At the time the British were engaged in building the first secondary school in the entire province, which had an enrollment of 56 students by 1966.[115]

The 1960s and independence brought significant changes to the educational system, mostly involving transformation of the Italian school system to the English medium. In the north, expanded educational opportunity was available. In 1968, the United States offered forty scholarships to Somalis for study in America and two for study in Kenya. The United Kingdom offered two scholarships.[116] Candidates were students at the two Somali secondary schools in the northern region, originally built by the British—Camuud and Sheekh. But despite this emerging school system, the English language did not flourish in colonial Somaliland. A British Commission of Enquiry into Unofficial Representation on the Legislative Council in 1958 estimated, according to Saadia Touval, "that there were only eight persons outside the civil service whose ability to use English was up to seventh-form [intermediate school] level."[117] This evaluation is partly borne out by the very low scores on the English-language General Certificate of Education examination that I mentioned earlier.

Italian Somalia was more widely exposed to English than was Somaliland to Italian. Lewis reports that during the British military occupation of the south, many politicians and senior officials had acquired some knowledge of English. He adds, however, that few knew the language sufficiently well to use it regularly as a means of written communication.[118] Furthermore, Britain had to recruit a gendarmerie to bring some degree of order in 1942 and 1943, and they had to choose one language in which to train their recruits. They decided to give a five-month preliminary training in English. The people who were in this course formed an early nucleus for the Somali Youth League. But with the return of the Italians in 1951, the medium of instruction in the south again became Italian, and the level of English, sank even lower. It was only in the Arab-supported schools that English was still taught in the southern region. Since Egyptian higher education is largely in English, students in Egyptian-supported schools got a fair English-language background.

Some English words permeated into the Somali language, especially in the realm of technical vocabulary. *Daktar* means doctor, *raadiyo* radio, and *telefonka* telephone. Most Somali poets and linguists mourn even this small intrusion, in a way they do not do with Arabic loan words. In a well-known poem, Salaan Carrabey alliterates in the letter L his complaint that modern poets are forgetting the Somali language and must therefore borrow English words to fulfill the alliterative requirements of the Somali poem. He uses the very technique he scorns in order to make his point: "Some people recite words as foolish and nonsensical as the European's 'lectures' / And still keep at it imagining themselves successful." Here Carrabey coins the Somali word *lagjar* to mean lecture and also to make his alliteration. Using the same technique he calls these lazy poets *loofari*, loafers.[119] Somaliland to the British was the backwater of the empire, a gawdy nuisance which should have been ignored. There was no hoped-for glory in a Somali colony (as there had been in the Italian view); Somaliland was merely a cog in the British imperial wheel. It was most surely to Somaliland's benefit that little effort was made to transform Somali culture, religion, language, or economy; and that the Somali people emerged from the British colonial experience barely subjugated. It was to the credit of many British civil servants to recognize this and to admire the Somalis for resisting the kind of subjugation they themselves would surely resist.

Conclusion

At the time of independence (1960), the traditional Somali social structure was very much intact. Although modern political parties began to proliferate in the years preceding independence, those parties very much reflected the nature of the traditional clan structure. Most of the parties were explicitly clan-based, as for example the Marreexaan Union, the Abgal Youth Association, and the Hisbia Digil Mirifle. And even those parties which claimed to be pan-Somali, such as the Somali Youth League, the Greater Somalia League, and the Somaliland National League, were built up and maintained on clan foundations. The nationalism of the parties "is not so much a complete surrender to a national patriotism transcending lineage loyalties as merely a realignment of lineage and tribal interests at a new level."[120] The parliamentary structures, built in 1956 and 1957, were still quite fragile at the time of independence. From the earliest stages of national government, politics, even for those political actors who scorned tribalism, involved careful "ethnic balancing" to assure that all Somali clans had national representation.[121]

Although the civil service was the haven for educated Somalis who had supposedly developed national consciousness, the administration in the emergent Somali Republic was "a consortium of rival lineage and clan interests which people regard in terms of the number of kinsmen they can count in its ranks."[122] Each ministry developed what might be called clan empires, and it would be known throughout the republic which clans had power, hired their own people, and allocated other resources to their people in each ministry. That leaders such as

Cabdirisaaq Xaaji Xuseen, when he became prime minister, attempted to rid the republic of these empires demonstrates a keen Somali understanding of their presence. The civil service, instead of transforming the traditional structure in the years preceding independence, was in fact molded by the social structure.

The most significant influence of national electoral politics has been to widen the clan alliance system. Where early in the century the most salient level of political membership was that of the diya-paying group, in independent Somalia the primary lineage level and even the clan family level has taken on much wider significance. Party politics has stressed membership groups such as "Daarood" or "Rahanwiin," and tended to override in its recruitment the intra-clan family fissions. This phenomenon is comparable to the political effects of the Dervish wars. The scale of Maxamad Cabdille's activities forced alliances which far transcended the diya-paying group. Although modern politics did create wider loyalties, those loyalties were based on the same criterion—agnatic lineage—as in the diya-paying group. Foreign influence may have increased the size of the political groups within the republic, but it did not transform the structure of the traditional political system. A further manifestation of this, which will become clearer in the following chapter, is that there was little tension between the "traditional elites" and the "modern elites" in independent Somalia, a tension that was quite prevalent in other African states. The traditional elites fed nicely into the "modern" political system.

Well over 95 percent of the Somali population, if you consider those who grew up before the trusteeship years, had never gone beyond a few years of Qur'anic training. And whatever changes were brought about in the Somali economy by the colonial governments were of the same scope. Approximately 85 percent of the Somalis at the time of independence were still pastoral nomads or seminomads. The plantation system created by the Italians employed mostly the Bantu populations along the Shabeelle River, and these people have remained somewhat outside the traditional political system. While many more Somalis have been participating in commerce, these people have remained part and parcel of their reers. Somalia remains a pastoral society.

In an important sense, Islam is one of the defining characteristics of the Somali identity, and the Somali protonationalists, such as Axmed Gran or Maxamad Cabdille, clearly saw themselves primarily as Muslim. Yet adherence to Islam as a universalist religion has not prevented the Somalis from maintaining many of their pre-Islamic religious practices. More important, Islam has not merged totally with Somali secular institutions to transform them. The shir, based on agnatic kinship, and consolidated by secular contract, xeer, has given the Somalis a clearly defined secular politics. The men of religion, the wadaads, are no more influential in the shir than the warriors, the warranle.

The Arabic language spread along with the Qur'an, and although few Somalis can understand the words in the Qur'an, they have some familiarity with those words. A small but effective educational system in the Arabic medium has created a small elite literate in Arabic; and certain men of religion have pursued their theological studies to an extent where they too are highly literate in Arabic. The influence of Arabic is about the same in both the north and the south of the Republic. English has had its greatest influence in the north of the Somali Republic and in the Northeastern Province of Kenya, but, with miniscule educational structures and almost no British settlement, the penetration of the language was very limited. Italian had exposure only in the southern region, but, because of the ease of learning Italian and the more aggressive Italian administration once Somalia became its Trust, that language had some currency outside of the school system. Both English and Italian, unlike Arabic, were almost unknown away from the towns.

An important consequence of low levels of foreign penetration was that the emergent political elite in Somalia was not markedly Westernized. In dress, in manner, and in preferences, those Somalis who had been exposed to education were not manifestly alienated from their own people. They were neither obsequious to Europeans nor scornful of their illiterate brothers. Though they did speak English, Italian, or Arabic, and had studied science and mathematics, they were still intellectually stimulated by Somali poetry and art. Never has "modernization" in Somali meant becoming more "Westernized." The call for modernization has been, for the Somali political elite, a call for more water for the nomad, for the eradication of malaria and tuberculosis, and for the writing of the Somali language. This is true for both the members of the Somali Youth League, the first explicitly nationalist organization, and the new military elite. Neither of these two ruling elites ever sought to replace "tradition" by "modernity."

In his speech announcing the writing of the Somali language, military leader Maxamad Siyaad Barre even suggested that the preservation of the Somali literary tradition is the fundamental goal of a revolutionary movement. We now turn to the long political controversy among the Somalis concerning national language and national script. With the collective inability to agree upon a script, the newly formed Somali republican government had to decide which of the three foreign languages should be used for state business.

4 Language Politics in Somalia
The Politics of Nondecision

Our ancestors ... scorned the man who attempted to be superior to his fellow men, and quelled the ambitions of potential dictators. Compromise and tolerance brought peace, prosperity, and happiness.

President Aadan Cabdulle Cisman
Muqdisho, 1962[1]

Two of the more important items on the political agenda of the Italian Trust Territory of Somalia were a national orthography and an official language. The future Somali Republic would have elites literate in three different foreign languages but no elites literate in the national vernacular. A common written language was deemed essential for a modern bureaucracy and an educational system. Over the ten-year trusteeship period, and in the first nine years of independence, these questions were discussed in many forums—the national assembly, the territorial councils, the government and independent press, indigenous commissions, and commissions of foreign experts. Despite a nineteen-year period of relatively free speech and free assembly, the Somali values of "compromise and tolerance" which President Aadan extolled, along with the institutional democratic forms transferred from Italy and Great Britain, seemed inadequate to deal with these critical questions. The Somali people therefore suffered the consequences of a nondecision, as Arabic, Italian, and English were all considered official languages of the new republic, while the Somali language itself remained unwritten. Why did Somalia, having perhaps the most propitious language situation for administrative efficiency in all of Africa (with at least 95 percent of its citizens understanding the same indigenous language), fail to take advantage of it?

The general explanation for the choice of a set of foreign languages as the official ones was that the Somali people were unable to agree on a script for their language. It was not that Somali had never been reduced to written form, but rather that a number of powerful individuals and groups were each advocating different scripts and vociferously opposing the scripts that were not theirs. Any attempt by one group or individual to write Somali engendered strong opposition. The different groups often divided on clan lines, and so it was a controversy that went to the very center of the Somali political universe. Somalia's democratic institutions were unable to handle effectively an issue of such importance where compromises did not seem possible.

Toward a Written Somali

The first attempt to foster literacy amongst Somalis was by Sheekh Yuusuf bin Axmed al-Kawneyn, who came to Africa's Horn in the thirteenth century from Arabia and devised a Somali nomenclature for the Arabic vowels in order to teach the Qur'an to Somali youth. In teaching Somalis the intricacies of the Arabic vowel point system, known as the *harakāt*, Sheekh Yuusuf needed to distinguish Arabic from Somali sounds. In so doing, he was the first person to study Somali phonology in a scholarly way. Variations of Sheekh Yuusuf's script flourished in Somalia and became known as "wadaad's writing," a style of writing Arabic that became widely used throughout Ethiopia and the Horn. It was used by merchants and by others for the writing of letters. Sheekh Yuusuf's attempt to bring about mass literacy in Arabic amongst the Somalis planted the seeds for a written Somali.[2]

Other attempts were made centuries later to adapt the Arabic script for the Somali language. The problem is that the Arabic language and script are vowel-poor, while the Somali language is vowel-rich, and that in Arabic, vowels can often be omitted without loss of meaning, whereas in Somali, vowels are critically important for meaning. Nonetheless, in 1887 Captain J. S. King of the Indian Army attempted, in two articles in the *Indian Antiquary*, to salvage the Arabic script for Somali by mixing it with Hindustani, thereby capturing the nuances of the Somali phonetic system.[3] In 1919 Sheekh Uways ibn Maxamad al-Baraawi applied the Bravenese Arabic script to the Somali language. The Chi Miini language of Brava is a Swahili dialect, and Swahili had both a standard Latin as well as a standard Arabic script. Sheekh Uways published *qasidas*, poems in praise of the Prophet, in Somali with his revised Arabic script. Finally, in 1938 Sheekh Maxamad Cabdi Makaahiil, a member of the Isxaaq clan in northern Somalia, disregarded the adaptations of "wadaad's writing" and published a book, *The Institution of Modern Correspondence in the Somali Language*, using the standard Arabic script. But ambiguities abounded in King's, Sheekh Uways's, and Sheekh Maxamad's attempts, due to weaknesses in their vowel systems.

In 1954, Muuse X. I. Galaal, soon to be one of the chief protagonists for the Latin script but at the time doing research at the School of Oriental and African Studies in London, published some Somali poems and proverbs in the *Islamic Quarterly* in a radically altered version of Arabic script.[4] This script was quite accurate, with few ambiguities resulting. But it was sufficiently different from Qur'anic Arabic for the wadaads to ignore it, and sufficiently close to Arabic for the nationalists to reject it.

The young Somali nationalists in the twentieth century felt it of utmost importance to have a national script, but their nationalism was decidedly non-Arab. In order to assert their independence, many felt that the Somali language, unique in the world, ought to have a unique script. They seized upon the script written in about 1920 by Cismaan Yuusuf, a Majeerteen Daarood. It had been recorded that Cisman, while writing letters to his family in Somali with the unsuitable Arabic script, said to himself: you are Somali, you speak Somali, why don't you have Somali letters?[5] He then developed his own script, which bore little resemblance either to Arabic or to Latin, and began to teach it.

The Majeerteen people are centrally situated in the Horn and have had considerable influence in Somali nationalist politics. Being Daarood, the most geographically dispersed clan family, the Majeerteen had great opportunities for leadership. They were influential and numerous in the early organization of the Somali Youth League and got the party in its original party platform officially to accept Cismaaniya, the script of Cismaan Yuusuf, as the national script for Somalia.

Other indigenous scripts developed independently of Cismaaniya. In 1933 Sheekh Cabduraxmaan Sheekh Nuur of the Gudabiirsi clan devised another orthography. Sheekh Cabduraxmaan was a teacher of religion in British Somaliland, followed his father's footsteps as qadi (judge) of Borama, and eventually became the qadi for the whole northern region of British Somaliland. His script, although highly accurate phonetically, has "languished in obscurity," probably because the Gudabiirsi are a small clan, somewhat outside the main clan structure of Somali society. They were widely respected for their educational achievement, however, and the script had some currency around Borama. Sheekh Cabduraxmaan had few illusions, and in his small publication using the script he explained, "I publish it here with no intention of attempting to contribute to the already abundant confusion in the choice of a standard orthography for Somali."[6]

In 1952, Xuseen Sheekh Axmed Kaddare, an Abgaal (Hawiya clan family) from near Muqdisho invented still another script. The technical commissions that evaluated scripts were in general agreement that the Kaddare script was the most accurate indigenous script for the Somali language. By 1966, a UNESCO commission had evaluated no less than ten "unique" Somali national scripts.

Concurrent with the development of the Arabic script for Somali and with the numerous attempts to devise a national script, was the slow and steady development of Latin-based orthographies for Somali. Missionaries were the earliest pioneers. In 1897 the Reverend Evangeliste de Larajasse and the Venerable Cyprien de Sampont wrote a *Practical Grammar of the Somali Language*. In their preface they announced, with a touch of irony: "The great desire, not to say the will, of the Propaganda of Rome being that Roman characters should be used for all classical works which Missionaries publish on the languages of the peoples they are sent to, we therefore, for writing Somali phonetically, employ ... the Roman characters with their Latin pronunciation."[7]

Somali tradition has it that one of the young boys at the French Catholic mission once ran across Maxamad Cabdille Xasan; when asked his identity, the boy replied, *"reer fadda,"* "the clan of the Fathers." This incident is said to have sparked the Sayid to his wars against the anti-Muslim Europeans. Whether true or apocryphal, it was in the wars against the Sayid that the Latin script developed further for use in the Somali language. J. W. C. Kirk, while serving with the Somali troops in 1902-4 against the Dervishes, attempted to learn and record the Somali language in his spare time. He wrote *A Grammar of the Somali Language with Examples of Prose and Verse and an Account of the Yibir and Midgan Dialects* in 1905.[8] He used an apostrophe for the Arabic ayn (voiced pharyngeal fricative), *hh* for the unvoiced pharyngeal fricative, and *gh* for the uvular plosive. Although this worked fairly satisfactorily, Kirk made no distinction between long and short vowels, a distinction of vast semantic consequence for the language, and his texts were rife with ambiguities.

In 1938 the British attempted to introduce a written Somali with the

Latin script in one of their primary schools in Burco. The attempt led to demonstrations in which three Somalis were killed. The wadaads saw the British action in much the same light as Maxamad Cabdille saw the Roman Catholic efforts, and the plans were dropped. In the south, despite the fact that most of the indigenous scripts were from clans in Italian Somalia, the wadaads were less influential, and the Latin script achieved moderate currency. By 1955, in a Muqdisho conference concerned with a Somali script, a permanent committee was formed, and called itself *Kulanka Afka Somaliyed* (The Somali Language Meeting). This use of the Latin script evoked no public outrage.

Italian scholars such as Enrico Cerulli, Martino Moreno, and Mario Maino had published Somali extensively in the Latin alphabet (and other alphabets as well, notably Cismaaniya). In 1956 Muuse X. I. Galaal and B. W. Andrzejewski published *Hikmad Soomaali (Somali Wisdom)*[9] using the Latin script. But in the case of the Italian and British scholars, use of the Latin script for the Somali language was developing in Europe rather than in Somalia. Only occasionally, as when R. C. Abraham's forthcoming Somali-English dictionary,[10] to be published in Great Britain, was announced in Somalia, did the Somali public react to Western scholarship. Publication was long delayed because of Somali negative reactions to the use of the Latin script.

At the time of Somali independence and the unification of British Somaliland and Italian Somalia into the Somali Republic in 1960, no unified script had been agreed upon. With northern civil servants, literate only in English, moving to the new capital city, Muqdisho, only chaos could result. Knowledge of only one of the three official languages was required for recruitment to the civil service. Since Italian bureaucratic procedures requiring many officials to agree and sign the same document were carried over into the Somali Republic, administrative inaction resulted. Civil servants were reluctant to sign even the most routine circulars when they could not read the language. The government needed to hire (foreign) translators at very high salaries in every branch of the civil service. In a country as poor as Somalia, this was a great hardship. The choice of any one of the nonindigenous languages as the language of the civil service would have brought strong objections from those literate in the other two languages.

The way out of this linguistic chaos would have been to agree on a script for the language they all shared. But this obvious solution began to seem unreachable. Instead of agreeing on a script, the Somali government quietly, by administrative decree, accepted English as the medium of instruction for the intermediate and secondary levels throughout the republic, with the intention of instituting English instruction one year at a time in the southern (Italian-language) schools. Eventually, or so it was believed by the minister of education, English would become the sole language of the Somali bureaucracy. This decision for the educational system seemed to be easier for the young government than agreeing on a script for the Somali language.

Evaluation of Three Scripts

In order to understand the difficulty of choosing a suitable script, we shall examine three of the competing scripts—Cismaaniya, a modified Latin, and a modified Arabic (see figure 1, p. 2) —using technical, political, and religious criteria.

Cismaaniya

Competent linguists have considered the Cismaaniya alphabet to be technically sound. Martino Moreno, in his book of Somali grammar and texts, *Il Somalo Della Somalia*, claims that Cismaaniya is "an excellent alphabet, because it is phonetic, with accurate distinctions of all the sounds—consonants and vowels, both long and short."[11] Both he and Professor Mario Maino have presented texts in the Cismaaniya script written by Yaasiin Cismaan, son of the inventor of the script. B. W. Andrzejewski, British linguist and today the foremost Western scholar on the Somali language, agrees that the Cismaaniya script is accurate.[12] Furthermore, adherents of the Cismaaniya script were able to procure typewriters that could reproduce Cismaaniya.

The 1966 UNESCO commission, however, noted that many of the signs bore a close resemblance to each other, which would be a great source of confusion if the script were nationally diffused. The costs of originality, the scholars argued, involve seriously reducing the number of easy to distinguish yet easy to form signs. Second, the scholars found that some letters were written from right to left and others from left to right. This, they felt, would make the development of a cursive system much more difficult. They were of the opinion that a cursive system is necessary for educational purposes, because students need to write fast. A third technical consideration, related to the first two, was the educational burden of having to learn three different scripts. Religious instruction involved the Arabic script; any involvement in the world culture, scientific or political, involved knowing a Western language and therefore the Latin script. It is clear that the educational costs of having to learn yet a third script would be high.

The Cismaaniya script had one great advantage politically. It was a truly indigenous script, and it emerged at a time when Somali national consciousness was beginning to crystallize. I. M. Lewis believes that the Cismaaniya script served as a catalyst, for it was "associated with perhaps the most prized of all things in the Somali national heritage—the Somali language."[13] Xersi Magan Ciise, one of the leading advocates of the script, has underscored this point. As a student in America, where he received a bachelor's degree in linguistics at Columbia University, he visited a secondary school accompanied by other foreign students. The teacher asked them all to write "good morning" in their native tongue on the board. The Arab, Indian, Japanese, and Somali visitors all used their "national" scripts. The Ugandan student, who had to use the Latin script, "was so humiliated and felt inferior to the rest of us."[14] In a time of developing national awareness, many borrowed institutions seem to become a source of humiliation. The Cismaaniya script helped some Somalis overcome that humiliation and reinforced their feelings that Somalis are indeed unique, and are a separate "nation."

The main political problem that the Cismaaniya script faced, ironically, was that it really was not a national script. Like nearly all political issues in Africa's Horn, the script became enmeshed in clan politics. Nearly all the advocates of the Cismaaniya script were reer Cismaan Maxamuud (Majeerteen; Daarood), and many of the young nationalists who were of different clans resented the tactics of the more ardent proselytizers of Cismaaniya. If Cismaaniya was supposed to make Somalis feel superior to foreigners, it was asked, won't it then make Cismaan's clan feel superior to other clans?[15] This feeling was one of the reasons, as we shall see later, that the Somali Youth League withdrew its support of Cismaaniya in favor of a "national script."[16] Nevertheless, the Cismaaniya script had wide political support among the early nationalists, especially when it was perceived as a "Daarood" script rather than just a "Majeerteen" or a "Cismaan Maxamuud" script, for the Daarood are a large clan family, spanning former British and Italian colonies, the Ethiopian Ogaadeen, and Kenya's Northeastern Province. They would have been a weak minority in either an independent British Somaliland or an independent Italian Somalia, but they saw themselves as a strong force in a united Greater Somalia. They were therefore the only clan family with a real stake in pan-Somalism. Because Somali national consciousness that overrode colonial boundaries was initially a Daarood phenomenon, the development of a national script was of greatest interest to the Daarood clan family. And so the Cismaaniya script was used as an ideological tool in fostering national consciousness.

The basic popularity of the Cismaaniya script is difficult to ascertain. The only public opinion data available are ambiguous. A poll of civil servants and students in Muqdisho gave only 17 percent support to Cismaaniya; and another poll of residents of Muqdisho gave Cismaaniya only 9 percent support. Yet both of these polls reached the literate elite, people who were well aware of the technical difficulties of instituting a third script, and neither accurately factors out "popularity" from "feasibility." In the only attempt to get at "mass" opinion, Xuseen Adam, who ran the surveys, went to the village of Afgoy. Xuseen found that the Cismaaniya script was almost completely unknown. After one man asked, "Cismaaniya? What is that, a new religion?" he decided to give respondents a choice between Arabic, Latin, and "a Somali script." A plurality (45.5 percent) chose "a Somali script."[17] This group was obviously unaware of technical factors, as demonstrated by the very meager support for the Latin script. The fact, however, that few people in Afgoy had ever heard of Cismaaniya tells us little about its diffusion, for Afgoy is a town where the dialect is af-Rahanwiin, and it would have been unusual if the residents there were familiar with literary developments in the Somali language.

On the religious level, the Cismaaniya script was relatively neutral. Many of the wadaads felt that it would weaken the attachment of the Somali people to Islam, but they reserved their energies to combat the Latin script—a much more serious danger, they thought. Adherents of Cismaaniya were very careful in their proselytization to give due regard to Islam and to make it clear that Arabic would remain the language of the Qur'an. The national script would be used for secular purposes only.[18]

Latin

From a phonetic point of view, the Latin script is easily the best suited to express Somali. Although the Somali vowel system is complicated, the Latin characters can handle it moderately well. The ten basic vowel sounds can be handled by the five Latin vowels standing alone or doubled. The only major problem concerns the "front" or "back" quality of each of the ten vowels, forming two "harmonic groups."[19] The Latin alphabet cannot account for these differences without resorting to diacritics, and there are strong technical reasons against the use of diacritics. Although some significant ambiguities can result from ignoring this distinction, most linguists are of the opinion that such ambiguities would nearly always be resolved by context.

A number of linguists have been able to work successfully with variants of the Latin script, and a large literature has developed in Somali with the Latin script.[20] The script considered best by the two linguistic commissions was the one designed by Shire Axmed Jaamac. It involved no new signs and no diacritical marks, using the letter *c* for the Arabic ayn (voiced pharyngal fricative), *x* for the unvoiced pharyngeal fricative, and *q* for the uvular plosive. Somali names in this text have been written in a modified form of Shire's script. That no diacritics were needed was an advantage, not only because of the historical tendency for diacritical marks to be eliminated in print, but also because of the reduced costs of printing and typewriting.

In both the political and the religious arenas, however, the Latin script faced much opposition. Riots would often break out when its ugly letters appeared in public. The British met with rioting when they employed the Latin script in Burco. And in 1957, when Cabdillaahi Ciise, prime minister of the internally self-governing Italian Somalia, put out a page in the local newspaper in Somali using the Latin script (*Wargeyska Somaliyed*, "The Somali Messenger"), intense public pressure forced him to abandon the attempt after two issues.[21] The Latin script was considered "foreign" and therefore, to many Somalis, unworthy of the Somali language. Moreover, it was the script of the colonialists. As one Somali intellectual, Ibraahiim Xaashi, writing (in Arabic), put it, "Somalia came in contact with the Latin script as a result of colonialism. We were compelled to learn it. Now that we are free, we must get rid of all colonial roots—and Latin would just remind us of the dark deeds of the colonialists."[22] Furthermore, adoption of the script would mean, at least according to Muuse Galaal (in 1954), unequal linguistic development throughout Somalia, favoring the cities over the bush, and the secular over the religious. The Latin script, he said, "is likely to create an exclusive class of literate men, in fact a ruling minority, and this might in the long run bring a great deal of unhappiness to Somaliland."[23]

The Latin script did muster some political support, nonetheless. Thirteen years after his *Islamic Quarterly* article favoring the Arabic script for Somali, Muuse Galaal became an ardent supporter of the Latin script. In a panel discussion at the Somali Institute of Public Administration, he argued that adoption of the Latin script was tantamount to an identification with "progress," and that since Latin was the script of the most modern countries, using it for Somali would put Somalia in the camp of the "modern" world.[24] Muuse was probably overstating his case for effect. Still, the choice of the Latin script would enable the great majority of civil servants to be able to communicate with each other in writing, with little retraining needed. As former Prime Minister Cabdirisaaq Xaaji Xuseen said: "We have over 60,000 people in our schools, administration and the armed forces. These people could read and write their language immediately should we adopt the Latin script with which they are already so familiar."[25] The Latin script seemed to enjoy firm support among the administrative elite. In Xuseen's opinion survey of 106 Somali civil servants in Muqdisho, 78 percent favored the Latin script when given an open choice for a script for the Somali language.[26] In the general survey of the capital city, with a bias toward the professional elite, 55 percent of the 1,486 respondents (1 percent of Muqdisho's population) claimed to favor Latin.

Politically, then, I discern a mixed record for the Latin script. The script engendered hostile feelings from some segments of the nonliterate population, was indeed associated with the colonial experience, and would enhance the emerging linguistic inequalities of Somali society. Nonetheless, those people who were literate, and who were deriving some political and economic benefit from their knowledge of a Western language, gave the Latin script their (latent) support.

Because the Latin script was closely associated with Christianity, the religious elements of the Somali community were unyielding in their attempts to obstruct its use. They developed a powerful slogan, a play on words, which was used again and again: *Laatiin waa Laa Diin*, "Latin is without God." Most wadaads who fought against the Latin script feared that its use would gradually erode religious values among young Somalis. One supporter of the Arabic script put the issue this way:

> I have changed my mind about two or three times on this issue. The more I have read and thought about the subject, the more I have encountered newer complexities and dimensions. While writing a thesis for the University of London in 1948, I paid considerable attention to Islamic societies—Turkish, Iranian, Afghanistan and Pakistan. When I look at Turkey and Pakistan, I would say that Pakistan is more religious than Turkey. This is partly because Pakistan uses Arabic characters to write Urdu while Turkey opted for Latin at the rise to power of Kemal Ataturk. Somalis today do not take their religion half as seriously as the Pakistanis. What would happen to us twenty years from now if we were to use Roman characters?[27]

In an impressive attempt to defuse the religious issue, the UNESCO team of linguists, in their 1966 report, attempted to demonstrate common derivation of the Latin and Arabic script from the North Semitic script. While the Latin script came from the Phoenician branch of the North Semitic script, they wrote, the Arabic script is derived from the Aramaic branch. The linguists presented a historical table of script evolution to give substance to their claim. But this report was never circulated publicly, and intensely negative feeling toward the Latin script in the religious community did not subside.

Arabic

The Arabic script is known to nearly all Somalis through the training they have received in the Qur'an. Whatever the script decision in regard to the Somali language, the Arabic script would still be taught to Somali youth, for no group in Somalia has any intention of translating the Qur'an. The Arabic script, too, can be adapted to the phonetic needs of the Somali language. However, the extensive use of diacritical marks and other changes in the script in order to adapt it makes it difficult to use even for those who know the Arabic alphabet well. And the existing office machinery for the Arabic language is practically useless for the adapted Arabic script. At the very least, a number of dead keys would have to be installed in typewriters. A technical adviser to the linguistic commission formed in January, 1971—a scholar who had done all his research in the Arabic language and was preparing translations of the new Somali script into the Arabic language—told me that "although I have already published philosophical treatises in Arabic and I know the language quite well, I could hardly read Somali when it was in the Arabic script. It would have taken me years to read Somali in the Arabic script with any fluency. And yet, even though my English is far worse than my Arabic, it took me only weeks to read Somali fluently in the Latin script."[28] The 1966 UNESCO linguistic commission expressed similar misgivings. They feared, furthermore, that the extensive system of Arabic diacritics usually ignored when Arabic is written, might eventually be left out for Somali, leading to "orthographic chaos."[29]

The Arabic script is even regarded as technically unsuitable for the Arabic language itself. A number of Somali intellectuals who had studied in the Arab world were well aware of the ferment within the intellectual community in the Arab world concerning their own script. One leading advocate of the Latin script argued that it would indeed be ironic if Somalia invested heavily in the Arabic script only to see the Arab world adopt the Latin script. While it is held by certain Islamic theologians that the Arabic script is a "divine gift," Egyptian scholars such as 'Abd al-'Aziz Fahmi have deplored the need for the diacritics and the lack of a permanent vowel system. Fahmi has gone as far as to recommend the use of the Latin script, which "would eliminate the greatest obstacle in learning the language."[30] One Western scholar has suggested that the built-in ambiguities of the Arabic script, and the fear of bringing about any changes in it, have seriously impeded scientific advance.[31]

Politically, the Arabic script fared much better. First of all, acceptance of it, as opposed to the Latin or even the Cismaaniya scripts, would have been compatible with Somali feelings about equality. Knowledge of the Arabic script spanned city and bush, north and south. No region, no clan, and no economic group could claim special privilege if the Arabic script were accepted.[32] Unlike Cismaaniya, the Arabic script was not associated with any particular clan; and unlike Latin, it was not directly associated with the colonial experience. Since knowledge of the script is so widespread in Somalia, it has been reasoned that mass literacy would be a realistic goal in Somalia if the Arabic script were chosen.

A second political factor favoring Arabic is that it would tend to reinforce economic contacts with the Middle East and reduce such contacts with Europe. Many of the most ardent supporters of the Arabic script, people such as Xaaji Yuusuf Cigaal, Xaaji Diiriye, and Xaaji Cabduraxmaan Garyare, were wealthy merchants engaged in the import-export business with the Arab world. These men formed the "Xaaji group" in the ruling Somali Youth League, putting constant pressure on the party to adopt the Arab script.[33] The feeling that a country trades with those countries with which it can "communicate" is not at all unsophisticated, nor was the feeling that acceptance of the Arabic script for Somali would enhance communication with the Arab world and reduce it with Europe. Related to this are considerations of Somalia's international position. Many Somalis see Ethiopia as a natural enemy, not only because it includes much land which rightfully, in terms of self-determination, belongs to Somalia, but because of a "natural" enmity between a Christian and an Islamic state. It has been argued that Somalia will have to rely on the Arab world for support in any future conflict with Ethiopia; and that any political gesture by Somalia to show solidarity with the Arab world would ultimately be beneficial.[34]

A third political factor favoring the Arabic script was that Maxamad Cabdille Xasan, the Somali nationalist hero, not only wrote poems in Arabic but used the script for his Somali poetry. There is reason to believe that Maxamad was less a "Somali" nationalist than he was a "Saalixiya" or an "Islamic" nationalist. He rarely called himself a Somali, and when he did use the term, it was often in a pejorative manner. If a new nationalist identity were created based on "Islamic" rather than "Somali" values, then the Arabic script would clearly have greater nationalist appeal.

The Arabic script faced one enormous political liability. As we saw in chapter 3, whatever the origins of the Somali people and whatever the origins of the Somali nationalist movement, most Somalis have a great antipathy for Arabs. Much of the nationalist activity in the postwar era was directed at freeing the Somali "nation" from any other definition than "Somali." To have accepted the Arabic script would have been, for many Somalis, to give up their unique identity. In Xuseen Adam's survey of two hundred Somali civil servants and students (with only seven of the ninety-six students coming from the Arab school system), 59 percent supported Latin and only 20 percent Arabic. In the statistical survey of Muqdisho, 55 percent supported Latin and only 33 percent Arabic. And in Xuseen's more random survey in the less cosmopolitan town of Afgoy, only 34 percent favored Arabic.[35] Though not a completely reliable test of public opinion, these data do not support the view that the "masses" overwhelmingly favored the Arabic script. At the best, the Arabic script has been politically neutral in Somalia.

In the religious field, the story is different. If some religious men thought that a written Somali language, even if written in Arabic, would reduce interest in the Sharī'a, the body of sacred Islamic law, and would "defile the alphabet of the Holy Qur'an,"[36] the Arabic alphabet was clearly the choice of those who did want to see the Somali language written, and who were most concerned about the impact of literacy on religion. The technical problems put the religious criteria severely to the test, however. Since the script would require transmogrification in order to suit the needs of the Somali language, and since the Arabic script had been deemed sacred and eternal, religious supporters of the Arabic script often found themselves in the contradictory position of advocating an Arabic script for Somali, while assailing every attempt to make the Arabic script consonant with the Somali language as a desecration of the Arabic script. It was this problem, I believe, that forced most supporters of the Arabic script into the position of supporting Arabic as the national language. And in the debate over the script, most supporters of Arabic chose to condemn the Latin script as godless (*Laa Diin*) rather than to champion the Arabic script.

The National Debate

In the substantive debate in Somalia concerning a national script, different values seemed to suggest different choices. Each script was preferable on one of the three criteria. Technically, Latin was the best choice. From a political point of view, Cismaaniya had the advantage. From a religious standpoint, the Arabic script was optimal. Table 3 may be used as a handy reference for my ensuing discussion of the *form* of the nineteen-year national debate.

Table 3   Evaluation of Three Scripts

Scripts:	Criteria		
	Religious	Technical	Political
Cismaniya	0	0	+
Latin	−	+	0
Arabic	+	−	0

+ Benefits outweigh costs
− Costs outweigh benefits
0 Costs and benefits balance

The Trusteeship
Period (1950-60)

The return to Somalia by the Italians after the Second World War, this time with Somalia as a United Nations trust territory, marked a new era in Somali politics. The Italian trust administration was required to "foster the development of free political institutions and promote the development of the inhabitants of the territory toward independence." To this end the inhabitants of the territory were to be given "a progressively increasing participation in the various organs of Government" and to be guaranteed "complete freedom of speech, of the press, of assembly and of petition, without distinction as to race, sex, language, political opinion or religion, subject only to the requirements of public order."[37] For the first time in Somalia's history, there would be a political center to which opinions could be freely expressed.

Despite some contentions that the Italian fiduciary administration was favoring Arabic and giving Somalis "the erroneous impression that our language is not adaptable for use in modern expressions,"[38] the Italians were by and large open to Somali opinion on the language issue. As early as 1949 an anonymous article appeared in *Nuovo Giornale*, "Il problema della lingua somala," in which the author, a high Italian official, claimed that the government program was essentially to allow Somalis themselves to study the issue and decide it for themselves.[39] The Italians did have a policy of calling congresses to discuss the issue with Somali leaders. It should be noted, however, that the Italian administration was willing to put together an education curriculum teaching any language in any script that the Somali elite requested, so long as it was secondary to Italian. The Italian administration put this question before the Territorial Council: "What ought to be, besides Italian, the official language, which languages, besides Italian, ought to be learned in school, and in which languages ought teaching be imparted?"[40] Whatever their predilections, the Italians had to tolerate free speech. And because the educational system and civil service which would take Somalia into independence in ten years were beginning to be formed, the issue engendered much heated discussion.

Most of the debate occurred within the Somali Youth Club (later called League), which formed in 1943. The fourth point in its program was "to develop the Somali language and to assist in putting into use among Somalis the 'Cismaaniya Somali script.'"[41] It was Yaasiin Cismaan Yuusuf Keenadiid, the son of the inventor of the Cismaaniya script, who was the guiding light behind the Somali Youth League language policy in those years. Yaasiin was born in 1919 in Obiya, where he went to Qur'anic school. He moved to Muqdisho when he was fifteen and studied in both Arabic and Italian schools. During the British military occupation he learned English as well. It was in this period that Yaasiin became active in the propagation of his father's script, helping to found the Society for the Somali Language and Literature. In 1949 Yaasiin set down the purposes of his organization, which was conceived as a cultural adjunct to the Somali Youth League:

1. To search out and collect books which deal with the Somali language, to study and to publish them....
2. To study the improvement of the Somali script.
3. To use Somali in all social connections....
6. To translate into the Somali Language the best foreign books....
9. To use Somali as a cultural language for teaching.
10. To acquire the material necessary for the publication of books written in Somali characters.[42]

But, unfortunately for Yaasiin, the movement for Cismaaniya was beginning to be challenged. Power in the SYL was slowly diffusing, and the Daarood clan family, which could not by itself muster a majority in the trusteeship, began to lose its hold on the SYL. In May 1949, Xaaji Maxamad Xuseen, a member of reer Xamar—a small group from Muqdisho which was outside the main clan structure of the Somalis and was closely related to the Arabs—became president of the SYL; and Cabdillaahi Ciise, a Hawiya, became secretary-general. Neither of these two leaders had any commitment whatsoever to the Cismaaniya script, and they were to bring substantial changes into the SYL.

Xaaji Maxamad Xuseen, though in office only for three years, had a profound influence on Somali language politics, as his thinking and beliefs were closely tied to the Arab world. Eventually he would be going to Cairo, where he would spread anti-Western propaganda on Radio Cairo. His influence in the SYL explains the fact that by 1950 the party was no longer in favor of Somali as the national language with Cismaaniya as its script. In April 1950 the SYL wrote an official memorandum to the Italian administrator Fornari, recommending that Arabic be the "international language" of Somalia. The memorandum claimed (1) that the SYL secretary had traveled through the country, could get no agreement concerning a standard Somali dialect, and found no objection to a "uniform" Arabic which would be understood throughout the Islamic world; (2) that the Arabic language is rich in vocabulary, whereas "it is extremely difficult to express oneself sufficiently well in the Somali language"; (3) that the Arabic language is vital and growing, whereas "it is difficult, if not impossible for the Somalis to make their language better at this time"; (4) that Arabic would enable the Somalis to speak a world language, and thus enable them to "embark on an ocean of culture which has no limits"; (5) that the Arabic language is already a lingua franca in Somalia; and (6) that the Arabic language will facilitate the cultural and political alliance of Somalia with our brother Muslims who all believe "in ALLAH, in HIS SACRED PROPHET, MOHAMMED, and in the SACRED QUR'AN."[43]

Xaaji Maxamad and Yaasiin Cismaan brought their disagreements into the open in a series of letters to the *Corriere della Somalia*. Yaasiin attempted to get translators at official gatherings where Arabic was to be spoken; and Xaaji responded by insisting that Arabic was not a foreign language, and then accused Yaasiin of agreeing too often with his "European friends."[44] In his reply, Yaasiin agreed that Arabic was the language of their religion, but insisted that it was still a foreign language. The Central Steering Committee of the SYL then saw fit to respond to Yaasiin with this public statement: "The Arabic language is the official language of the Somali Youth League and of all the population; the Arabic language is that which God has given to these Somali people which is an integral part of the Islamic world."[45] And in 1951, when the Italians brought the issue to the Territorial Council, there was unanimous agreement that both Italian and Arabic should be the official languages of Somalia. The call for the immediate writing of Somali in Cismaaniya was no longer sounded. The agreement merely said that all efforts should be made to put the Somali language in "its rightful place."[46]

In this period of Somali national development, the organizational forces of the Islamic community were strong. Since the Egyptian government had an interest in maintaining the Arabic language in Somalia, the Egyptian member of the United Nations Consulting

Advisors demurred when his team encouraged the development of the Somali language. He thought that time would be wasted in substituting "a new language."[47] The Muslim League was by that time active in Somalia, and it too advocated the development of Arabic as the official language. Other organizations, such as the Somalia Conference and the Xaaji Group, were also actively advocating Arabic as the national language.

In 1952, Xaaji Maxamad Xuseen went off to Cairo, and the Hawiya wing of the SYL became more powerful. In the 1956 elections, the last to be held under direct Italian supervision, the SYL maintained its dominance, and the Italian administrator appointed Cabdillaahi Ciise as the first prime minister of an all-Somali government. This signalled another change in SYL's character, for Cabdillaahi and the then SYL president, Aaden Cabdulle Cismaan, were both on good terms with the Italian administration.[48] In a party statute of 1957, it was agreed that while Arabic should have predominance in teaching, there should be "Somali characters" in writing Somali. The statement forbade any party member from writing the Somali language with foreign characters,[49] which demonstrated some change from Xaaji Maxamad era but did not accurately reflect the thinking of the SYL leaders. For it was in 1957 that Prime Minister Cabdillaahi attempted, unsuccessfully, to include in the government newspapers a regular weekly page of Somali using the Latin script.

The major debate throughout the trusteeship years was between those who favored the Somali *script* and those who favored the Arabic *language*. Yaasiin carried the flag for Cismaaniya both in the early 1950s (when the debate was inaugurated by the Italian administration) and after 1956, during the heated election campaign. In both periods he maintained his usual scholarly manner. In one newspaper article[50] he distinguished Somalia from most other new states in that the Somalis do share a language. He then went on to compare the Somali experience with the historical experiences of the English, the French, and the Italians in order to demonstrate that the national vernacular, however vulgar it appears to the intellectual elites, seems to prevail. Third, he compared Somalia with other Islamic countries such as Pakistan and Iran in order to demonstrate the feasibility of having a language of religion concurrent with a national language. Finally, he argued that to teach children a foreign language first means to develop in them an "unnecessary affection for that language and culture, their heroes, their history." He pointed out that those who learn Italian first see the Somali language as "brusque and unrefined"; those who learn Arabic first see Somali as "unholy and sinful"; and those who learn English first see Somali as "poor and inferior."[51] Yaasiin was then making a plea for the Somali language, for he felt at the time that the main threat came from those who wanted Arabic or Italian as the national language.

By 1956, Yaasiin was in Italy studying philosophy, philology, literature, and linguistics. Nonetheless, he was still participating in the national debate. In another of his erudite tracts, Yaasiin began to argue that Language and culture are inseparable: "Without language, community would not be realized ... [it] is a great force necessary for human community." He related this to Somalia where he felt "the leaders of the Somali people" were to blame. "Almost all the difficulties and obstacles which hinder the rapid course of progress in all fields," he wrote, "derive exclusively from the negligence of this sacrosanct duty toward their mother tongue. It is logical that a nation ought to find itself in an embarassing situation when it neglects such a fundamental duty."[52] Yaasiin then related what he saw to be Somali backwardness in the trades, in agriculture, in livestock breeding, in fishing, in weaving, in leatherwork, and in carpentry, and blamed it all on "ignorance," on the inability to read, and on the inability to learn new ways of doing things. He went on to criticize his main opponents, the wadaads:

> Why ... have I never found a Somali "wadaad," author of a book of a few pages, on any argument of natural religion? The answer is simple. They cannot write such a work either in Italian or in Arabic, while they consider their mother tongue disgraceful and impure.... Then if the wadaads are in such a condition, how will the masses be made to learn the most elementary notions of religion.... They do not know the spirit of Islam, its history, its civilization, its prayers and its philosophy.[53]

A considerable number of letters and articles appeared in the Italian language newspapers directly confronting Yaasiin, and in support of the Arabic language. The same points were made by many correspondents: (1) that nearly all Somalis know Arabic; (2) that it was already chosen by the Territorial Council, and it is now time to work for independence, and not to reverse the Territorial Council's decision; (3) that since there are a number of Somali dialects, each region would demand its dialect to be the national one, and agreement would never be reached; and (4) that there is no disagreement about standard Arabic.[54]

By the time of the 1956 election, however, most Somalis in the literate community were utterly frustrated by the whole debate. The overwhelming number of letters to the editor of the *Corriere della Somalia*—the recognized forum for political ideas—demanded that some script should be chosen for the Somali language. These letters were from people who thought any script would be better than having education and politics conducted in a foreign language, and they did not specify their preferences. One correspondent argued that Somalia would never be truly united until its inhabitants could agree on their national language. Another argued that "only with our language can we distinguish ourselves as Somalis from the rest of the African populations, and we can instruct our children and our wives and the masses only with the Somali language." He mourned the fact that students were learning the history and cultures of other peoples and neglecting their own, ensuring that "Somalia will be canceled from world history." Still another correspondent affirmed that "if a people does not know its own language it cannot have complete independence and cannot compare itself to the other civilized peoples," and warned, as did many supporters of Somali as the national language, that "the Somalis must not confound religion with the official language." One correspondent seemed to sum up the level of frustration of this sector: "The most urgent and necessary thing," he pleaded, "is to begin."[55] None of these correspondents mentioned his preference for a script; it was clearly implied that any script was better than indecision.

It was in the period right after the 1956 election that some voices recommending the use of the Latin script began to be heard. Although this support would grow, never again in the parliamentary years would it be politic to advocate the Latin script in public. In March 1957, Sheekh Maxamad Cumar Cabdi, a deputy in the Legislative Assembly, wrote to the *Corriere della Somalia* urging the adoption of the Latin script. He conceded that Arabic was a more beautiful language, but held that more Somalis knew Italian than Arabic, so that the Latin script was more widely known.[56] Another correspondent a few issues later also argued that Arabic was minimally known. A teacher, he thought that the Latin script, since its characters were universally known, easy to learn, and already available on office machinery, would be the best choice.[57]

In that period, Shire Jaamac Axmad made his first public statement in favor of the Latin script. Shire was born in 1936 in Wardheer, in the (Ethiopian) Ogaadeen province, of the Marreexaan (Daarood) clan. He had done exceptionally well in Qur'anic school there, and continued his Arabic education in Muqdisho when his father brought him there. From 1945 to 1951 he attended a teacher training course at a school organized by the British military administraion, and thereby learned English. With the return of the Italians, Shire switched his education back to Arabic, and eventually won a scholarship to study at Al-Azhar University in Cairo in 1955. While in Cairo he spent considerable time studying modern scholarship concerning the Arabic language, and especially the criticisms of the script. It was there, he reported, that he became convinced that Somalis would be making a grave error if they opted for the Arabic script.[58]

Shire returned to Somalia in 1957 amidst the lively debate concerning national language and national script. He was especially impressed with the page of Somali in the Latin script that appeared inside the *Corriere della Somalia*, and wrote a letter of appreciation. The tone of his argument was rational: "Our aversion to the West ought not to be directed to its culture since culture is a different thing from politics." He compared the Latin script to electricity, pointing out that Somalis do not deny themselves the advantages of electricity just because it comes from the West. He gave examples of non-Western societies that used the Latin script such as Turkey and Indonesia, and reiterated that scripts are creations of men, not of God, and that it is not a heresy to use the Latin script.[59]

There were a few adherents for Italian as the national language and for the Arabic script for use in the Somali language in this period. But most of the energy came from four groups: those who favored the Cismaaniya script, those who favored the Arabic language as the official language, those who favored the Latin script for Somali, and those who wanted Somali as the national language in any script. The result of all this activity was government inaction; the least costly way to act was to do nothing. In 1955 the Italian administration and the department of instruction of British Somaliland organized a conference in Muqdisho in an attempt to develop a unified Somali script that would make unification of the north and the south administratively possible. There was almost no follow-up, however. No national script was agreed upon; and students in the south continued to learn Italian while students in the north were learning English. The obvious problems that would be created by unification of the Somalilands were not being faced. The issues involved were too basic, for on the decision about script the very nature of the national identity would be determined. One script, or one language, had to be the official one, and no compromises seemed possible. Most participants in the debate were already impatient. Little did they know that the debate had just begun.

The Period of
Independence

Often in the trusteeship years, political spokesmen would argue for the status quo because any change would have delayed independence. Since language was a national issue, it should wait until Somalis alone could decide for themselves. On 1 July 1960 the independent former British Somaliland joined with Italian Somalia to become the independent Somali Republic. Even though foreign policy suddenly became the dominant political issue, as the problem of unredeemed Somalia took on new import once two of the five regions were free, the question of a national language and a national script remained salient. Unfortunately the politics of nondecision and no action continued as it had during the trusteeship years.

In the third month of independence, the National Assembly made a formal request that the government appoint a committee to undertake the investigation of the best means of reducing Somali to writing. In October, the minister of education, Cali Garaad Jaamac (Dhulbahante; Daarood, from the north) appointed the nine-man committee. Although Cali Garaad favored the Arabic script,[60] he chose the members of the committee on judicious criteria: knowledge of linguistics and the scripts, representation of the different Somali dialects; support by the various interest groups; and equal representation for advocates of each of the major scripts. Among committee members were Muuse X. I. Galaal, Yaasiin Cismaan Keenadiid, Ibraahiim Xashi Maxamuud, Shire Jaamac Axmed, and Xuseen Sheekh Axmed Kaddare. They were instructed to "investigate the best way of writing Somali, considering all the aspects of the language, with a special eye on the technical side, and submit a report to the Government by March, 1961."[61] The phrase "with a special eye on the technical side" suggested the choice of Latin. The committee chose to review nine scripts on seventeen criteria. Sixteen of the criteria were "technical" (Is it phonetic? Is it simple in its lettering? Have its letters any diacritics? Has it any sign which has more than one function? Has it any letters which are difficult to distinguish? Has it any printing machines available? Is it economical? Has it a good cursive value? etc.); one was "political" (Is it unique?); and none was religious. The committee was explicit about this overloading, claiming that "the political, the religious and the social aspects of the problem have been left for the Government, the Parliament and the public to decide."[62]

Three important members, including Yaasiin Cismaan and Ibraahiim Xashi, left the committee before it finished its work, highly critical of its mode of operation. They could see that, by the criteria explicit in their charge, the scripts they favored (Cismaaniya and Arabic) did not stand a chance. The final report was signed by only six members. Its conclusions, given the charge and the final membership, were no surprise:

> According to the answers shown against the queries set in the seventeen guiding principles the most advantageous script has made itself crystal clear. It is the form of Latin Script ... submitted by Shire

Jaamac Axmed and later on improved by the Committee.... In short, it is the script that offers the best prospects to us, as a growing nation, and as a Committee of men who not only know about their language but who understand the difference between their emotions and personal pride and their real needs, we recommend it for adoption as a matter of first choice and the Somali script devised by Xuseen Sheekh Axmed Kaddare as No. 2 on the list. This committee could not recommend any other Scripts.[63]

Cali Garaad received the report and promptly filed it, marked "confidential," in the archives of the ministry. It was never published, nor brought to the attention of the National Assembly. Rumors abounded concerning the work of the commission, but few seemed to have certain knowledge.

Shelving the issue as Cali had done did not obviate the need to take some action in regard to language. Most important, a unified educational system was a primary goal of the new republic. In November 1961, shortly after the minister of education received the committee's report, he issued a major educational policy statement which had as its "ultimate aim ... to raise the standard of living and achieve nationwide literacy" and sought "to promote only that kind of education which is based on our distinct Somali National character, racially and religiously." With that in mind, it could well have been a deep disappointment to the minister to make the following recommendations in regard to the language issue:

The major problem with which this Ministry is faced is the integration of the media of instruction in the whole Republic. At present both the educational systems and the methods and mediums of instruction of the South and of the North are very different.... It is absolutely imperative that both the educational systems and the medium of instruction should be unified immediately if we are to implement our development programmes effectively. We must choose now the language we shall adopt, and on that decision proceed to plan for the future.

After a careful study of the problems and the needs of the country, we propose that English should be gradually brought in as the common medium of instruction throughout the whole Republic. However, we propose that this transition should be done quite practicably and with the least possible hazard to the established order. At present English and Italian are introduced at the third year of the Elementary and gradually become the medium of instruction during the following years. Now all those pupils who are learning Italian will learn and finish their education in Italian. Beginning this year, however, Italian will not be taught in new third year elementary classes and English will be introduced instead.

> Those pupils who have already started studying Italian will be saved from the necessity of changing to a new language, while the beginners will commence their studies in English..According to plans, the Italian language will gradually recede down into the horizon and English will take over completely over a period of six to seven years. At the end of this transitional period English will be the medium of instruction in all our schools except the elementary in which Arabic will remain the main language.[64]

Interestingly, and significantly, this policy was quietly implemented by the Ministry of Education without being presented for debate in the National Assembly. The communities most affected by the policy were unaware of its implications for a few years (see next chapter). Most people's attention was on the question of national orthography.

The minister of education stated that the English-language policy was derived from the recommendations of the conference of UNESCO and the Economic Commission for Africa in Addis Ababa in May of 1961. However, a UNESCO team of educational scholars was only then preparing a report based on a fairly extensive study of Somalia's dual educational system. The report, distributed from Paris in August 1962, made clear that the dual language system was economically and socially wasteful, and it recommended that English be the language of international communication because it is much more widely known throughout the world than Italian. But the authors, from both a cultural and an economic point of view, argued that Somali should be the medium of instruction through at least the secondary school level. Culturally, they contended, it would be harmful for a student's creative development and for his understanding of his own milieu if he had to express himself in a foreign language. Economically, they argued that an educational system in which a foreign language was the medium of instruction would be overly reliant on expatriate teachers, which would be too expensive for any country, particularly one as poor as Somalia. Without studying the script issue, they implied that Latin should be the orthography.

This report was largely ignored in Somalia. Occasional pious utterances would emanate from the government, but the question of a national script, for all intents and purposes, became a dormant issue. In 1963, the new minister of education, Yuusuf Ismaaciil Samatar, speaking at the Somali Fair, said, "It is necessary that an early decision is taken about the script for the Somali language."[65] And in March 1964, Cabduuraxmaan Cabdishakuur, head of the adult education program, spoke at a literacy conference at Abidjan, Ivory Coast. He told the conferees, "It is realized that the launching of a world literacy campaign is an excellent opportunity for making a decision on the script and it is possible that the Somali government may decide this question after the general election of March 30, [since the] report of a special committee entrusted with the task of recommending a script has been before the government for some time."[66] But official statements on the script issue became rare. Government stagnation is partly explained by the stagnation within the ruling party, the Somali Youth League. The Cismaaniya script became a "clan" issue. With SYL in bitter internal debate, only the military and the police seemed immune from the politics of inaction. They began to train their recruits in Somali, using the Latin script.[67]

Despite the primary importance of international concerns, the language issue still evoked letters to the *Somali News*, the government (English) weekly newspaper.[68] In August 1962, during the historic visits of Jomo Kenyatta and Ronald Ngala to the Somali Republic, when the future of Kenya's Northern Frontier District was discussed with some candor and public awareness of the frontier issue was brought to new heights, a major "Opinion" article appeared in the *Somali News* by Maxamad F. Jaamac "Shiine," dealing with the technical difficulties of adapting the Arabic vowel system to Somali.[69] During the short 1963 war with Ethiopia, with an important election coming up, a letter by Xuseen Sheekh Maxamuud mourned the fact that the Somali language had been "pathetically forlorn" and suggested as a national motto: "He who is not proud of speaking Somali is not fit to live in Somalia."[70] When national attention was most concerned about the Ogaadeen Somalis who were clearly "pathetically forlorn" under an uncaring Ethiopian administration, it is of some significance that at that time the same feelings would be publicly expressed about the language.

As in the trusteeship period, most people who did write letters to the newspaper just wanted a decision, without specifying a script. One correspondent, H. Cismaan, discussing a UNESCO project in Niger where scripts were being developed for its five languages, added that since Somalia has only one such language it is a "national disgrace" that it cannot agree.[71] Another letter to the editor, this one by H. Cali Shiddo "Dighe," expressed similar sentiments: "Unless the mother tongue is taught in adult classes, our masses will continue to swim in an ocean of illiteracy which of course, breeds apathy, prejudice, ignorance, disease, poverty, tribalism, laziness, inferiority complex and all other social evils which hinder the progress of human society."[72] A *Somali News* editorial in 1965 urged a written Somali language as "a matter of vital importance," but no script was mentioned.[73] And in 1964 the minister of the interior, Maxamuud Cabdi Nuur, was reported to have said to an SYL meeting: "There can be no hope to fight down illiteracy until a Somali script is adopted.... A choice must be made."[74]

The 1966 Commission

After the 1964 elections, President Aaden Cabdulle Cismaan, with considerable parliamentary difficulty, was able to get Cabdirisaaq Xaaji Xuseen as his prime minister. Cabdirisaaq was an effective public speaker, and was most interested in using his energies to improve the Somali civil service. He spoke out forcefully against corruption in the bureaucracy and against the sinecures that most civil service jobs seemed to have become. In turning to these issues, he defused somewhat the irrendentist issue. And in turning to bureaucratic efficiency, he could not avoid the language issue. His goal of bureaucratic efficiency in part determined his biases on language.

> I can see how easy it is for those who do not have to take lecture notes, draft memos, type letters, write reports and so on—at least not every day in their lives—I can see how easy it is for them to advocate Cismaaniya or Arabic for chauvinistic or pseudo-religious reasons. But we have to be pragmatic. We have to look from the angle of the man who is forced to use the written language almost daily in his life. To such a man, a script is not like an ornament, like the Somali rugs we hang in our houses, for decoration.[75]

Not lost to most spectators of Somali politics was that Cabdirisaaq, although Daarood and Majeerteen, was of the reer Cumar Maxamuud, a subclan known for its long-term rivarly with the reer Cismaan Maxamuud, the subclan of Cismaan Yuusuf Keenadiid, the inventor of Cismaaniya.

Cabdirisaaq, soon after assuming command, endorsed the plan of his minister of education, Axmed Yuusuf Keenadiid, to invite a committee of UNESCO-sponsored experts to form a linguistic commission. The experts, B. W. Andrzejewski, S. Strelcyn, and J. Tubiana arrived in Muqdisho in March 1966, only to meet demonstrations by groups favoring Arabic. Some Somalis were arrested, including the well-known businessman Xaaji Diiriye, one of the founders of the Xaaji Group. The political situation at the time was tense; supporters of the Arabic and Cismaaniya scripts were well aware what the results of the commission would be, assuming that they would make recommendations solely on technical criteria.

In this period the national debate attained ever higher levels of acrimony. Muuse X. I. Galaal stirred up the intellectuals with a letter to the UNESCO commission sent through the minister of education. In it he recommended the script of Shire Jaamac Axmed as both "practical" and "objective." Muuse is a scholar, a nomad, a wit, a poet, and a gadfly, and it is therefore difficult to assess the seriousness of some of his claims. In 1954 he wrote a scholarly article for the *Islamic Quarterly* supporting the claims of the Arabic script. In the 1955 cultural conference of educationalists from the north and the south, Muuse spoke out in favor of the Cismaaniya script. And as chairman of the 1961 language committee he recommended the Latin script. Muuse enjoys taking controversial stands, and enjoys rebutting the torrent of criticisms which come his way. During the independence years, Muuse traveled widely, including trips to the Soviet Union and China, to study the linguistic situation in other countries. He always wrote long, insightful but controversial letters to the newspapers reporting his findings.

Muuse began his communication to the commission by stating his qualifications, reminding the members that when it comes to issues concerning linguistics, broadcasting, printing, shorthand, telegraphy, he might not know much, but he knew far more than any other Somali. "I remember," he wrote, " once coming across an English saying that, 'In the country of the blind, the one eyed man is the king.' I think I am not boasting if I consider myself as the 'one eyed man' among the Somalis in the study of our language and traditions."[76] Then, after paying due respect to Islam and stressing the necessity to study the Qur'an in Arabic, he launched a diatribe against the United Arab Republic. He accused *Al Ahram* and other Egyptian papers of being behind the movement to bring the Arabic script to the Somali language. He agreed that while the UAR government had been friendly, and had given technical assistance, it

> is vigorously, though covertly [opposing Somali writing, through a Muqdisho religious society with] a facade of Somali leadership [but] it is generally believed that this society has been established by U.A.R. officials in this country, and that it is currently financed, organized and dictated to by them.
>
> This society arranges the delivery of wrathful sermons by enraged fanatical Somali theologians in Mosques and religious gatherings against certain proposed forms of scripts.... In fact, it has submitted memoranda warning the Government that riots (presumably organized by them) and bloodshed will ensue should certain forms of alphabet be adopted.
>
> The pulpit is also used by this society for subversive utterances against Government policies and measures which are viewed with disfavour by the Government of the U.A.R. As the spokesman of the society usually quotes passages from the Holy Qur'an in support of their lop-sided arguments they endeavor to impress on the ignorant

masses which constitute about 60 per cent of the population, that it would be heretical to reject their exhortations....

[Some] observers are convinced that the U.A.R. is determined (perhaps less hopefully since the appointment of the present Somali Prime Minister) to reduce this country to the status of a satellite and to dominate it through intensive cultural, ideological and religious influence. It is generally believed by discerning Somalis that, through such influence, local U.A.R. Officials had at one time even hoped to transform the Somalis into an Arabic nation and to substitute Arabic for Somali as their mother tongue.[77]

Muuse went on to accuse the UAR of "neo-colonialism" and of policies against "which the U.A.R. as an elder brother constantly warns this and other developing countries." Finally he accused some of the Egyptian UN experts of being active in promoting these policies. The rest of his memorandum, less polemical in tone, explained the technical weaknesses of the Arabic and Cismaaniya scripts.

A short and unequivocal document almost immediately appeared in the *Corriere della Somalia*, coming from "The Somali Government." "From the point of view of the Somali Government," it read, "the affirmations contained in the memorandum against the United Arab Republic are completely unfounded, prejudicial, and prefabricated in order to create misunderstandings on a problem which is purely cultural in all of its aspects."[78] The political atmosphere became heated. The assistant director general of the Ministry of Education, Maxamuud Xaaji Axmed Cali, put out a memorandum on 22 March, stating his "personal" views. He argued that the use of the Roman script in Berbera at the turn of the century was the principal cause of the twenty-one-year Dervish war, and implied that if the present government attempted to propagate the Latin script, a similar fight would ensue. He claimed to be arguing on technical grounds, but his advocacy of the Arabic script was based on cultural and religious criteria: "Let us all frankly admit that the use of the Roman script for the Somali language will definitely change the culture, perhaps finally the religion and certainly the future history of the Somali people."[79] His greatest fear, he said, was that the Qur'an would be translated into Somali with a blasphemous script if Latin were chosen. He was kinder to Muuse Galaal than the government was, calling him "an intimate friend ... a true Somali to the bone"; but he argued that Muuse's mistakes stemmed from "his shallow knowledge of the Qur'an and equally poor knowledge of the Arabic language."

Public statements were also made in support of Cismaaniya. Dr. M. Jaamac Maxamad "Afballaar" downgraded the Arabic script, arguing that only religious fanatics supported it. And if the issue is between

Cismaaniya and Latin, both technically sound, he argued, only Cismaaniya could be a force for national unity.[80]

A few days after the strongly worded note against Muuse appeared, the Somali government published another statement, this time against the other camp. Reviewing the old arguments on the need for a written Somali, it then referred to rumors that certain elements would demonstrate in public and disturb the public order if a language choice were made "against the national religion." The statement reminded its readers that article 1 of the Somali constitution provides that "Islam is the State Religion," and article 50 that "the doctrine of Islam is the founding principle of the laws of the State." Thus all Somalis, it claimed, were well protected by their constitution. The government then emphasized that the elected representatives of the people and not "instigating elements" are the defenders of the constitution. They strongly advised that the mosque remain a place of prayer and not become transformed into "a platform for political propaganda."[81] After dissociating itself from the embarassing accusations of Muuse's memorandum, the government tried to prepare the public for a decision that would be consistent with Muuse's principles.

The technical orientation of the commission did indeed determine its outlook. It gave as its criteria: "A script must be treated as a tool and be chosen accordingly: it must be simple, sturdy and as economical as is consistent with its other good qualities."[82] Although no specific recommendation was made, the commission found numerous problems in choosing any of the indigenous scripts, or Arabic either, but "found no valid objections to the Latin script on technical or scientific grounds."[83] When the time came for implementation, however, Cabdirisaaq's cabinet had fallen. The new president was Cabdurashiid Cali Sharma'arke, who is said to have once exclaimed, "As long as I am in power I shall never permit the adoption of Latin characters for Somali."[84] His prime minister, Ibraahiim Xaaji Cigaal, shelved the 1966 report just as the 1961 report had been shelved.

Just after the submission of the 1966 report, Xersi Magan Ciise decided to terminate his academic career in the United States to return home to proselytize for the Cismaaniya script. Fearing a choice favoring the Latin script with the support of UNESCO, Xersi wrote to U Thant, then secretary general of the United Nations:

> Under the name of UNESCO, Mr. Akhtar Husain [Pakistani; head of the UNESCO mission in Muqdisho] has been secretly collaborating with certain foreigners: Americans (elements of the United States Information Agency), Italians and some pseudolinguists of British origin to suppress the native script and romanize the Somali language....

Moreover, in Muqdisho, the intensive rumor is that the Somali language will soon be romanized, and the expenses for the enterprise will be met by UNESCO! People question, "If UNESCO provides some aid to the reduction of the Somali language into a written form, why in Roman and not in the native script?" Such rumors can hardly be leveled.[85]

Upon return to Somalia, Xersi Magan wrote a stinging attack on Latin. He mentioned that Mark Twain and George Bernard Shaw both scorned the Latin script. He pointed out that the Japanese, the Chinese, and the Russians have made great technological advances without the Latin script, while Spain and Portugal, both users of Roman letters, remain backward. Finally, he discussed the problem of front and back harmonic groups in Somali, pointing out ambiguities that the Latin script could not overcome. He then emphasized the cultural advantages of the Cismaaniya script.[86]

Xersi was active in other ways. As president of the Society for Somali Language and Literature he arranged to get more typewriters in the Cismaaniya script, and was able to procure a Somali printing press. He wrote letters to the SYL and the National Advisory Congress urging them to make use of the new Cismaaniya office machinery. He told them, "You can buy tanks and MIG fighters, but never cultural elements such as script, music and fine arts."[87] Although Xersi was able to procure office machinery, he could never escape being considered part of the Cismaan Maxamuud clan, and fighting a reer rather than a societal cause. His were to be the last sparks in the half-century of life for the Cismaaniya script.

The SYL at this time was moribund due to extensive internal division. During the celebrations for its twenty-fifth anniversary, Cali Maxamad Hiraabe, the secretary general of the SYL, spoke on the language issue. "The Somali language script problem must be faced once and for all," he urged, "and solved, cost what it may, even at the risk of unpopularity. Children, at least in elementary school, must be taught their mother language, and must not be psychologically retarded by the teaching of a foreign language, whatever it may be."[88] The real political issue, which script to use, was still being avoided by the leading political party.

The final years of the period of parliamentary democracy closely resembled the trusteeship years and the early years of independence. After the 1969 elections, the prime minister announced his new program, with only the following cryptic message about the language issue: "Last but not least, my Government will devote its utmost attention to the most important task of tackling the difficult problem posed by the lack of a script for the Somali language."[89] And when asked why he had been so quiet on such an important issue, he is said to have responded, "We did not see any fresh contribution to make on the subject."[90] The government continued to accept the status quo.

The inability to resolve the issue reached comic opera proportions in September of 1969, a month before the coup d'état which would terminate the nine-year period of civilian rule. The government gave considerable publicity to International Literacy Day: posters were put up throughout the country, and speeches around the republic by government ministers urged greater efforts to eradicate illiteracy. Various self-help schemes (*iskaa wax u qabso*) were organized to combat illiteracy. Yet there was very little said about what language this new literacy would be in. While the minister of education, Aaden Isxaaq Axmed, did state the problem clearly and committed his ministry to working as hard as possible to bring about literacy in the official foreign languages until a national script should be agreed upon, most speakers ignored the fundamental problem.

The editorial in the government's newspaper, the *Somali News*, tried to remove the blame from the government.

> The absence of a written mother tongue makes it impossible to launch a successful massive attack to eradicate illiteracy quickly. Education officials contend that without a written mother tongue, a massive attack no matter how big, will fail to produce the desired results in the time required. To teach an adult how to read and write in a foreign language is a time consuming matter apart from the huge expenses involved.
>
> Many people wonder why then doesn't the Government have our mother tongue written? The truth is that the people have been the major obstacle to government efforts to decide which script to use. Whenever the matter is raised, foreign elements appear to be at work: the people split into factions—some supporting Somali scripts for prestige reasons, some supporting Arabic script on religious grounds, and others advocating Latin for economic or technical reasons.
>
> We hope that the Government will make a break-through of this mounting pressure to decide which script to use for our mother tongue before it is too late.[91]

The sense of urgency expressed in the editorial was paralleled in many of the written statements of the 1950s. Ten years of trusteeship with free discussion, followed by nine years of parliamentary democracy with relatively free speech, and a free people could not decide on an issue that was fundamental to the definition of its political system. In 1966, Saciid Yuusuf Samantar wrote a letter to the *Somali News* asking why public discussion seemed to be over and why the 1966 UNESCO report was not made public. He urged quick action. "We cannot go on hoping," he wrote, "that a benevolent deity will wave a magic wand and give us a well-developed script with no effort on our part."[92]

National debate on the language questions seemed to do little but postpone any action. And a nondecision, the intellectuals began to recognize, was very much a decision. The Somali Republic was learning to live with a babelian bureaucracy and a school system increasingly unresponsive to the needs of its students. The last choice of nearly every politically aware Somali—the recognition of Arabic, English and Italian as official languages, and the use of Arabic as the medium of instruction in the early years of school, with English used in the later years—became, by default, the national policy. The Somali government was becoming increasingly separated from its people, all in the name of preserving democratic institutions. It is no wonder, then, that a Somali intellectual would publicly express the need for a "benevolent deity."

On 21 October 1969, the deity might be said to have arrived. A few days earlier, the president, Cabdurashiid Cali Sharma'arke, had been assasinated. The National Assembly was in confusion and unable to agree upon a new leader. The military intervened, and Maxamad Siyaad Barre became the head of a Supreme Revolutionary Council. Under his rule, all democratic institutions were disbanded. The parliament was closed, and free speech was choked. Three years after the coup, however, President Siyaad was able to announce that the Somali language would be written in the Latin script, and he was also able to rely on public support.

5
Decision and Political Consequences

> In the history of the world, our Language was taking no part;
> But the sunrise appeared uncovering our Language from darkness;
> The fence was cleared, so the livestock could graze.
> Give me your pen, the words I write for you.
> It is not a Foreign Language; the tongue does not slip,
> Like milk, it can be swallowed smoothly.
>
> Song on Radio Muqdisho,
> heralding written Somali

Fifteen months after the October 1969 revolution, the Supreme Revolutionary Council (SRC) took the first steps necessary to fulfill their goal of establishing a written Somali as the official language of the Somali Democratic Republic. A new linguistic commission of twenty-one members was appointed in January 1971. A discussion of the commission's charge, its composition, and its work, put into focus by an analysis of the political climate of postrevolutionary Somalia, will enable me to explain why, after twelve years of independence, and twenty-two years of national debate, a decision on a written Somali could be reached.

Unlike the previous one, the new commission was asked only, (1) to write textbooks for elementary schools, (2) to write the Somali grammar, and (3) to work out the compilation of a 10,000 word Somali language dictionary.[1] The members were not asked to choose a national script. The military council made clear that the choice of a script would be a political decision, and that any discussion by the commission in regard to a script would be out of order.

Most of the language protagonists of the parliamentary era were appointed to the new commission. Yaasiin Cismaan Keenadiid became an active cooperating member; with the burden of advocating the Cismaaniya script off his back, he involved himself in lecturing his fellow members on the fine points of linguistics. Xirsi Magan Ciise was also present, giving the commission another of the most vocal advocates of the Cismaaniya script. A third member was Xuseen Sheekh Axmed Kaddare, whose script, it will be remembered, was considered the best indigenous script by both the 1961 and the 1966 commissions. Ibraahiim Xaashi Maxamuud, then the leading advocate for the Arabic script, served for six months until his death in July, 1971, when the commission lost a vast store of erudition. Muuse X.I. Galaal, who had already begun to advocate the Latin script, was also appointed; but his humor and good will were often absent, as he spent months contending with jaundice. Shire Jaamac Axmed, whose Latin script had been chosen by the 1961 and the 1966 commissions as technically the best, was absent from the initial stages but joined the group at a later stage. Unlike the 1961 committee, the new commission included a number of appointees who were not only qualified but were uncommitted concerning script.

In the early stages, there was much bickering among the members concerning prospects. Some of the old hands were quite cynical about the whole matter and saw the commission as evidence that this government, like its predecessors, would avoid the political issue through the appointment of a commission. Muuse Galaal, as always, was the most explicit on this point. He wrote a letter to the secretary of the commission stating his reservations:

> The reference of this problem of written Somali to a Commission like ours at this time is, in my opinion, very inappropriate for the following reason; research on the choice of script for Somali took about fifty long years. In this long process, some thirty different systems were devised by the national research groups and individuals.... Having managed to reduce the number of those multitude of ... scripts from thirty to four the past researchers have in fact done well. This is obvious.
>
> It then became the duty of the Government to finalize the problem by choosing one ... for adoption. Is this done? No.
>
> Instead, the ball is thrown back to its old stand still position, for no other reason than a sheer lack of decision.... There was no need for further research.... The key problem is not yet solved.[2]

If the old hands were cynical at first, they were soon aware that this was a rather different enterprise. The acting president of the commission,

Axmed Cali Abokor, clearly recognized the problems of the past: "The fate of the language became a game of contest between the parliament and the Government, and the nation was given the position of a referee. The *musuqmaasaq* [corrupt] state of affairs which had crept into the machinery of previous Governments exalted to the extent that it made the national language to suffer and as a result be regarded as a dead issue."[3] Axmed Cali was determined to keep the issue alive, but not burning. Within the first few months the appointed members had produced four language books using the Somali language, six books in mathematics and science, two books in geography and history, and one basic Somali dictionary with 10,000 words recorded and defined. A set of subcommittees had been set up to deal with the various problems: language, mathematics and science, geography and history, dictionary, and terminology. Each subcommittee arranged regular sessions with individuals and groups outside of the commission to gather information on neologisms and on foreign words lacking a good Somali translation.

Since the office machinery was borrowed from the Ministry of Education, which had been operating primarily in English, commissioners were virtually confined to the Latin script. They did report that they wrote some things in Cismaaniya, but none of their mimeographed materials could be in any script but the Latin. The twenty-one books that the commission produced at the end of its first year were, according to Axmed Cali, "submitted in one script, the Roman script as a matter conceived by the Commission to be .... convenient."[4]

The military government, unlike the parliamentary governments, kept a careful eye on its commission. In February of 1971, President Siyaad's secretary of state for education, Major Cabdirisaaq Maxamuud Abobakar, spoke to the members in these terms: "I need not emphasize the importance that the SRC attaches to this national effort which you agreed to undertake.... It is logical to treat the question of developing the National Language this time, in a different approach—and devote our energy in providing instructional materials before the issue of the 'Script' comes up. This is different and it merits its own time."[5] And in April, President Siyaad himself invited all the commissioners to his home in order to demonstrate his interest in their project. By then, most of the Somali population had been successfully intimidated by the new regime. The SRC had already established a reputation for locking up, and even killing, its political enemies. Politicians, students, and wadaads were all being treated harshly when they attempted to defy the new military government. The era of free speech was over. Members of the language commission were genuinely afraid of discussing the script issue even among themselves. From discussions with some of them, I gathered that the issue of script did not arise, even in private.

The acting president of the commission did not mourn the end of public debate or private bickering over scripts. He was impressed with the output of such a divergent and formerly contentious group in only one year's time:

> The success of the Commission in this work is largely due to the fact and as in agreement with its term of reference not to discuss the question of "Scripts" or anything *that may lead* to that effect. It has been clearly understood that the finalization of the Script to be adopted rests entirely with the Supreme Revolutionary Council and so members on the commission, particularly Script supporters, were cautioned to refrain from any activity that may arouse suspicion in propagating one orthography against another in public places or elsewhere.[6]

Throughout 1972 the commission plodded along, still having no idea whether its work would ever be made public, or in what script. The SCR never openly discussed its ideas, not even with members of the commission; and only pious statements concerning the need for a national script and for hard work by the commission were made public. Meanwhile, the idea of a Latin script was cautiously being promoted. The important group to win over were the wadaads, the religious leaders who had so strongly favored illiteracy over latinization. Members of the SRC began to visit the Qur'anic schools in order to put these schools, for the first time, under some sort of secular control. Major Cismaan Maxamad Jelle, the Extraordinary Commissioner of Muqdisho, spoke to a group of religious leaders and teachers of Qur'anic schools in April of 1972. He threatened to confiscate the free land given to the Qur'anic schools and to eliminate their subsidy unless they "modernize and change the face of the Qur'anic schools and adjust it to the state of affairs."[7] The following week Lt. Ismaaciil Barood met with twenty-four Qur'anic school teachers and urged them to modernize themselves and to prepare their students for the continuation of their education. Both speeches were reported in the government weekly *Dawn*, and the threats inherent in them were only thinly veiled. The wadaads were told that whatever their religious legitimacy, they had better not challenge the military government.

Perhaps the SRC needed to convince the entire population that their script decision, like the wadaads' objection to it, came from the heavens. In any case, on the third anniversary of their coup d'état, in the midst of the celebrations and to the surprise of even the members of the commission, the results of the government's decision did indeed come from the skies. The government newspaper described the event with some exuberance:

> Unlike the night of October 20, 1969 when the Somali nation was full

of uncertainty, gloom and despair and the Capital city was dark and dead, last night was full of life and colourful illuminations everywhere.

As everybody was taking his position in order to secure a clear vision of the parade, a helicopter flew low and dropped multicolor leaflets. People who were accustomed to grab the printed speech of the President quickly scrambled to snatch the leaflets, but they soon frowned when they immediately realized that this was not Arabic, nor Italian, and nor English. they began to fight with their tongues to read the new writing. Few might have given up hope to make sense out of the thing but many managed to read and got the key to the thing.

This was Somali! And Latin has been adopted in order to get it written, a fulfillment of the promise of the Revolutionary leaders and an implementation of the First Charter of the October Revolution.[8]

And the president spoke:

But we face some obstacles [one being] the language problem. By this I mean the language in which the children are taught. This is not our language.

We cannot be free in our thinking, in our behavior and in our way of living when many parts of us are tied up to political and social values in which we have nothing to share. It will not benefit our culture and our traditions when our children are taught methods and systems which have no meaning to us.

We have to face and solve once and for all the question of script for our mother language, which goes back historically to our very beginning. It is rich in literature and poetry and can compare with the best languages. Through verbal transmission our ancestors have handed down to us a rich heritage to safeguard and develop.

The imperialists and the colonialists maintained the divisions. They put Somali against Somali, alphabet against alphabet, and tribe against tribe.

If we had a written language this would not have happened for as long as it did. Because of this 90 percent of our people are illiterate. As dedicated revolutionaries we must now ensure that what has been handed down to us over the centuries is no longer lost.

You are aware that in 1971 we formed a special committee to prepare the necessary materials for the teaching of the Somali language in our schools, and to collect all relevant material relating to our history and our literature. This committee has completed the first part of its task and handed over to the Minister of Education the results of their researches and the books they have compiled. I am therefore happy to announce, in accordance with the First Charter of the Revolution, these decisions which have been long awaited by our people. It is the accomplishment of a Revolutionary pledge.

a) The Somali language will be adopted, starting from today, as the only official language of the country. After careful study it has been decided to adopt the Latin alphabet as the script of our language. Under separate regulations, provisions will be made for the practical introduction of the language in every sector of our national life....

We are not unmindful of the difficulties that lie ahead but this action has been necessary and could no longer be postponed.[9]

The government did meet with some criticism. Letters were addressed to the editor of *Dawn* attempting to demonstrate that the script was not yet perfect, and to suggest alterations. One correspondent, Muuse Bashiir, although joyous about the decision, made a number of constructive suggestions and argued that "the fact that other languages have the same defects cannot be an excuse for unnecessarily complicating our language."[10]

The secretary of state for education handled the more complex problem concerning the objections by the wadaads. He spoke to them and told them that they had never objected when the nomads put *x*'s on their livestock, and then asked why they objected when Somalis put *x*'s on paper. The lead editorial of *Dawn* also tried to put down potential criticism when it declared that "the 'Alphabet War' with all its divisive undertones has been snuffed for good." They went a little far, though surprisingly did not add fuel to the wadaads' fire, when they summed matters up this way: "This was indeed crossing the Rubicon into the immortal pastures of austerity for Somali."[11] That final malapropism served well as an epitaph for the English language in the Somali press. *Dawn* would soon disappear, as would the Italian and Arabic weeklies, and *Xiddigta Oktobar*, "The October Star," would soon appear as the national (government) daily paper, all in Somali.

The chosen script, that of Shire Jaamac Axmed, involved no diacritical marks and was fully usable with no changes necessary in any office equipment. The government was thereby able to decree that all written messages in the civil service were to be in the Somali language within three months. The choice of the Latin script was made, I believe, on technical criteria. It was the only script that could have been legislated into existence in a matter of months. With the government essentially putting the damper on all political activities, and intimidating the religious community, a purely technical decision could be made.

No decision made in the Somali Republic, however, is without its implications for clan politics. However committed the present government is to the eradication of clan divisions from Somali society, clan considerations can rarely be avoided. The president of the Supreme

Revolutionary Council comes from the Marreexaan clan of the Daarood clan family. The Marreexaan stand somewhat apart form the heart of the Daarood—the Majeerteen, the Dhulbahante, and the Warsangeli clans—those three forming the Harti sûbbranch. The oral history of the Daarood clan family suggests that Sheekh Daarood, the clan founder, sent Marreexaan away to the south, telling him that he would always be surrounded by war. The Marreexaan clan was indeed split up and always surrounded by groups of Hawiya, of a different clan family.

The military coup d'état had been a blow to the Majeerteen clan. Cabdirisaaq Xaaji Xuseen, the former prime minister, was Majeerteen, as was the former president and prime minister, Cabdurashiid Cali Sharma'arke who had been assassinated days before the coup. The Majeerteen saw themselves as the backbone of the Somali struggle for independence. They looked down on the Marreexaan as "'bush people," and many of them scorned the new military regime. The president's lack of enthusiasm for the Cismaaniya script may have been based on notions other than technical and economic infeasibility, since it too was a product of the Majeerteen clan.

That Shire Jaamac Axmed is also a Marreexaan probably had little bearing on the decision. Shire's script, for one, had little of his personal stamp on it. He used it in his scholarly and popular publications, but he was not fanatical about it. It was never really seen as Shire's script, but rather as the Latin script. Furthermore, for a government intent on bringing about universal literacy and changing the life style of the nomadic existence, the institutionalization of the Arabic script would have been a painfully slow process. Those who were technically trained, and on whom the government was forced to rely, were usually only minimally literate in Arabic. And even those who were literate in Arabic could not easily read their language in the Arabic script. Once the Cismaaniya script was elimated from contention, partly for political reasons, the choice of Latin was based, I would guess, on largely technical considerations.

Popular support for the decision, in light of general governmental intimidation, cannot be accurately assessed. But there are factors which do suggest widespread approval, or at least acquiescence. The great majority of the participants in the national debate, as I pointed out in the previous chapter, emphasized that although they might have their preferences about which script would be best for Somalia, some decision was better than no decision. The protracted battle, most thought, was sapping the energy of the Somali nation, and many recognized that if a decision were to be made, it would have to be somewhat arbitrary. This pervasive public feeling was one reason why many Somalis, committed to democratic institutions, were so enthusiastic about the military coup d'état itself. After the decision had been made, *Xiddigta Oktobar* was circulated throughout the capital city, and nomads from the bush came into town and watched intently as their literate brothers read them the news in Somali. The song which heads this chapter, although broadcast on government radio, seemed to reflect the public mood. The parliamentary system brought into focus and perpetuated public differences on the issue of a national script, whereas the military council, on the same issue, was able to draw on the solid basis of public agreement.

Consequences of Nondecision: Democracy

The first nine years of Somali independence were characterized by some solid achievements in democratic institutionalization. A number of free elections had been successfully contested, with only small outbreaks of violence. Two peaceful changes in government occurred, with the losing presidential candidate assuming the role of loyal opposition in both instances. Political parties flourished, and only a few were suppressed. The independent press, while not permitted to say everything it wished, was given wide latitude in which to criticize the government. And the government press permitted in its pages letters which were quite critical of the government's performance.[12]

Perhaps just as important, advocates in the debate, from all sides, were advancing publicly relevant arguments in support of their positions. The advocates were presenting arguments which would support their own interests, but in terms of some greater public interest. It is only with a sense of public interest that compromise and concession, so very important to democratic institutions, can take place.[13]

Those appeals to what was best for Somalia often took the form of appeals to the Somali Parliament to come to some determination on the language issue. By challenging, imploring, or ridiculing the government, these political actors were giving at least their implicit support to government institutions as the places where a decision should be made. And by expressing their ideas in the government newspaper, they were implicitly granting legitimacy to the notion of a national forum for ideas. In an important sense, then, the extended period of language debate was putting more and more Somali citizens into the position of acknowledging the legitimacy of Somalia's democratic institutions.

The growth of democratic institutions in the first decade of Somali independence was paralleled by two contradictory trends: the erosion of the Somali democratic social structure and the emergence of new regional fissures. The extended language debate, while enhancing the legitimacy of Somali democratic institutions, was beginning to erode the very social structure that would make those institutions viable.

Social Stratification

In the early part of this century, Sheekh Axmed Gabyow of Muqdisho ended a poem with these prophetic lines:

> Before the end of the world,
> The Somali shall be divided in three:
> One will live in a place surrounded by his guards,
> One will continue living in the bush,
> Drawing sustenance from the sale of milk,
> Which he will carry to town in his *tunji*;
> One will die in the dusty street crying,
> "Somalia!"[14]

Most Somalis are proud of their egalitarianism and eschew any manifestation of emerging social stratification. Any Somali who gets rich at the expense of other Somalis is usually put up to public ridicule. Nevertheless, linguistic competence, which was beginning to be a necessary condition for political power, was creating a privileged group. While it is true that the president of the National Assembly in the final years of the parliamentary era spoke only Somali, it needs to be kept in mind that nearly all jobs in the modern sector required writing, and literacy was available only to those who spoke a foreign language. Ability to speak and write a foreign language was a necessary condition for nearly all employment in the modern sector.

Since the Somali government in the mid 1960s needed more teachers, clerks, and administrators, it had to expand intermediate and secondary education because competence in English was still insufficient by the end of the primary course. This decision involved the relative slowing down of primary education. The ideology of "mass literacy" gave way to an ideology of sufficient literacy for a small elite.[15]

From the school year beginning 1966 to the school year beginning 1970, enrollment in elementary school as a percentage of population of elementary school age increased by only 1 percent (see table 4). Expansion in the intermediate and secondary levels was only slightly greater, but the investment for each increase in the latter levels was greater than the investment for increases in the elementary level, because the higher stage of education requires more specialty equipment, more textbooks and library facilities, and more expatriate teachers. The data further suggest that those likely to have linguistic competence in a foreign language in the following generation would be less than 10 percent of the total Somali population. And a program to foster universal literacy would have involved putting the budget for education at a level commensurate with the national revenue. The chances for any nonliterate Somali to acquire the necessary skills for participation in the modern sector were small. It is clear that the linguistic elite would maintain itself, as there was only the most limited opportunity for most Somalis to have linguistic mobility. And this, for the Somalis, was perhaps their first experience in real social stratification.

Table 4 School Enrollment, 1966-70

	School year	
	1966-67	1970-71
Percentage of total age group enrolled in:		
Elementary (ages 7-10)	7	8
Intermediate (ages 11-14)	3	5
Secondary (ages 15-18)	1	2
Expenditure on education as percentage of national revenue	6.5	7.2

Figures derived from Somali Democratic Republic, *Current Statistical Trends in Somali Education* (Muqdisho, 1971), pp. 19-21.

Attempts to combat linguistic stratification through adult literacy campaigns were doomed to failure. In 1957, a UNESCO-funded technical assistance program permitted a group of teachers to go out into the Somali bush to organize a literacy campaign. They were able to recruit twenty students and taught them one day a week in Italian. The course lasted three months, until the rains came, when students disappeared. Camillo Bonanni wrote up a report on this campaign while waiting for his students to return. No reports followed, however.[16] Little changed over the next ten years. In 1967 another UNESCO expert, A. R. Siddiqi, returned to India, believing that his adult education program "suffered greatly on account of the non-availability of simple literature specially prepared for this purpose in the local language of the people. He considered that the foremost step in the strengthening of the existing adult literacy programme rested in the decision on the adoption of a script for the Somali language."[17]

The officials in Somalia's Ministry of Education were not unaware that they were administering an education program designed to stratify their people on criteria other than merit. In 1967 the director general of education, Maxamad Axmed Sheff, was quite explicit on this. "Adult education," he wrote, "has not been tackled satisfactorily and the problem still exists. No mass literacy for adults could be offered by the Ministry of Education without the Somali language being written. For the same reason, no simple suitable reading material could be prepared for the masses."[18] The annual reports of the ministry always detailed the implications of having education through the English medium. Their experts wrote that "linguists have found that it is easier for a member of a preliterate group to achieve literacy in the dominant language of the nation-state if he first learns to read and write his mother tongue."[19] And in their 1968 report it was noted that "the Curriculum unit . . . is seriously hampered by a lack of a script for the Somali language, without which we cannot launch a mass literacy campaign or even reconcile the differences between our cultural heritage and the foreign languages in which we try to convey it."[20]

Muuse X. I. Galaal also recognized the implications for social stratification of the politics of no decision. In an article in the *National Review*, a journal published by the Ministry of Information, he summed up the issue in this way:

The following are some points of fact showing that no development scheme of any kind is likely to achieve any results in our country, unless the question of writing our language is first settled:
  a) About 90 per cent of our public is totally illiterate;
  b) About 80 per cent of our people can speak only Somali;
  c) To learn a foreign language would take one at least a year full time, while to become literate in Somali only about two months would be sufficient.
  d) As a result of the absence of a system of writing our language, education is too expensive for the poor—only the well-to-do families can afford to keep their children in the schools for seven long years.[21]

And to become well-to-do most often required knowledge of a foreign language. In that way a linguistic elite was beginning to perpetuate itself.

The official use of foreign languages was also exacerbating urban-rural stratification, favoring the urban areas. It is not surprising, then, that the Somali revolutionary government, which gave its full support to the enchancement of the vernacular, has also stressed development of the Somali bush. The government, for instance, has insisted that first priority of all programs is for the Somali nomad, and students have therefore been compelled to go out into the bush to teach as a sort of national service after finishing intermediate school and before entering secondary school. The government has given priorities to projects which involve education to the nomad, as well as policies which would enhance his ability to procure water. Schools which travel with the nomad, and a major road from north to south with an extensive network of wells, are already public commitments.

Furthermore, the military regime seems to be committed to the reduction of some of the rural-urban inequalities in public investment which marked the parliamentary years. Although capital expenditures are only a rough indicator of the resources actually made available to Somalis in the bush as opposed to the cities, investments in projects with a rural focus, such as agriculture, fisheries, forestry, animal husbandry, and irrigation, seem no longer to be giving way to investments in industry. In the five-year period before the coup d'état (1963-68), industrial investments were nearly twice as high as rural investments—214 million Somali shillings as against 142. The three year period following the coup (1971-73) demonstrates the reverse: industrial investments were down to 87.8 million shillings, but rural investments were up to 220.3.[22] The rural-urban gap, which I hypothesized (in chapter 1) would be reduced if the language of politics were the language of the people, has indeed been confronted by the Somali regime, contemporaneously with the language change. The military regime, then, has begun to erode the emerging linguistic and urban-rural stratifications.

Emergent Regionalism and Separatism

Independent Somalia had succeeded in amalgamating two disparate political structures: the former Italian Somalia and the former British Somaliland. Efforts of this sort have rarely succeeded and are filled with difficulties. The political ingenuity of the Somali elites was remarkable, and they deserve much credit for having made that transition a relatively smooth one. To be sure, there were problems. The north, for instance, voted strongly against the 1961 constitution. They were against permitting political activity of civil servants—a normal occurrence in Italian democracy but scorned in the British tradition. But by far the biggest division was based on official language policy. As the national school system became increasingly anglicized, an increasing number of jobs were made available to northerners, and educated students in the south found their linguistic skills to be in desuetude. As the first decade of independence progressed, enmity between the north and the south began to grow. As more northerners migrated south to the capital city of Muqdisho and were able to land more and better jobs, southerners became increasingly aware of a "southern identity." The unity of Somalia was beginning to shred, this time not on clan lines (which had little corrrespondence with colonial borders), but on regional lines.

Ismaaciil Jimcaali Cosoble, editor of the independent journal *La Tribuna*, castigated the Ministry of Education for deciding "that all Somalis must speak the language of Shakespeare, without considering that a majority of the Somali people speak Italian as a foreign language." He argued that Somalia had always been considered a democratic country, yet the northern minority in this case was able to impose its will, and language, onto the south. He suggested that both north and south should at least continue using the language of their choice, "without interference, without pressures, without hateful intervention."[23] Ismaaciil, incidentally, had received a law degree in Italy, and there is little doubt that he saw the (English) handwriting on the wall.

Nuovi Ovuzzonti, another Italian-language independent journal, protrayed this same problem in this humorous dialogue between a director general (DG) and a recent graduate (Grad) of an Italian University:

Grad: I have come back from Italy, where I completed my studies. Through suggestions of friends, I have come to you as a contact.

DG: In what field did you major?

Grad: Jurisprudence.

DG: Do you speak English?

Grad: Enough to understand others, and to be understood.

DG: That's too bad, too bad, my son.

Grad: But I didn't major in languages.

DG: I didn't mean that, but anyway, forget it.

Grad: But Mr. Director ... my degree is internationally recognized. Do you doubt that I have a legal right to it?

DG: Well, what did you come for?

Grad: I am impelled by the desire to put my services at the disposal of the state of the nation.

DG: Well, I don't think I can help. All the posts are occupied by Indians and Pakistanis.

Grad: But I am a Somali, and I have preference

	over these foreigners ... I'm curious ... from which university did you graduate?
DG:	From Berbera ... Sheekh University.
Grad:	I'm sure you had excellent university teachers.
DG:	Sure, they are English.
Grad:	Farewell to Somalia.
DG:	Farewell to your Italian degree![24]

That Sheekh is a secondary school and not a university only compounded the irony. The graduates from the Italian system felt more and more frustrated as English became more important than Italian in the educational system and civil service.

The fact that students from the north were in a better position to succeed in modern Somalia was amply demonstrated in 1971, when the Ministry of Education administered its first centralized examination for students completing their eighth year of school. The students who passed would be eligible for a secondary school education, and so this examination was of considerable importance to all participating students. From a total enrollment in standard 8 of 1,178 from the north and 1,695 from the south, 1,038 (88 percent) of the northerners passed, whereas only 907 (54 percent) of the southerners did.[25] When it is recognized that the south has approximately two-thirds of the population of the Somali Republic, the figures take on added significance. Linguistic skills are critically important in examinations of this nature, and there is little doubt that students from the north had better opportunities to learn English than their compatriots in the south.

In the southern region of the newly independent Somali Republic, the process of assimilation was being outpaced by the process of social mobilization. That is to say, since English was emerging as the most important official language of the state, a decreasing number of Somali citizens from the south could communicate effectively with their government. Consequently, they were unassimilated into the official political culture of the new state. The (English-speaking) political culture was a new and different political culture, into which these citizens were being told to assimilate. As assimilation foundered, however, the rate of political demands (social mobilization) was probably increasing. The level of political frustration that a social situation of this type engenders is high. As Ismaaciil's editorial in *La Tribuna* and the humorous column in *Nuovi Ovuzzonti* suggest, a new "southern consciousness" was beginning to develop. This type of regional issue is especially problematical because the cause of the complaint (that Engish was becoming the language of power and influence) was also the very reason that those who were disadvantaged could not act productively to remedy the situation (low linguistic resources). The influence of Somalis from the southern region, due to linguistic stratification, was disproportionately low given their population relative to the north. Such a social situation violates the democratic principle of equality.

The military coup of 1969 and the 1972 decision to make Somali the language of the state and the bureaucracy and, eventually, of the schools changed the political configuration of the republic completely. Now that Somali had become the official language, there was a different political culture in which to become assimilated. Since nearly all people in the Somali Republic were capable of participating in the Somali language, and since universal literacy became a realizable goal, the great bulk of the population would soon be assimilated. Politics in Somalia was likely to become less region-oriented and less subject to basic threats to the survival of the political center.

One way in which this may have already manifested itself is the irredentist issue. I would suggest that the cohesion of the Somali Republic in the 1960s was built upon a common national purpose to regain the then still foreign-controlled territories of the Somali nation. The only issue which held together the north and the south was the common desire to bring Kenya's Northern Frontier District, Ethiopia's Ogaadeen and Hawd, and France's Territory of Afars and Issas into the Somali state. Those concerns were at fever pitch throughout most of the first decade of independence. The military regime, although no less desirous to incorporate these territories than its parliamentary predecessors, has been far less vocal about "unredeemed Somalia." The new rulers have not faced regional fission, and their use of authoritarian control only partly explains why they have not. Their attempt to build a Somali nationality in the Somali language rather than one in the English language is, it seems to me, part of that explanation. Somalia's regions were united on a domestic issue, and common external enemies were no longer necessary to maintain Somali unity.

Thus, while it is true that the military coup of 1969 did abolish all the democratic institutions of the Somali Republic, it is also true that the new rulers stopped the process by which Somali social and regional egalitarianism was being eroded. That the Supreme Revolutionary Council has seen fit to use capital punishment on its political enemies, to use preventive detention and house arrest with virtually no constraints, to permeate the country with political informers, and to militarize every Somali institution can only distress observers of the Somali scene. Yet the revolutionary government does seem to be restoring the social requisites for democratic society.

I need to make two important qualifications, however. First, when I argue that some form of revolutionary or nondemocratic movement was a necessary condition for a future democratic society in which all groups and individuals would have a relatively equal opportunity in which to further their political ideas, I do not want to imply that it is a sufficient condition. Second, when I argue that the military regime has rooted out a structured inequality in Somali society, and has dislodged an entrenched elite, I am unable to assess or predict whether other forms of social stratification have emerged or will emerge. Since I have focused on only one area of emerging inequality - linguistic competence - other evidence that looks at other areas of social division could contradict what I have to say.

In traditional Somali social structure, as we have seen, both society and polity were characterized by a sort of direct democracy, where each man could be, and most men were, politically active. Freedom of speech needed no safeguards, because no one questioned any other person's right to speak his mind. No man's word carried more weight than another man's merely because of a special political role—no man had more right to speak in the name of the people, with few exceptions, than any other man. Traditional Somali social structure is, then, a paragon of democratic social equality. But the development of a centralized state which abandoned the traditional council (shir) and replaced it with a representative parliament and civil service, and which abandoned the Qur'anic school (dugsi) as the core educational institution and replaced it with the colonial educational system, began to stratify the Somali population, giving some Somalis educational, linguistic, military, political and financial resources which made them "more equal" than the others. The social egalitarianism of traditional Somalia was beginning to wane.

Political independence in 1960 brought free elections, a parliamentary system, a relatively free press, and a multitude of political parties. Somalia was thereby believed to be continuing and preserving its democratic traditions.[26] Indeed the development from shir to national assembly did give the impression that Somali society was keeping to its democratic tradition. But the institutional transfer of modern democratic institutions from Britain and Italy to Somalia was not in keeping with the Somali democratic tradition, since the imported representative institutions bore little resemblance to the indigenous direct democratic institutions. Although inter- and intra-clan fusions and fissures that were prevalent before independence continued as part of parliamentary politics, the vital questions—Who could speak in the name of the people? Who could have access to the relevant decision-making bodies?—had different answers in the modern institutions from those in the traditional institutions.

The most important change, perhaps, is that the modern state, due to its size, scope, and complexity, must function through written communication. So while traditional society can be democratic with universal illiteracy; modern society requires universal literacy to attain democratic institutions.[27] Literacy, which had been a skill of the religious elite in traditional Somali social structure, began to emerge as a skill of the political elite in the modern Somali state. That fact alone has had vast consequences for the relationship of the Somali citizen to his government.

The representative institutions in newly independent Somalia reflected all aspects of Somali society: Daarood, Isxaaq, Hawiya, and Rahanwiin; north and south; town, farm, and bush; and wadaad and waraanle. Yet this pluralism hampered effective decision making. On the language dimension, the Latin script was violently opposed by the wadaads; the English language was opposed by southern representatives, the Italian language by the northerners; the Arabic language and script were opposed by many of those from the cities and in the civil service; and the Cismaaniya script was opposed by many of the non-Cismaan Maxamuud subclan and most of the non-Daarood clan family. The issue was too fundamental, too much involved with the basic definition of the Somali state, to lend itself to compromise, even though the relevant political actors did make appeals to a wider public interest. Nondecision in regard to script and language of the polity was assured. Since the language of the people could not be written, literacy would remain an elite skill; and general participation, as the state expanded and became more reliant on written communication, became less and less feasible. Somalia, by virtue of allowing all voices to be heard, by virtue of accepting democratic forms, was unwittingly on the path toward becoming an elitist, stratified, substantively undemocratic society.

It is ironic that a military revolution which has abolished all democratic institutions could be restoring the possibility of equal opportunity to participate, and has advocated the goal of universal participation through universal literacy. On the day that the language decision was announced, Major General Maxamad Siyaad Barre announced that the civil service would have three months to learn the new script; and all intrabureaucratic communication from that time would be in Somali. In March 1973 Siyaad further announced a "cultural revolution" which would bring literacy to all Somalis by 1975. While this was a dream, there can be no doubt that with a common language and script in this relatively homogenous language community, universal literacy is a realistic medium-range goal. That the government has closed all secondary schools for a year in order to send its students out into the bush to teach literacy to the nomads demonstrates Siyaad's seriousness.[28]

The irony remains: democratic forms (national assembly, free speech, free press) put Somalia on a course where democratic substance (social equality and general participation) would be substantially limited. The unintended consequence of the linguistic nondecision nearly assured by pluralistic representation would have been to reduce social communication and to have made Somalia a society which would be ruled by those few literate in English, mostly from the towns and from the north. One of the consequences of a clearly nondemocratic revolution was the restoration of one of the social prerequisites for substantive democracy.

Barrington Moore, Jr., has argued that certain inequalities, especially when they involve an entrenched elite, can be overcome only by revolutionary means.[29] While the costs of revolution are staggering, the costs of neglecting great social inequalities are even higher. It is perhaps the burden of the Supreme Revolutionary Council to make the enormous personal and political costs of their policies ultimately worthwhile to the Somali people.

Consequences of Nondecision: Political Culture

The political culture of a community is, in Verba's phrase, its "subjective orientation to politics";[30] and one seeks to understand a political culture through the examination of the root beliefs of its members. I have suggested that language policy could have two separate yet related effects on political culture in the African context. First, the acceptance of a European language as the official language of the political community may help create a "client state"; that is to say, a state which "borrows" its political institutions, values, and beliefs from that of the former imperial power, with a feeling that all borrowed institutions are better because the society from which they are borrowed is, in general, better. The political culture in that case would be one of dependency. Dependency would manifest itself in the continued close relations between the former colony and the former colonizer, even when relations of that sort no longer served the interest of the former colony. In terms of the recent literature on interdependence, dependency manifests itself when there are low or negative opportunity costs in following a course of political, economic, or social autonomy.³¹ Second, the acceptance of a European language as the language of the society may well induce, in the speakers of the borrowed language, a change in their basic understanding of the world. This new world view may reorient their root beliefs and values—a point that I shall develop in part 2 of this study.

There is some evidence that, in its first decade of independence, the Republic of Somalia was becoming increasingly dependent on the English speaking world. Many Somali intellectuals saw this phenomenon as foreshadowing the demise of Somali culture. The cultural department of the Ministry of Education wrote in an annual report that without a national script, "there is every danger of the national culture being completely lost to posterity."³² In a survey of opinions in Muqdisho, respondents saw "immeasurable cultural consequences" and "a gradual but definite disintegration of our Somali culture and the Somali personality" as the consequence of not writing the Somali language.³³ After the revolution, Col. Ismaaciil Cali Abokor, vice-president of the Supreme Revolutionary Council, criticized the widespread belief in Somalia that someone was "uncivilized" unless he spoke a foreign language.³⁴ Some lines from the poet Maxamad Ismaaciil best sum up this attitude:

> Protesting children are compelled to learn foreign tongues;
> And make a universal cry for that sweet flower: their own native speech;
> Now 'tis being forgot and one may behold its parts disappearing;
> The old poets and tellers of tales who preserved it, are passing away one by one;
> And its most descriptive subtleties already vanishing are more numerous than the blades of grass in the fields;
> The out-cries you hear, like the grumbles of thirsty camels, are really those of the language itself;
> For revival, it now appeals to the leaders of the state;
> It is a beacon which could lead us to the right path;
> It does not deserve deaf ears from its own people;
> Who, by rejecting it, insult the breast of their own mother;
> And any proverb or vital word which disappears from the language is gone forever.

> It resembles the falling teeth of an aged man, and the blame is ours.
> Like a person bereft of clothing, it holds not its beauty.
> Its sweet smelling expressions are losing their meanings.
> The torch of wisdom, like the long introductions to our verses, has departed.
> We are ignoring the foundations of our very existence;
> And all you (neglectful) Somalis—you cannot perceive the best paths for your life.[35]

Indeed, Somali intellectuals were beginning to ignore their own cultural tradition and to rely on the English tradition. The use of the General Certification of Education in the school system was one indicator of intellectual dependency. As Somalia anglicized its educational system, it planned to have all of its students take the secondary school examinations set in Cambridge, England. The British educational system was therefore setting the criteria for an educated person in Somalia. In order to get a job in the modern sector in Somalia, it was beginning to become essential to be certified by a British board of examiners. A secondary effect of this system is that it prepares Africans (and students all over the world in the former British Empire) for jobs in the British economy—and the British intellectual community becomes their obvious reference group.

When education is in a European language, it is logical and economically efficient to borrow the school texts from the European country. One geography text book still used in places in Africa for preparation of Cambridge "O" level (secondary school leaving) examinations discusses the tropical African climate, and tells the student that "the high temperature, heavy rainfall, and humid atmosphere make white labour impossible.... Hence .... their development [is contingent] on coloured peoples who can work in such climates, and white people are generally engaged in the work of organization."[36] In Somalia, the decision to use Somali as the medium of instruction in all levels of education has already entailed the phasing out of the Cambridge examinations. Already it has meant the introduction of textbooks which discuss aspects of Somalia's wealth such as the rich variety of animal and plant life, rather than dwelling on its economic poverty. Its newly written history text for elementary students is also Somali-centric, and it is doubtful that any Somali in the future will think that it was *his* ancestors that crossed the English Channel in 1066. Furthermore, the use of a recognized Somali script has encouraged Somali intellectuals to publish scholarly and artistic works in their own language. The encouragement of a lively cultural environment is surely one way in which formerly dependent countries can contain its intellectuals.[37] If a colonial mentality was a byproduct of Western education in Africa, a switch to the vernacular could bring about significant change.

Dependency is manifest in economic affairs as well. It has been hypothesized that in economic affairs country A is dependent on country B if the trade between those two countries is a significant percentage of A's total trade but a relatively insignificant percentage of B's total trade. Any discontinuities in the trade pattern, then, would have substantial impact on the economy of A but a not very noticeable impact on the economy of B. A would therefore be more vulnerable to threats from B than B would to threats from A; thus A would be beholden to, or dependent on, B.[38] Since trade with African countries has always been a relatively negligible portion of Europe's total trade, while trade with Europe has always been a substantial percentage of most African countries' trade, most newly independent African states, at least in trade, were dependent on their former imperial rulers. Italy and, to a lesser extent, Great Britain were significant trading partners for Somalia at the time of independence. If my analysis of the relationship of language to dependency carries over to the economic sphere, then as the official importance of the English language waxed in Somalia, economic dependency on the English-speaking West ought to have waxed as well. Conversely, as the official importance of the Italian language waned, trade dependency on Italy ought to have waned.

Trade data, however (see table 5), lend only partial confirmation to the view that trade relationships, and therefore the possibility of political dependency, follow or vary with language policy. Somalia, even at the time of independence, had not been brought into the trading spheres of its colonial rulers to the extent other new African states had. Over a quarter of Somalia's trade in 1961, the first full year of independence, was dispersed among a plethora of states outside the colonial sphere. By 1971, trade with these other states accounted for nearly half of Somalia's total trade, and that in itself acts as a buffer against trade vulnerability. Because Somalia was never really colonized, its trade was not closely tied to the states which purported to rule the territory.

Nonetheless, there is some degree of correspondence between language and aggregate trade. In the 1960s the Arabic language continued to be the language of religion and the language of early education, but receded in importance as a political language. Corresponding to this trend, Somalia's trade with the Arab world increased steadily in

Table 5 Dependency as Measured by Trade (Each figure represents a percentage of Somalia's total imports and exports)

Trading Partner	1961	1962	1963	1964	1965	1967	1968	1969	1970	1971
Italy	43.1	38.6	34.6	33.2	36.7	32.6	31.9	29.3	28.1	25.4
United Kingdom	7.3	5.3	4.9	7.7	3.7	3.8	4.4	5.8	3.9	4.3
United States	2.8	5.2	2.5	2.3	3.6	4.1	6.0	7.4	4.9	4.4
United Arab Republic	2.8	3.4	3.3	3.9	1.9	1.4	2.0	.2	.8	1.5
Arabian Peninsula	16.3	19.1	18.3	18.9	18.6	26.6	25.7	31.4	28.5	21.3
Other	27.7	28.4	36.4	34.0	35.5	31.5	30.0	25.9	33.8	43.2

Sources: 1961-65 data are from the United Nations Yearbook of International Trade. The 1966-71 data are from the Yearbook of International Trade Statistics, 1970-1971.

importance over the decade; but with the UAR, the principal political influence in the Arab world on Somalia, the percentage of trade declined. Over that same period, the English language continued to grow in importance in the Somali Republic. A slow increase in the relative importance of trade with the United Kingdom and the United States is perceptible in that period, reaching its peak in 1969, the year of the revolutionary coup.

Somalia's trade with Italy, however, does vary significantly along the predicted lines. In 1961, 43 percent of its imports and exports were with Italy. By 1969, that percentage was down to 29. The 1960s saw a parallel decline in Somalia's use of the Italian language.

Although no unambiguous relationship can be established between language policy and political dependency, the evidence presented in part 2 does show that the use of English as the language of the state, if continued, would have had a significant independent influence on changes in Somalia's political culture.

Somali
The Language of Politics

2

6

Linguistic Relativity
A Theoretical Introduction

Birds perched together on the same tree
Call each their own cries,
Every country has its own ways,
Indeed people do not understand each other's talk.

Anonymous Somali poem[1]

Linguistic Relativity: The Theory

Franz Boas was perhaps the first American anthropologist to suggest the close interrelationship between culture and language.[2] Having worked in Berlin and being therefore aware of the seminal work of Wilhelm von Humboldt a century earlier, Boas speculated in 1911 that "purely linguistic inquiry is part and parcel of a thorough investigation of the psychology of the peoples of the world ... and human language ... would seem to belong naturally to the field of work of ethnology."[3] Boas's fieldwork, however, went in a different direction. In 1912 Edward Sapir attacked the Boasian formulation, arguing that while culture can and does change, language remains quite stable, so that "the forms of language will in course of time cease to symbolize those of culture."[4] This contention helped lay Boas's idea to rest for a decade in American anthropology.

Yet it was Sapir, whose views of language and culture developed considerably over the next two decades, who helped revive Boas's theory. By 1921, in his brilliant *Language*, Sapir could affirm that "language and our thought-grooves are inextricably interrelated,"[5] and as evidence he pointed to possible differences between languages which express conditions of time, object, and mood *before* the verb (as the Bantu languages do) and ones which do so *after* the verb (as Eskimo does). He suggested that speakers of Bantu see the world as having "an architectural diagrammatic quality" and that the Eskimo world is more diffuse, having "a quality of pruning afterthoughts."[6] He further argued that "it must be obvious to any one who has thought about the question at all or who has felt something of the spirit of a foreign language that there is such a thing as a basic plan, a certain cut, to each language. This type or plan or structural 'genius' of the language is something much more fundamental, much more pervasive, than any single feature of it that we can mention."[7] And that is why, somewhat dissatisfied with his conclusion, Sapir mourned that "it is so difficult in practice to apply these elusive, yet important distinctions."[8]

But another concern held Sapir back from pursuing notions of linguistic relativity much further; and that was his concern to demonstrate that no language was "inferior" to another, and that native Americans did not belong to an inferior culture. "As there is nothing to show that there are significant racial differences in the fundamental conformation of thought, it follows that the infinite variability of linguistic form ... cannot be an index of such significant racial differences.... The latent content of all languages is the same—the intuitive *science* of experience."[9] True to his academic training, Sapir advises that, until patterns of relating language with culture can be discovered, "we shall do well to hold the drifts of language and culture to be noncomparable and unrelated hypotheses."[10]

By 1924, however, Sapir introduced the notion of "relativity" of concepts between languages. In a 1929 paper he suggested that "human beings do not live in the objective world alone, nor alone in the world of social activity as ordinarily understood, but are very much at the mercy of the particular language which has become the medium of expression for their society.... The 'real world' is to a large extent unconsciously built up on the language habits of the group.... We see and hear and otherwise experience very largely as we do because the language habits of our community predispose certain choices of interpretation."[11] By 1931 Sapir was suggesting that different languages are akin to different mathematical systems, and that study of language categories would demonstrate "the tyrannical hold that linguistic form has upon our orientation in the world."[12] These speculations were subject to two major problems. First, anthropologists feared that studies in linguistic relativity would lead to invidious comparisons between European languages and "primitive" languages, leading to charges of "ethnocentrism." Second, neither Boas nor Sapir was clear as to what kind of evidence was needed to demonstrate the interrelationship of language and culture. It was Benjamin Lee Whorf who was able to make progress in both of these areas.

While Sapir was training university students to be linguists, Whorf, trained as a chemist, was working as an insurance inspector. His job was to visit the factories of his company's clients to see if they were complying with fire safety standards. In one factory, he noticed workers, during one of their breaks, smoking cigarettes in a room filled with "empty gasoline drums." Whorf recognized that even though these drums, because of the fumes, were more dangerous than drums filled with gasoline, the workers chose to smoke next to them. Because in English we perceive containers that are filled with only fumes as "empty," these English speakers intuitively felt that they would be safe. Whorf concluded from this experience that "people act about situations in ways which are like the ways in which they talk about them." Similarly, he attributed the cause of one fire to careless behavior around "spun limestone," a very inflammable substance but considered safe because the notion of "stone" implies noncombustibility.[13]

On his own initiative, Whorf began to study native American communities, and did studies in the Hopi and Shawnee languages. To enhance his understanding of linguistics, he studied under Professor Sapir. From his own intuition, his work with native American informants, and his study under Sapir, he developed—and argued in a number of provocative essays—the "language relativity theory." The theory, according to Whorf, "holds that all observers are not led by the same physical evidence to the same picture of the universe, unless their linguistic backgrounds are similar, or can in some way be calibrated"; and "that *users of markedly different grammars* are pointed by their grammars toward different types of observation and different evaluations of externally similar acts of observation, and hence are not equivalent as observers but *must arrive at somewhat different views of the world.*"[14]

In one of Whorf's more suggestive examples of linguistic relativity he discusses the Hopi notion of "time," for he considered Hopi to be "a timeless language." The Hopi do not distinguish between past, present, and future, as we, speakers of SAE (Standard Average European), do, but demand that the speaker indicate what type of verification the speaker is employing. For instance, *wari* can be translated as "Running, statement of fact" and mean (to us), "He ran." *Warikni* can best be translated as "Running, statement of expectation" and means (again to SAE speakers) "He will run." Finally *warikngwe* is translated as "Running, statement of law" and means (to SAE) "He runs" (e.g. on the track team). The Hopi therefore have a concept word "running" and modify it according to the mode of confirmation, rather than by its position in a sequence of events, as we do.[15]

Whorf then speculates: "How would a physics constructed along these lines work, with no T (time) in its equations?" Interestingly enough, he answers immediately, "Perfectly, as far as I can see, though of course it would require different ideology and perhaps different mathematics." Velocity would have to go, and in its stead perhaps we might have "I," intensity. Instead of acceleration, we might have "V," standing for variation. After constructing this new reality, Whorf muses:

> A scientist from another culture that used time and velocity would have great difficulty in getting us to understand these concepts. We should talk about the intensity of a chemical reaction; he would speak of its velocity or its rate, which words we should at first think were simply words for intensity in his language. Likewise, he at first would think that intensity was simply our own word for velocity. At first we should agree, later we should begin to disagree, and it might dawn upon both sides that different systems of rationalization were being used. He would find it very hard to make us understand what he really meant by velocity of a chemical reaction. We should have no words that would fit. He would try to explain it by likening it to a running horse. We should try to show him, with a superior laugh, that his analogy also was a matter of different intensities, aside from which there was little similarity between a horse and a chemical reaction in a beaker. We should point out that a running horse is moving relative to the ground, whereas the material in the beaker is at rest.[16]

Whorf even suggests that theories of (physical) relativity could be more easily expressed in Hopi. That Einstein, in order to present his theory of relativity, had to push the language of physics and mathematics into a new realm, unemcumbered by the limitations of the conventional SAE distinctions, lends some credence to Whorf's speculations. One of Einstein's biographers notes that Einstein was a late language learner and was always ill at ease listening to talk. Perhaps it took a man who could escape from the strictures of his own linguistic background to reformulate our conception of our physical universe?

Another of Whorf's more attractive examples concerns the differential association of concepts in different languages. For this, he takes two English sentences: "I push his head back" and "I drop it in the water and it floats." He then translates them into Shawnee, and demonstrates that the two sentences are nearly the same. Whorf then draws a pictorial essay of these two events for the English speaker and the Shawnee in order to show how differently the two speakers perceive the two events. The key to this puzzle is that the Shawnee speaker sees "pushing back" against some "force" to be the verb in both sentences. The thing in the water is not "floating" but rather is being pushed back to the surface of the water. And if the Hopi concept of time is more amenable to Einstein than SAE is, the Shawnee concept of force is more consistent with Archimedes than SAE is.[17] Whorf was therefore able not only to give fascinating and provocative examples of linguistic relativity but also, by showing where native American conceptualization was superior to that of SAE, to avoid the charge of ethnocentrism.

The work of the linguistic relativists has nonetheless met with much criticism. For one, although Whorf wavered between a "linguistic relativity principle," which argues that the language one speaks *influences* how one perceives the universe, and a theory of "linguistic determinism," which argues that the language one speaks *determines* one's conception of the universe, the latter formulation (in which he says speakers of different languages "*must* arrive at somewhat different views of the world"—my emphasis) is clearly the more exciting one. However exciting, it is unprovable, and any (understandable) evidence is necessarily self-contradictory. In order to prove a theory of linguistic determinism, Whorf would have had to show two languages, L_1 and L_2, with different "grammars" and therefore different "views of the world" whereby observers in L_1 "must" see things in a different way from observers in L_2. The only way this could be done is to make a statement about the world in L_1, call it S_1, and demonstrate that it could not have been seen in L_2. But in order to make that demonstration it would be necessary to translate the statement into L_2 and to determine whether such an observation were possible. If S_1 could not be translated, then speakers of L_2 (that is, the scientific community to which the linguist is showing his research) could not evaluate the evidence as to whether they could have made the observation. If, for instance, Whorf took a proposition from Hopi and claimed that (a) he understood it, and (b) he could not translate it into English, his audience would have to take his word for it that the hypothesis was proved. But the device would only show that Whorf could not translate a particular Hopi phrase, and not that a particular Hopi observation statement could not have been made by a speaker of English.

If in fact Whorf could translate S_1 into S_2, even if it took some circumlocution, then he would have to prove that statement S_2 could not have been arrived at by a speaker of L_2. But in a sense as a speaker of L_2, Whorf, or any linguist, would have just made the observation. If Whorf said it in L_2, it could well have been said before. The grammar could not have militated against S_2 being said before if it is being said now. The problem is this: if no translation is possible, then there is no evidence that the principle has been confirmed; if translation is possible, then that very translation is evidence against the theory of linguistic determinism. The only way to confirm the principle is to be unable to give an example—a process that can hardly be called confirmation. Returning to Einstein, we can say that although he had difficulty overcoming the hurdles imposed on his thought by SAE, he eventually was able to talk about relativity in an SAE language. So not only do we not have evidence supporting a theory of linguistic determinism, but there can be no evidence.[18]

Abandoning the more exciting determinist theory, I can now examine the criticisms of the "relativity" theory, and question the nature of the evidence that Whorf used. Whorf seems to have assumed, at least in the Shawnee example, that synonymous concepts are somehow deeply associated in the mind of the speaker. Because a Shawnee speaker uses the same verb for "pushing" (back a head) as he does for "floating" (an inanimate object), Whorf assumed that the speaker "sees" the same thing happening, but with different subject and object. But must this be so? And should we necessarily assume that happens? John Carroll, once a strong supporter of the Whorfian hypothesis but now less sanguine about its prospects, reminds us that English speakers don't see "breaking a fast" as the same activity as "breaking a stick," merely with different objects. He therefore argues that the Shawnee example "is really no evidence at all; it merely points to the possibility of such differences in cognition that might be confirmed by appropriate investigation."[19]

Alongside his assumption that using the same word for two things or two actions means that the speaker of the language sees these things or actions as related, Whorf makes another assumption, equally questionable—that if one language has a word for something, speakers of the language can see that something, unlike the speakers of a language who have no word for that something. He suggests, for instance, that because the Eskimo has many different words for what SAE speakers call "snow," depending on its state, the Eskimo can see many changes occurring during a storm, while for us SAE speakers it is simply "snowing."[20] Whorf is assuming that to see something, or to have a concept of something, we must have a word for it.

This assumption, that the vocabulary of a language gives us an inventory of the cognitive capacities of the speakers of that language, also seems false. I am reminded of the experience I had so often in

Somalia, smelling the rain miles away in the desert, knowing that it would not reach us. We sometimes experience the smell of rain evaporating at a distance, but have no word for it. The Somalis do have a verb, *sexansaho*, which stands for that sensation. I do not believe that I experienced that feeling any less than the Somalis, although I had no single word to describe the experience. Or, to take Whorf's example, surely we can see the changes occurring in a snowstorm even if we cannot describe them as efficiently as the Eskimo.

Carroll attacks this assumption too. He suggests that farmers have been prying up stones in all cultures and in all eras, many of them without a verb "to pry," and most without the concept word "lever." Surely we don't need the word "lever" to suggest more efficient ways of getting stones off of our fields. These observations lead one to reject the assumption that for those languages which have no word for concept x, native speakers of that language do not perceive x.

This criticism becomes more compelling when we deal with concepts such as "trust" or "authority." What would it mean to say a language had no word for these concepts? Would it necessarily imply that the native speakers of that language do not have these concepts? Again, I think not. We usually experience a variety of situations which teach us concepts before we learn the words for them. "Put on your sweater," "Eat your vegetables," "Don't leave your room": only later do we find words to express the relationship—"authority"—implied in those contexts. To observe a society which has no word for "authority" and to conclude from that observation that the speakers of that language have no concept of "authority" would be foolhardy. Even more so if the religious leader is observed saying, "Let us pray," after which everyone prays. The same is true for "trust": "Tomorrow I'll take you to the zoo," "I promise I'll return it," and other contexts teach us what it is to trust people; and this learning can take place without using the word "trust."[21] While it is an interesting datum that language L_1 has no word for x, whereas language L_2 does, and while this should be cause for further investigation, by itself that datum is inconclusive.

A third criticism of the Whorfian hypothesis is that it is too static and does not provide for changing world views or modes of perception in one language community, or revision of concepts or creativity outside the boundaries of that language. In Western philosophy, users of SAE have been rationalists and empiricists, analytic and metaphysical. Descartes, Kant, Hegel, and Wittgenstein, philosophers of considerably different *Weltanschauungen*, were all speakers of SAE. Similarly, in the scientific community, there have been what Thomas Kuhn has called "scientific revolutions," where geniuses have been able to postulate new universes from the ones the scientific community had accepted, again all in SAE. In these scientific revolutions—from Aristotle to Galileo, from Ptolemy to Copernicus, and from Newton to Einstein—according to Kuhn, "the world itself changes" both for the creative genius and for the next generation of "normal" scientists.[22] These observations are in indirect criticism of Whorf's linguistic relativity theory, because Whorf does say that each language has linked to it a certain metaphysic, a certain way in which the world is perceived. And these observations suggest that in philosophy and in science a whole set of seemingly unrelated metaphysics is possible for the language community of SAE, and that these metaphysics are subject to change.

More generally, Whorf seems to ignore the role of creativity for man in all his communications. Through neologism or metaphor, speakers of any natural language are able to recreate their universes in multifarious ways. Eric Lenneberg, experimental biologist and one of the pioneers in linguistic relativity research, made this point in a recent reappraisal of the Whorfian hypothesis. Whorf, he suggests, had not really recognized that language "does not cripple or bind the speaker because he can make his language, or his vocabulary, or his power of word-creation, or his freedom in idiosyncratic usages of words do any duty that he chooses, and he may do this to a large extent without danger of rendering himself unintelligible because his fellow men have similar capacities and freedoms which also extend to understanding."[23] The point of these criticisms is not that interlinguistic differences in conceptualization or in lexical inventory are irrelevant or unimportant, but rather that insights of this nature are at best inconclusive.

Nonetheless, substantial numbers of philosophers, psychologists, biologists, anthropologists, and linguists have been sufficiently intrigued by Whorf's work to go out into the field and "test" the linguistic relativity hypothesis. These researchers must have gone into their work with feelings akin to those of philosopher Max Black, who, after reviewing Whorf's essays for *Philosophical Review* and making some of the criticisms discussed above, admitted: "I do not wish the negative conclusions reached to leave an impression that Whorf's writings are of little value. Often enough in the history of thought the unsoundest views have proved the most suggestive. Whorf's mistakes are more interesting than the carefully hedged commonplaces of more cautious writiers."[24]

Testing for Relativity

Attempts to test for linguistic relativity have yielded, on the whole, negative or trivial results. Joshua Fishman, a scholar who has helped found and develop the subdiscipline of sociolinguistics in America, has classified the various attempts.[25] To do so, he made two important distinctions. First, he considered the linguistic data that the field researcher used in order to hypothesize a possible difference between two language communities. He distinguishes between lexical/semantic differences and grammatical/syntactic differences. The former category refers to words that may exist in one language but do not in the other, or words that do not exactly translate across languages. Here the linguist is saying that differences in *meaning* are occurring. As for differences in syntax, the linguist would be pointing to such things as placement of adjective, requirements of distinction (say of gender), and requirements of tense. Here the linguist is saying that differences in *form* are occurring. This first distinction concerns what may be considered the "cause" of differential cultural patterns or world views.

The second distinction refers to the cognitive data used to support the hypothesis. Fishman says that the researcher either relates the language difference to cultural themes which are found to be in that language community, or he relates his language data to individual performance or attitudes. If the first distinction concerns "cause," this second distinction concerns the different modes of studying the "effects" of linguistic differences. By making these two distinctions—on the kind of evidence used to develop the hypothesis, and on the kind of evidence used to support the hypothesis—Fishman is able to distinguish among four different levels of empirical study. On level 1 there are the studies that relate lexical/semantic differences to differential cultural themes. On level 2 there are the studies which relate lexical/semantic differences to differences in individual attitudes and performances. Level 3 studies relate grammatical/syntactic differences to general cultural differences. And Level 4 studies relate grammatical/syntactic differences to differences in individual attitudes and performances.

I have already covered most of the ground on level 1, as this is the kind of study that Whorf himself often did. The great number of Eskimo words for snow (lexical difference) can be related to the importance of snow in Eskimo culture (cultural theme). On this same level, it has been pointed out that the French have only one word for both "conscience" and "consciousness," and this has been related to fusions in French philosophy of these concepts which seem odd or unclear to the reader of the English translation. Other lexical items, like the untranslatability of the German *Gemütlichkeit* into English, also fit at this level; although I am not sure whether proponents of this insight wish to suggest that German speakers are more or less *gemütlich* than English speakers, or if an English speaker can be *gemütlich* at all. Other than saying that translations are often hazardous, presenting great hurdles, I am not sure what can be gleaned from this level. These insights seem intuitively important, but by themselves they provide insufficient substantiation to a theory of linguistic relativity.

Level 2, the attempt to relate lexical differences to individual performance or attitude, has been the predominant mode of relativity testing, perhaps because the hypothesis lends itself to examination by experimental psychologists, who are well equipped to detect performance or attitude changes in chosen subjects through changes in the testing environment. Many researchers have centered their research design on "color" because the way we divide the color spectrum, or in fact the way any language divides the spectrum, is inherently arbitrary. We can therefore find considerable differences across cultures. That the Shona people in Zimbabwe have a name for what we would call "greenish yellow" (*cicena*), and another for "greenish blue" (*Citema*) does not mean that English speakers or Shona speakers are wrong, but different. What *we* see as a boundary line between colors, *they* see as a true color, and vice versa. Many psychologists have hypothesized that differences in the naming of colors can be related to different abilities or different performances in regard to color discrimination.[26]

In 1954, Brown and Lenneberg reported a significant correlation between codability (having a word for the color) and memory. Further they reported that recall of colors is faster with greater codability. They did not work cross-culturally, due to the difficulty of getting proper controls, but did note that some cross-cultural data were needed because the findings relating to codability and performance could demonstrate either that our names affect our perceptual abilities or that physiological factors have affected hue discrimination in certain parts of the spectrum.

But further tests weakened the Brown and Lenneberg finding. Other psychologists changed the setting slightly and found negative correlations between codability and recall or recognizability. So Lenneberg now suggests that if some studies found a positive correlation, and others a negative, surely, if the stimuli were chosen a slightly different way, zero correlations could be managed. And in experiments with deaf children, Lenneberg was able to demonstrate that no cognitive disabilities resulted from lack of language. In his retrospective analysis of this whole research program, Lenneberg cites the conclusions of Lantz and Stefflre, who tried to overcome some of the inconclusivensss of the previous testing. They found that, "codability ... predicts recognizability only in special contexts ... [and that] communication accuracy or efficiency will depend frequently on individual ingenuity rather than on the language spoken by the communicator." Lenneberg therefore concludes that "the semantic structure of a given language only has a mildly biasing effect upon recognition under special circumstances."[27]

Leonard Doob has attempted to carry out color tests cross-culturally. He used subjects with languages rich in color terms (the Luos of western Kenya) and attempted to compare them with peoples whose languages were relatively poor in color terms (the Ganda of Uganda and the Zulu of South Africa). He gave cardboard sorting tasks and Rorschach color plates to both groups, but was unable to find any consistent differences in performance between the subjects whose language was "rich" and those whose language was "poor" in color vocabulary.[28] Psychological testing of the Whorfian hypothesis, in an attempt to relate color vocabulary to various types of performance, has, in sum, been a failure. Where some successes were found, the results were trivial.

Still on level 2, but not concerned with color, Carol Scotton has done extremely suggestive work on Swahili political words in her research in Tanzania.[29] When Swahili became the national language of Tanzania, various new words had to be coined to fit the needs of a modern state. One such word was "citizen," for which Swahili, never before a language of state, had no counterpart. Prime Minister Julius Nyerere chose to use the word *mwananchi*, which literally means "child of the land." Scotton did some informal and unsystematic interviewing of Swahili speakers. She found that most people, when asked in Swahili, thought it odd for Asians or for others not born in Tanzania to become *mwananchi*, even though many in these groups were already legal citizens.

Here Scotton has taken a lexical item (word for "citizen") and found that the assumptions concerning who can become a Tanzanian citizen were influenced by that lexical item. It ought to be made clear that the testing here was quite informal, and today Scotton feels, for a number of reasons, that this point is not worth pursuing. Nonetheless, she has shown that a lexical item can mold attitudes, which seems to be an element of confirmation of the Whorfian hypothesis. But only partly. Nyerere, in choosing the word *mwananchi*, was not attempting to find an exact translation of "citizen" in Swahili but rather to influence his people's ideas about community membership. He could well have chosen *raia*, a much more neutral Arabic loan word for "citizen." What Scotton's work shows, then, is not that a Swahili speaker and an English speaker see different political universes, but rather that richly connotative words can be employed to form and reform mass attitudes and perceptions. This is a well-known political ploy: what one political actor calls "welfare" a second actor might call "social insurance benefits." How a political leader defines an issue will often be important to the way the public understands it.

Although most of the tests of the Whorfian hypothesis have been on the lexical levels (levels 1 and 2), Whorf fully intended to include the whole linguistic system, and especially the grammar of a language, in his principle of relativity. In fact, one of his more interesting examples, the one concerning Hopi concepts of time, was on level 3. He tried to relate the fact that the Hopi do not have tenses, only markers for mode of validation, and other aspects of "time" in their grammar, to cultural facts such as the "timelessness" of Hopi life and that duration and certainty of events is of greater importance to a Hopi than the time when the event occurred. The anthropologist Hoijer, working with the Navajo, was able to demonstrate that the Navajo link their verbs and subjects in such a way as to involve the subject in preexisting actions. Hoijer related this syntactical phenomenon to the passivity of the Navajo, and to their mythology, which suggests that individuals must adjust to a universe which is given to them.[30] Similar attempts have been made with Western languages, relating the propensity for inductive thinking among English speakers because they put their adjectives before nouns, and the propensity for deductive modes of thinking among the French because they put their adjectives after nouns.

The major problem with this type of analysis is that one is never sure whether the language is causing cultural differences or merely reflecting them. To show congruence between linguistic and other cultural norms is not to show cause.

Level 4, because it would require the researcher to demonstrate attitude change due to language change, would overcome this difficulty. Unfortunately, very little work has been done on this level. The most notable set of experiments was done by Carroll and Casagrande, reported in 1958, concerning differences in Navajo grammar from English grammar. In the Navajo grammatical system one cannot say, "Give me that object," alone; one must affix on to the verb some kind of specification of that object, such as long and rigid, or flexible, or flat and flexible, and so on. From this grammatical point, Carroll and Casagrande hypothesized the Navajo-speaking children "would learn to discriminate the 'form' attributes of objects at an earlier age than their English-speaking compeers."

The research design involved giving young monolingual Navajo children an "object triads test"; that is, the children were given three objects—say, a yellow rope, a blue rope, and a yellow stick—and were asked to choose the two that "went best" together. Since the verbs accompanying "rope" and "stick" require different affixes in Navajo, it was thought that Navajo speakers were more likely, in this case, to classify the different colored ropes as more alike, and that the English speakers were more likely to choose on the basis of color. The results were compared with the results of bilingual English-Navajo speaking Navajo children. Carroll and Casagrande got partial confirmation of their hypothesis, finding that the Navajo monolingual group classified in terms of shape at an earlier age than their bilingual counterparts. But as age increased, the differences disappeared.

The same study was replicated in a Boston suburb and in New York's Harlem. It was found that the Bostonians were more like the Navajo monlinguals and the New Yorkers were more like the bilinguals. Here it was explained that because the Boston children were more exposed to toys and puzzles, with an emphasis on form, than the ghetto residents of Harlem, they would be more attuned to shapes. With this evidence, however, Carroll and Casagrande were forced to conclude that the differences based on language abilities were significant but small, and could be relatively easily overcome.[31]

Unfortunately for those who want to find support for linguistic relativity, even their initial finding is highly questionable. They were, after all, not comparing speakers of language L_1 with speakers of language L_2, but rather speakers of language L_1 who had (presumably) no Western education with speakers of languages L_1 and L_2 who were (presumably) exposed to Western education. What this means is that a series of possible independent variables (socioeconomic status, exposure to education, literacy, bilingualism) could explain the differences found, and there is no special reason to accept the "grammatical differences" explanation as the cause of the differential results. But this criticism is moot, because in their replication they did find that other environmental factors, having nothing to do with language, have bearing on mode of classification in the "object triads test."

Given the nature of the empirical support of the Whorfian hypothesis, on each of the four levels, one cannot but agree with Fishman when he concluded that "although evidence favoring the Whorfian hypothesis exists at each level, it seems likely that linguistic relativity, though affecting some of our cognitive behavior, is nevertheless only a moderately powerful factor and a counteractable one at that."[32] And even John Carroll, in a similar review of the literature, was forced to conclude that "the linguistic relativity hypothesis has thus far received very little convincing support. Our best guess at the present is that the effects of language structure will be found to be limited and localized."[33]

Toward a Reformulation

The experimental data on the Whorfian hypothesis create a dilemma for scholars. On the one hand, the tests of the language relativity hypothesis show at best only limited verification; and on the other hand they have a lurking feeling that there is something true and important about the hypothesis. My experiences in Somalia led me to believe, albeit intuitively, that language could influence culture; yet the research tradition to which I referred seemed inadequate to analyze the dynamic effects of language on culture. I still felt that the idea of linguistic relativity was subject to empirical testing, that the results need not be trivial, and that for my purposes language change could be seen as an explanation for political cultural change.

It was through an understanding of the later philosophy of Ludwig Wittgenstein that I was able to reformulate the linguistic relativity theory to overcome some of the problems of untestability and triviality. Wittgenstein himself had very little to say about language relativity, despite the fact that he saw all metaphysical problems as language problems and was bicultural himself. In his *Philosophical Investigations*, he does suggest that "to imagine a language means to imagine a form of life," which has been taken by some interpreters as Wittgensteinian support for language relativity,[34] but if this is so, there is very little in the *Investigations* that goes into the subject. In his earlier *Brown Book*, Wittgenstein speculated on various translation problems one might encounter in visiting a "tribe" whose language one does not know, but he does not suggest the problems are insuperable.[35]

Wittgenstein's contribution, then, is less in what he had to say about linguistic relativity (even though support can be marshaled showing that he was amenable to such notions), than in how one can find out what it is that one really wants to know, and then how to design a way to get at it. My own reformulation of the linguistic relativity theory was made through a Wittgensteinian critique of its experimental tradition.

In relying on syntactic structures or semantics, the experimentalists under question have taken language "out of gear", out of its ordinary contexts. Presented in this manner, language appears more static than it really is, suggesting (incorrectly) that meaning is separable from worldly context. Linguists and philosophers sometimes distinguish (stable, rule-governed) meaning from changes due to context, and call the former "semantics" and the latter "pragmatics," but this distinction also has its limitations. Meaning is not like granite, refusing to yield to changing environments. We learn meaning from various uses, and the meaning of words often changes with changing external circumstances. Wittgenstein supplies a number of illustrations to demonstrate that the sense of a sentence is something more than (or different from) the meanings of the words in that sentence.

Suppose "is" is explained as "equals," as in "one plus one is two." What then would "the rose is red" mean? Wittgenstein asks.[36] Or, what about, "He is expecting me"?[37] In this latter sentence one will not know, just by examining each word, whether he is actively walking around thinking about my coming, or merely that he would be surprised if I did not come. Only the context of this utterance, "Why isn't he at the bar?" / "He is expecting me," can signal the meaning.

Elsewhere in the *Investigations*, Wittgenstein explores the notion of "judging a motive."[38] He demonstrates that in order to know what it is to judge a motive, one must know more than what "judging" is and what a "motive" is. Similarly with "determining a length": we don't learn what this means by learning the meaning of "length" and "determine," because "the meaning of the word 'length' is learnt by learning, among other things, what is to determine length."[39] What Wittgenstein is suggesting here is that we usually learn words in our language, not by looking them up in the dictionary, but by living and acting in our world. Words are learned in various contexts, and the meaning of an utterance is more than the sum of the meanings of each word and more than the grammatical configuration of words. The worldly context is part and parcel of the meaning.

Stanley Cavell has suggested a particularly lucid example. By looking in a dictionary, one might learn that "voluntary" meant something like "proceeding from the will, or from one's own choice." Consider now the situation where someone walks into a room, sees his friend, and says, "Did you dress that way voluntarily?" Is a philosophic question here being asked concerning "free will" in dressing? What is obviously *meant* here is that he thinks his friend is dressing in a peculiar or fishy manner. While some philosophers would want to relegate the notion of peculiarliness in this utterance to "pragmatics" as sort of a residual category that can affect meaning, Cavell—rightly, I think—would maintain that the pragmatics is as rule-governed as the semantics, and that in the context described, "Why are you dressing so peculiarly?" is the meaning of the utterance.[40]

The significance of these examples, from the point of view of criticizing the experimental tradition of linguistic relativity, is that the experimentalists too often took meaning to be stable and fixed, rooted out from any context. By claiming that in language L, when a speaker says x he means, "____," any researcher is playing unfairly with language. The pragmatics of an utterance works in dynamic interchange with syntax and semantics, and we cannot be at all sure of the meaning of any utterance unless we know what went on before and what followed. This criticism of the semanticists who see meaning as stable (influenced by context but not developed and molded by context) is the source of the philosophic call to the return to "ordinary language." Wittgenstein and his students have asked that we look to ordinary language, not because the butcher or the baker knows what words mean better than the semanticist, but because it is through an understanding of the use of our own language that we can begin to understand the "grammar," or set of possible meanings, of our words.

J. L. Austin's work in ordinary language philosophy is quite suggestive for research in linguistic relativity, in part because he understands that "use" is an important indicator of "meaning." In "A Plea for Excuses," Austin argues that through a study of ordinary language it is possible to find keys to our own morality "by examining what we should say when."[41] From an examination of unacceptable excuses, Austin attempts to define more rigorously his own standards, and the standards, he suspects, of his language community.

Although he is not explicit on this, one could derive from his discussion a guide to an anthropologist or ethnolinguist who came to study the English tribe. The anthropologist should notice that it is acceptable to tread on a snail "inadvertently," tip over the salt shaker "inadvertently," but *not* to tread on the baby "inadvertently." "Inadvertent" means, according to Austin, "a class of incidental happenings which must occur in the doing of any physical act," and is used when that incidental happening causes some (usually small) distress. Our foreign anthropologist, in learning English, might capture the sense of "inadvertence" as meaning merely "unintentional" (which, incidentally, is the definition in my dictionary). Suppose he does tread on a baby in one of the native's houses, and offers, "I did it inadvertently." And suppose the native returns with: "That wasn't inadvertence! That was pure callousness." What is our anthropologist to think? Is he getting a lesson in the English language (he used "inadvertent" when he should have used "callous"), or was it a lesson in morality (treading on a baby is far more egregious than treading on a snail; and for the former, a simple excuse is not sufficient)? In fact, what the anthropologist is learning is both the English language *and* the standards of misdeeds among English speakers (this will be pursued in a moment); but the point here is that only through *use* can our ethnolinguist learn the range and boundaries of *meaning*.[42]

Austin's plea was that we, who are interested in self-understanding, should begin to listen to ourselves speak. From listening to our language "in gear" we can get clearer insights into both our meaning and our morality. Many contemporary sociolinguists have already begun to do work on precisely this theme. Dell Hymes and John Gumperz have suggested that an "ethnography of communication" could find structure in the nongrammatical aspects of speech.[43] In any language-culture environment, their work suggests, certain things normally are said, and other things normally are not said. Social and cultural norms exist for language as well as for other aspects of human behavior, and these norms require careful study. Fieldwork involves regular observation of a language-cultural community with a search for linguistic norms.[44] Ethnographers of language and communication have not, to my knowledge, asked to what extent the language norms perceived by the ethnographer would transcend a change in language, and to what extent these norms are peculiar to the normal speech habits of the language studied. While the ethnograhers of communication have made a substantial step in seeing that pragmatics, as are syntax and semantics, is rule-governed, and part and parcel of what we mean by language, they have not, as yet, explored the relevance of this for the notion of linguistic relativity.[45]

How might it be possible to find "relativity" in world view from ordinary speech patterns? Would not this involve the collection and collation of endless data? Fortunately, other psychologists, working on other problems, have already shown that it would not. Jean Piaget's theories, seminal in our understanding of childhood development, were put to test by having children talk, sometimes without structure, sometimes with, but always in extended situations. He was able to find different conceptions of what a rule is between different age groups. He did this not by asking children, "What is a rule?" but by providing a clear context—the game of marbles—and asking them, "Who made up the rules?" What would be a good new rule?" and "What would be a bad rule?" While this work is not related to issues of linguistic relativity, it does suggest the fruitfulness of watching language as it is being used, to get insights into the world view of the speakers.[46]

Lev Vygotsky, a Russian psychologist whose work paralleled Piaget's, was more explicit on this point than Piaget. He believed that speech acts directly on thought, and can alter activity. He gave this example from one of his experiments:

> A child of five and a half was drawing a streetcar when the point of his pencil broke. He tried, nevertheless, to finish the circle of a wheel, pressing down on the pencil very hard, but nothing showed on the paper except a deep colorless line. The child muttered to himself, "It's broken," put aside the pencil, took watercolors instead, and began drawing a *broken* streetcar after an accident, continuing to talk to himself from time to time about the change in the picture. The

child's accidentally provoked egocentric utterance so manifestly affected his activity that it is impossible to mistake it for a mere by-product, an accompanyment, not interfering with the melody.[47]

What this research demonstrates is that there is a difference in kind between the language that the semanticist describes, in content, form and function, and the language that people speak. And that if language in any important way influences world view, it can only be demonstrated through the ordinary spoken language.

This is not to say that the insights from syntax or semantics are unimportant, or not useful in working with the linguistic relativity hypothesis, but rather that those insights should be taken as invitations to further inquiry. Differential conceptualization is not proof of linguistic relativity. Any attempt to isolate the conceptualization outside of language in some task will not lead to any proof of linguistic relativity. "Concepts," Wittgenstein suggests, "lead us to make investigations; are the expression of our interest, and direct our interest."[48] From these insights about any language, we ought to make investigations, and listen to the language as it is being spoken.[49]

My criticism of the research tradition attempting to validate the linguistic relativity theory has up to this point concerned itself with the possible causes of differential world views. According to Fishman, investigators have chosen either some lexical/semantic difference or some grammatical/syntactic difference between languages, and have then attempted to relate those differences to wider cultural differences. I have suggested that meaning is in part determined by use, and that the isolation of syntax and semantics from pragmatics has made researchers insufficiently attuned to meaning. And without clearer criteria of meaning, any statement of linguistic relativity would be suspect.

But then a second question arises. If, in doing experiments, one gets his subjects to talk, how can this talk be related to action or to behavior? The need to relate a linguistic difference to some cultural or behavioral difference was inherent in Fishman's classification. And to this problem, a Wittgensteinian approach can provide some direction. In his *Investigations*, Wittgenstein suggests that the distinctions between language and action, or between describing and performing, are untenable. Again and again in his later work he invites his reader to consider language as activity. "The *speaking* of language is part of an activity, or of a form of life," he tells us, and "words are also deeds."[50] To develop his point more fully, Wittgenstein quotes an appropriate passage from Augustine which describes how the author learned language. Augustine "confesses" that he learned language by learning the names of things, then by being able to utter the sounds, and thereby could make his wishes known.

Using Augustine as a foil, Wittgenstein aimed to investigate this "naming" or "label" theory of language learning. Words are not labels, according to Wittgenstein, but tools, and they perform manifold functions. If every word is a label to signify a thing, what do "Ow!" "No!" or "Help!" signify?[51] What about "this?" Is "this" (or "there") a name for a thing (or a name for a place)? What about words like "double" in Bridge, or "check" in Chess? What are they labels of? From words like these, and from an examination of many different types of language activities or "language games," such as "giving orders," "guessing riddles," "play acting," "making up a story," and "speculating about an event," Wittgenstein reminds his readers that most words in most contexts are not names of classes of things.

J. L. Austin has attempted to demonstrate that certain utterances *are* actions, and he called these utterances "performatives." When someone says, "I promise," after claiming that he will return the money he owes, he is not, according to Austin, describing a promise, or speculating about promises. Merely saying those words is what we mean by "promising." Or again, when a man and a woman each says, "I do" during a specific ceremony, Austin points out that they "are not reporting on a marriage, [they are] indulging in it."[52] These performatives demonstrate that at least in certain areas, the distinction between speech and action is nebulous.

But Austin is not able to distinguish these "performatives" from many other types of (language) activity. First of all, it is not clear whether performatives are sufficient criteria for the action. If I say, "I promise," and in my own mind I have no intention of returning the money, am I *really* promising, or am I just saying I'm promising? "Promising" may require some further action, such as intending to keep the promise, in order for it to be a (real) promise. And second, many other "language games" have a "performative" element about them. If someone asks me, "Will you return the money?" and I come back with, "You can count on it," in some contexts my utterance is a promise, yet it doesn't contain what Austin meant by a performative. The clear distinction between speech and action that Augustine proposed was clearly false; and even the distinction between "acting" words and "descriptive" words that Austin attempts to uphold is not tenable.

Hanna Pitkin, in explicating both the Wittgensteinian viewpoint and Austin's contribution, identifies another class of speech, which she calls "quasi-performatives," maintaining that this class entails "much or perhaps all of language." A quasi-performative is an utterance which, while it "may not always be performing the action named in the speech, ... is always performing an action for whose consequences the speaker is responsible."[53] Take, for example, the word "fair," in "That's not fair." The speaker of this utterance is not only describing an attribute of an (unfair) action but may be judging an action as well. This judgment, like many public actions, entails certain responsibilities, for the speaker may be called upon to justify his judgment. Thus, in the proper context, "That's not fair" entails a commitment to justify oneself if called upon to do so. Pitkin's point is that although there is a descriptive element in the quasi-performative utterance, elements of responsible action and commitment are also part of its meaning. Thus part of the meaning *is* action.

Of course, speaking itself is an action.[54] But the notion of quasi-performatives suggests that the act of speaking usually entails manifold classes of actions: judging, claiming, evaluating, condemning, assessing, reproving, and objecting. Surely, just by listening to a person speak, an investigator can determine how the speaker judges actions, assesses opportunities, and evaluates alternatives. This observation seems to obviate the duality between language data and performance data that pervades linguistic relativity research. And once that duality is abandoned, the performance tests on which most investigators seemed to rely (color coding, classification of objects) become an unncessary encumbrance. Just by having subjects talk, an investigator can get sufficient "action" or "performance" for experimental purposes.

Political and Linguistic Relativity

Political words, unlike words in other language domains, are inherently murky. Consider first the word "green." If we are told that in language L the word for green is y, and then hear a native speaker of L referring to things we call green as v, and referring to things we call yellow as y, we are not apt to conclude that when *we* see *green*, a native speaker of L sees *yellow*. Rather we would conclude that we had been given the wrong translation from English to L. Now it is possible for color words to divide the spectrum differently, but one feels assured that with a little discussion between a speaker of English and a speaker of L, the two could work out an adequate arrangement for translation. This is because there is something "out there" (colors) to which the speakers of both languages could regularly refer and find out what label refers to what color.

But this would not and could not occur with political words like "justice," "responsibility," "representation," "authority," "legitimacy," "legal," "obligation," "equality," and so on. One is hard put to think of giving an ostensive definition for one of these terms as we would do for "green." Could you point to a man in an electric chair and say, "that's justice" to a child or a foreigner and expect him to understand what justice is? Certainly not as easily, although not itself without problems, as you could point to a piece of cloth, an artichoke, a pippin apple, and say, "that's green." Pitkin, in distinguishing between the grammar of words like "green" or the grammar of object words (words that can be taught through ostensive defintion) and social and political words, makes this same point:

> The interdependence of words and the world, the determining and limiting role of concepts on what is perceived as reality, will generally be most intensive with respect to human, social, cultural, and political things. Here, even more than in our language for the conceptualization of the physical world, what we see and what is there for us to see will depend on the concepts we bring to our experience. For actions and relationships and feelings and practices and institutions do not walk up to us like elephants and stand there, gently flapping their ears, clearly distinct from their surroundings, waiting to be inspected and named.[55]

The referents of political words, unlike those of words more susceptible to ostensive definition, are not so clearly "out there" in the world. In politics, corresponding words or intercultural understanding might not be found. Furthermore, the ambiguity of political words and concepts enables a bilingual to live in two different worlds, without clearly seeing the different world views implied by each language.

Interestingly, Lenneberg's conclusions are consistent with this. He found in his color experiments that only in the most ambiguous areas in the spectrum was the significance of language differences detected. "These experiments," he concluded, "show that the semantic structure of a language may influence cognitive structuration where our physiological equipment allows for a range of alternative solutions."[56] While not physiologically harder to perceive, political concepts, are especially ambiguous and rarely have clear empirical referents. If language relativity could be demonstrated in any cultural arena, it would seem to be in the arena of politics.

Furthermore, it is difficult to conceive of what "politics" might mean without language. I think it would be possible to understand what "love" or "economics" or "religion" are without language, but not "politics." "The employment of language to sanctify action is exactly what makes politics different from other methods of allocating values," says Murray Edelman, and for him, politics is quintessentially talk.[57] He distinguishes among various language "styles" in politics and attempts to explain how a language style shapes a political activity. That legal language should be vague and ambiguous, allowing for various interpretations, is necessary for a functioning legal system, according to Edelman, because if laws were clear and noninterpretive, then the judicial system could not effectively operate. Edelman's main argument is that in order to understand politics, one must understand how language functions.

The notion that "politics" and "speech" are inseparable is a core element in Hannah Arendt's *The Human Condition*. "To be political, to live in a *polis*, meant that everything was decided through words and persuasion and not through force and violence. In Greek self-understanding, to force people by violence, to command rather than persuade, were prepolitical ways to deal with people characteristic of life outside the *polis*."[58] This understanding of what it is to be political reinforces my argument that language relativity, if it exists, must operate in the realm of politics. As Arendt says in her Prologue: "Wherever the relevance of speech is at stake, matters become political by definition, for speech is what makes a man a political being."[59]

Much speculative evidence on the relationship of language to politics is readily available. Thucydides, in his inventory of the horrors of the Peloponnesian war, noted that "words had to change their ordinary meaning to take that which was now given them." Only in a revolutionary era, Thucydides thought, would "reckless audacity" be considered "courage" or would "prudent hesitation" be considered "specious cowardice."[60] And George Orwell, in similarly dark times, argued "that the present political chaos [the 1940s] is connected with the decay of language, and that one can probably bring about some improvement by starting at the verbal end."[61] The degeneration of language, according to Orwell, was a signal for the degeneration of politics.

Other political commentators, in other contexts, have also reported what seemed to be language-related political phenomena. R. Cranford Pratt, a scholar able to observe the presidential office in Tanzania, has commented on the differential effects of Swahili versus English as the language of cabinet meetings. Before Zanzibar joined Tanganyika, the cabinet in Tanganyika used English as the medium of discussion. But since Zanzibari officials were not fully competent in English, and Tanganyikan officials were competent in Swahili, Swahili became the medium after the two republics united. Pratt noted that the more complete political vocabulary in English facilitated clear, precise decisions, and the decisions were therefore more "bureaucratic" in tone. Swahili, on the other hand, the language of political life, with "an expansive style of exposition which was often imprecise" led to less clear decisions, more "political" in tone.[62] The notion that different political styles can lead to different political content, as Pratt is here suggesting, complements Edelman's analysis of language styles in politics (and will be discussed more fully in chapter 8).

Anthony Nutting describing the 1952 coup d'état in Egypt, offers the following anecdote. On the eve of the coup, "Nasser came over to one of his close associates, overflowing with emotion, and said to him, in English, 'Tonight there is no room for sentiment; we must be ready for the unexpected.' His associate asked him why he had spoken in English, and Nasser replied, with a laugh, that Arabic was not a suitable language in which to express the need for calm."[63]

Other observers have examined the language of politics in various settings and speculated on language differences and possible concomitant political differences. Ali Mazrui, for one, has reflected on the very word "politics," its derivation from the Greek word for "city," and the fact that political consciousness in Africa seems to be inversely related to level of urbanization. Swahili, which had no root word for "politics" at all, had to borrow the Arabic *siyasa*. But *siyasa* has connotations of "justice at the discretion of the Muslim ruler," that is to say, the residual decisions in a community which are not directly religious.[64] So while "politics" has connotations of dealing with issues that concern the whole community, *siyasa* has connotations of dealing with residual, less important decisions for the community. Can the very connotations of the word you use to name the enterprise affect that enterprise? Mazrui does not answer this question.[65]

The Nyakusan word for "politician," according to Mazrui, is literally "a man who works against the government." In Tanzania, the Swahili word for "socialism" is *ujamaa*, literally "the concept of the family." In Luganda, the word for "capitalist" is *munyunyusi*, literally "one who sucks." And in Russian, the words for "hard" and "labor" both come from the same root, *trud*, making the statement "labor is hard" seem tautological. One cannot, in good faith, conclude very much from these insights until one observes how these words are used in multifarious political contexts and whether they direct discourse in certain regular patterns which are interculturally different. Politics may well be a realm of human activity in which a search for the possible effects of language on culture could yield fruitful results.[66]

7

Linguistic Relativity

An Empirical Formulation

The theory of linguistic relativity states that the language a person speaks to some extent influences the way that that person perceives and acts in his world. If this theory were to be confirmed, then the choice of a national language would entail a choice between differing behavioral patterns. Because political and social concepts seem to be the least rigid in all of our language domains, and are therefore most subject to differential conceptualization across language-culture groups, the choice of a national language can influence political relationships, political thought, and political culture. Moreover, the theory of linguistic relativity could furnish a partial explanation for the persistence of colonial values and institutions in independent Africa.

The Somali language is structurally quite different from what Whorf called Standard Average European, and it developed in a nomadic desert environment also different from Europe. Although many Somalis learned European languages, other aspects of European culture, such as urbanization, industrialization, secularism, and division of labor had very little influence on Somali society. It was therefore possible for me to find bilingual subjects in Somali-English who were relatively uninfluenced by Western culture, I could thus isolate the effects of language on thought and action from other possible independent variables. Moreover, the Somali language seemed appropriate for a case study because the Somali people (at the time I first went to Somalia) had been in the throes of an interminable debate concerning the language of politics, and the eventual choice was still a matter of doubt until October of 1972. English had begun to compete with Somali as the language of political discourse, and had already established itself as dominant in administrative discourse. The secondary effects, in terms of political thought and action, of language choice in Somalia were therefore politically relevant. Many multilingual African states have been forced to settle for a European language as their official language. And if the Somali case study were to yield results that confirmed the theory of linguistic relativity (in one context), those findings would suggest that the acceptance of a European language in other African states as the language of politics, based solely on efficiency criteria, may be having some as yet unconsidered secondary effects.

Still, the methodological hurdles to test adequately for linguistic relativity have been immense. Africa is a continent jealous of her knowledge; and scholars cannot go to Africa to harvest knowledge, as if it were a mango, from a tree. The Western scholar is like a blind man in Africa, and in reporting his findings he often sounds like a blind man describing the color green.

Personal Commitment to the Theory

In 1969 I went to the Somali Republic as a Peace Corps volunteer. The Peace Corps had a rather efficient language teaching program, and I received over four hundred hours of Somali language training, in groups ranging from two to six pupils. I was still far from fluent in the Somali language, and even now I can only use the language to convey and receive information. I am not able to converse extensively or freely in the language. My assignment in the Peace Corps was to teach and organize a high-intensity English-language program for qualified secondary school graduates of the Arabic and the Italian schools. These students were promised lucrative teaching jobs if they were certified by our program as having sufficient ability to transmit their subject matter to students in English.

It was through these experiences of learning Somali and teaching English that I developed ideas of linguistic relativity. I felt that there was a different social dynamic occurring among my students and colleagues when they were conversing in English and when they were conversing in Somali. I did not think that this difference was explained by their relative fluency in the languages, because I saw the same dynamic operating among Somalis who spoke English fluently, perhaps more fluently than Somali. And to a lesser extent (because my learning was much slower) I felt I myself was operating in a somewhat different world when I was speaking in Somali. Being a student of political theory, I began to relate the phenomenon I saw operating to ideas of cultural autonomy and political dependency. Could language be seen as a social institution which has its independent effects on other social institutions? Could the "colonial mentality" be formed and perpetuated, unbeknownst to the colonizers and the colonized, through the social institution of language? These were the seminal concerns of my research.

Upon return to the Univeristy of California after my Peace Corps service was over, I attempted to equip myself with the theoretical and methodological tools to give substance to some of the inchoate ideas I had developed while in Somalia. The literature cited in chapter 6 reflects my intellectual development after having experienced what I felt to be manifestations of linguistic relativity. Because of the nature of the research questions, I self-consciously designed a method that would attempt to find those areas in Somali and English where differences existed, and with behavioral implications. I was looking for examples of a language change fostering an attitudinal or behavior change, all other things being equal. I was not looking for examples of commonality, where language would have no effect, but for examples of language as a social variable which could explain some variance. I was not neutral concerning the theory.

The Testing Site
The military coup of 1969 in the Somali Republic has led to a government intent on changing the character of Africa's Horn. The Supreme Revolutionary Council has instilled fear in the hearts of most urban Somalis and has brought about a state of affairs where much work is being done. The rulers were able to get public acquiescence on the choice of a national script, and they have changed the Babelian administrative structure into one where Somali is the sole medium of inter- and intrabureaucratic exchange.

Unfortunately for me, however, the coup seriously curtailed my study. A few months after the coup, the military council decreed that the services of the Peace Corps were no longer needed and that Somali graduates were fully able to carry out our assignments. I therefore had to leave Somalia eight months after arrival. Some three years later, much to my surprise, and this time as a private citizen, I was granted a visa to the Somali Democratic Republic. I was granted research clearance shortly after my arrival, and some of the material that went into chapters 4 and 5 of this study was procured at that time. But the Somali government had evidently not been aware that the person to whom they granted the visa had been a Peace Corps volunteer there, even though I had mentioned it on my application. This time I was asked to leave two weeks after my arrival.

What I had always seen as Somalia's irredentist problem now became my personal opportunity. I applied for permission from the Kenyan government to do my research on linguistic relativity among the Somali population in Kenya's Northeastern Province. Although wary of working in what had until recently been a war zone, I was treated with utmost cordiality by both Somali and non-Somali Kenyans. That I did my research outside the boundaries of the Somali Democratic Republic, and in Waajeer in particular, presented both problems and opportunities.

The Northeastern Province has received very little scrutiny by scholars trained in anthropology and linguistics, and one cannot accept all the generalities about the Somali culture and language developed in areas to the north and to the east. Because Waajeer is in the southern part of the Somali lands, and migration has been north to south, the population of Waajeer is mixed and of somewhat recent arrival. No one Somali clan is dominant, and the population consists of Ogaadeen (Daarood), Dagodiya and Ajuraan (Hawiya), and various groups such as the Gurreh and the Murale, outside of the central clan divisions. Lewis suggests that the Ajuraan are closer to the Boran people (many Ajuraan to the west of Waajeer speak only Boran) than to the Somali, and that the customs of the Dagodiya diverge greatly from those of the other Somali clans, in that they have been only slightly Islamicized and their system of blood compensation is different from the Somali. Andrzejewski has suggested that the Gurreh are perhaps closer to the Galla people than the Somali, but are at best, on the fringe of the Somali nation.[1] Since Waajeer is in a penumbral area of the Somali nation, the language and the culture of the people there have been influenced by different, albeit closely related, cultures.

Furthermore, since the present-day Northeastern Province has been administered through the Kenyan administration for most of this century, the Swahili language has permeated the town. The few British administrators before Kenyan independence, and the larger number of "up-country" Kenyans present after 1963, all communicated with the Somali clans through the medium of Swahili—a relatively easy language in which to become moderately fluent. Official business in the Northeastern Province is usually carried out in that Bantu language.

Many Swahili words have thereby entered the Somali language of Waajeer, so that the language has lost some of its purity. Waajeer is a long distance from the former British Somaliland, where the classical Somali language is spoken and has developed. It has been subject to influence from languages of related peoples as well as from Swahili. The Somali language that my subjects spoke was a language somewhat different from classical Somali, and that, I think, worked against the success of some of the tests.

But the Waajeer site provided a number of unexpected advantages over research in the Somali Republic. Of all the areas in Somali territory, the Northeastern Province was probably least subject to European influence. The closest paved road was in Isiolo, and there was almost no evidence of "European" amenities. The town serves as a watering spot for nomads of many clans, and as a center for some trade, but there was little else. Even under the rule of independent Kenya, this province has been "forgotten." I heard one district officer there tell his friends that he was going to "Kenya" the next day, and did anyone want anything. In a public lecture in Nairobi, former Luo politician Tom Okelo-Odongo mused that on one of his trips to the Northeastern Province, someone asked him, "Oh, sir, do you come from Kenya?"[2]

Some statistical evidence bears this point out. Whereas in 1969 some 8 percent of the eligible primary age pupils were actually enrolled in primary school in the Somali Republic, in that same year only 1.5 percent of the primary age population was enrolled in primary school in the Waajeer District of the Northeastern Province. And in 1970 there was only one four-year secondary school in the entire province, with a total of 136 pupils.[3] It was at that one school, the Waajeer Secondary School, built in 1965, that I could do my research, for it was the only place in the province where there were a sufficient number of Somali-English bilinguals from the same social and regional background. The school was some four hundred miles from Nairobi and Muqdisho, the closest cities.

Because of this isolation I felt that any change in values or beliefs or actions that emerged from the use of the English language that were different from what emerged from the Somali language could well be attributed to language as a social institution. For here the English language was one of the very few elements of Western culture experienced. (The school system itself, and the whole notion of secular education, was clearly another influence, and that will be discussed more fully later.) And much to my surprise, the level of English in the Waajeer Secondary School equaled or surpassed the level of English attained by most of the secondary school students in the Somali

Republic. In the 1972 form 4 examinations, the Waajeer school placed six students in division 1 and eleven students in division 2, for one of the better performances in the entire Kenyan school system. Not only did the Waajeer students speak better English than their fellow Somalis in the neighboring republic, but they were able to perform as well or better than many students who had been brought up in an English-speaking environment. This point will emerge clearly when I document some of the transcripts in the following chapter.

In sum, I had to settle for Waajeer as my site. Given the political situation in the Somali Democratic Republic and the educational development in the Northeastern Province, it was the only place where sufficient subjects could have been found.

Creation of the Tests

Hypothesis formulation. I attempted to develop a set of verifiable hypotheses in areas where I thought linguistic relativity might be operating with Somali-English bilinguals. I took lexical items, ordinary speech patterns, proverbs, and concepts in Somali that appeared odd from the standpoint of an English speaker. I then attempted to determine what I considered to be possible attitudes, values, or actions that might be influenced by those items. I then could hypothesize that when speaking Somali the bilingual would be influenced in one way, and when speaking English he would be influenced another way. (In chapter 8, the origins of the confirmed hypotheses will be explained.)

Writing the tests. Once having developed hypotheses, I attempted to write interview questions, develop role-playing situations, and create a composition exercise that would be sensitive to the phenomena I was after. I had a Somali informant translate each question into Somali. I then had a second Somali informant translate the Somali back into English. Only after each question was translated back into the original question did I feel that the translation was accurate. I had to redo many of the questions after getting to Waajeer because of the differences in the local dialect.

Training informants. The most enjoyable aspect of training informants was that I had to teach the Kenyan Somalis the new script for their language. To many of the Somalis there I was providing a key to their continued cultural contact with the Somali Republic. Once this was done, my informants were able to translate for me fairly effectively. I decided to use two secondary school students at the Waajeer school as the administrators of the tests, believing that their fellow students would be less shy about responding to their peers. I taught the two students the range of responses I was looking for, and they suggested some revisions. I had them practice on me a few times. I often gave irrelevant answers, and tried to train them to keep asking until they got relevant answers. In this I was only partly successful.

**Substance
of the Tests**

The interviews. The interview (see exhibit 1) was designed for two purposes. First, I used it to get basic data on my subjects, in order to show that in relevant characteristics they were a homogenous group. Second, I was interested in eliciting a set of attitudes and values. I thought that the early basic data questions might warm the students up and give them confidence for the later questions, which were more open-ended and discussion-oriented. I was highly influenced by the interview technique, made famous by Jean Piaget, of constantly pursuing the subjects on the same question and recording the responses. Just as Piaget was interested in seeing how children of different age groups would justify rules, and was able to develop clear and consistent ways to code answers depending on the mode of justification, I was interested in seeing how Somali students justified their answers in different languages, and I attempted to develop clear ways of distinguishing various modal responses. All interviews were recorded on tape, and I was not present.

The role playing test. Since I had been convinced that most researches had failed to find linguistic relativity because they tended to take language out of gear, or out of its ordinary use, I set up structured role-playing situations between two Somalis. I formulated three different "situations," which each pair of subjects was asked to "perform realistically" (see exhibit 2). In both the interview and the role playing, I had half the subjects perform in Somali and half in English. If systematic differences in approach could be discerned between the Somali and the English interviews, or between the Somali and the English role-playing sessions, that accorded with my hypotheses, I was prepared to argue that the change in language could be the only explanation for the variance. For the hypotheses which were tied to certain questions, see exhibits 1 and 2, and for the more general hypotheses, see exhibit 3.

The composition test. Unlike the interview and the role playing, the composition exercise (see exhibit 4, with the hypotheses listed in exhibit 5) was developed when I was already in Kenya. The Waajeer site offered one other opportunity that I have yet to mention, and that I exploited. The Somali inhabitants of the Northeastern Province are in a very ambiguous political situation. They are ruled by Kenyans and have Kenyan citizenship, yet they are the same nationality as the people who rule the neighboring state. An important question is whether these Somalis would ever consider themselves Kenyans, and under what conditions. In order to deal with this question, and to determine whether language has any influence on national conception, I decided to use one of the exercises developed by Leonard Doob in his work on patriotism and nationalism in the South Tyrol.[4] Unlike Doob, I was interested in the extent to which the language of presentation influenced the expression of nationalist values. I therefore presented the composition exercise to half the subjects in Somali and the other half in English.

The listening test. Like the other three tests, the listening test (see exhibit 6) was administered to half the subjects in English and to the other half in Somali. Unlike the other three, the language of presentation was found not to be a salient variable. In the tape recordings of different voices, there were English speakers and Somali speakers, and we asked each student to evaluate each voice. The only difference in the two formats was in the language of the administration of the test, the language of the names of the characteristics on the answer sheet, and the language of the other labels on the answer sheets. That is to say, I was not comparing a Somali-language environment with an English-language environment in this test, as I had in the other tests. The answer sheet along with the hypotheses are presented in exhibit 7. The passage which all the "judges" listened to came from an article in the *Daily Nation* and dealt with the appointment of an African pilot to East African Airways. This was translated into Somali for the Somali readers.

**Administration
of the Tests**

Pretesting. When I was first in Somalia I used the role-playing technique with my students as a method of teaching English, and my students, who were quite sophisticated, took part without embarassment and with great seriousness. I was therefore

Exhibit 1. The Interview

Question	Purpose
1. Where were you born? 2. How old are you? 3. Have you traveled outside of Waajeer? Where? 4. What is your mother tongue? 5. What foreign languages do you speak? 6. What foreign language do you speak best?	1-6, 8, 9: I used the data from these questions in this chapter to show the similarity of testing groups.
7. Do you ever speak English outside of school? 7a. What language do you speak to your friends in the dormitory? 7b. What language do you use when playing football? 7c. What language did you use with Mr. Xasan Guleed outside the class? 8. What language does your father speak? 9. How many camels does your father own?	7. Hypothesis: the subjects would more likely answer "English" when asked in English, and "Somali" when asked in Somali.
10. Do you think Somali should become the medium of instruction in Waajeer schools? Why?	10. Hypothesis: there would be more "yes" answers when subjects were asked in Somali than when asked in English.***
11. Can someone be a Somali and not speak the Somali language?	11. Hypothesis: even though all the students knew people who considered themselves Somali yet could not speak Somali, many more students would answer "no" when asked in Somali than when asked in English.***
12. What makes someone a good speaker of English? 12a. Who in your class speaks the best English? 12b. Why is he able to speak it better than the others?	12. In translation to Somali, I substituted "Somali" for "English." Hypothesis: students would attribute good English to "practice" and good Somali to "intelligence."***
13. What job would you like to have when you are thirty years old? Why?	13. Hypothesis: students would have more ambitions for personal advancement in English than in Somali.***
14. Some people say that we should be forward-looking and plan for the future. They say we should reduce the number of our camels by selling them so that there will be enough grazing land for the next generation. Do you think our view of the future should change our customs or traditions? Why?	14. Hypothesis: the subjects would be more reluctant to accept planning in Somali than they would be in English. This hypothesis was developed from an analysis of Somali "time" vocabulary.***

Exhibit 1. (continued)

15. If the Kenyan government announced a policy of "socialism," what would they do, and what policies would they follow?	15. Hypothesis: the understanding of socialism would be a function of etymology. The Somali neologism for socialism is *hantiwadaag*, which means, "the sharing of livestock." I expected answers in English to reflect policies of state ownership, and the answers in Somali to reflect policies of redistribution of wealth.***
16. The Somalis say "Rag waa raggii horay, hadalna waa waxay yireen" [said in Somali, roughly translated as, "the real men are the men of old, and speech is what they said"]. What does this proverb mean? Do you agree with it? [Here the informant was instructed to make objections and to ask the subject to continue arguing his case].	16. Hypothesis: there would be more agreement of the proverb which reflects traditional Somali values in Somali; and the subjects would have difficulty discussing it in English.***

(A triple asterisk refers to a hypothesis where the null hypothesis could not be rejected.)

Exhibit 2 Role Playing

Situation	Hypothesis
1. Name A: You are an elder of the clan Cismaan Maxamuud, and your clan has just been fined 10,000 shillings for some misdeed. It is your job to collect diya payment from B, a member of your clan who is now in Nairobi as an assistant minister. Name B: You do not want to pay this money, because Nairobi is a very big city and you want to separate yourself from your clan. You try to get out of paying your diya obligations. Name A: You may start now, and ask B to fulfill his obligations. Try to imagine how this situation might really happen.	1. The Somali word for clan is *tol*, which literally means "to bind together." A Somali proverb, *tol wa tolane*, "clansmen are bound together," appears to be an analytic statement when said in Somali and a synthetic statement when said in English. Breaking the obligations of kinship for person B would be more difficult in Somali than in English. I expected that in Somali the burden of proof would fall on B, while in English the burden of proof would fall on A.***
2. Name B: You are a student at secondary school. Today there is a very important exam, and you want to study this morning before the test begins. You have lent your copy book to A, however, and you are waiting for him to come to school.	2. In Somali, the students would attribute less personal responsibility to the person who forgot the book. I expected fewer demands for an excuse by B in the Somali dialogues.***

Exhibit 2 (continued)

Name A: You have borrowed B's book and promised to have returned it this morning. In the excitement of the exam, however, you have forgotten it, and won't have time to return home. You see B waiting for you, and you approach him.

Name B: You start now, and ask A for the book.

3. Name A: You are the headmaster of this secondary school; and you have written the final exam for English language. You feel the students are being treated too kindly by B, and you want them to get an exam beyond their abilities.

Name B: You are the English language teacher in this school, and you have just seen A's exam. You think it is much too difficult, and unfair to your students. You go into A's office to protest. You may begin your protest now. Try to convince him to rewrite the exam.

3. Since there are few words that express deference in Somali, and there are no stratified role relationships in Somali society, I expected that the headmaster, the person in the more authoritative role, would be shown less deference in the Somali sessions. I predicted that the weight of the headmaster's claim in the Somali dialogues would be more of a function of his substantive arguments than of his position.

Exhibit 3 General Hypotheses Not Linked to any Particular Question

1. When asked to justify answers in the interview or positions in the role-playing sessions, the students would more likely give what might be called "poetic" or "allegorical" responses in Somali, while they would more likely give "analytical" or "deductive" responses in English.***

2. In argument, especially in the role playing sessions, the students would be more diplomatic in their exchange in Somali and more confronting in English.**

3. In both the role playing sessions and the interviews the students would more likely invoke religious criteria when speaking Somali than when speaking in English. They would more likely appeal to religious values in Somali.

4. When asked to explicate the proverb, *Rag waa raggii horay, hadalna waa waxay yireen*, in Somali the distinction between "speech" and "action" would not be made as clearly as it would be in English.**

(A double asterisk refers to an hypothesis I developed after I examined the data.)

Exhibit 4	Composition

1. My father is a ____. He owns ____ camels. In my life I have traveled to ____. My people were colonized by the British. I am not British, I am ____. Between history and geography, I prefer ____. Between the Somali language and the English language, I prefer ____. Between old age and youth, I prefer ____. Between my family and my school, I prefer ____. Swahili is spoken by ____. Arabic is spoken by ____. I think the land here is ____. I think the people here are ____. My favorite radio station is ____.

2. Write a paragraph entitled: The People of Kenya

3. Age: ____
   Class: ____

Exhibit 5	Composition Hypotheses	
Question	Expected English Answer	Expected Somali answer
I am not British, I am ____	Some responses of "Kenyan"	Fewer responses of "Kenyan"
Between history and geography, I prefer ____	Geography	History
Language preference	more "English"	more "Somali"
Age or Youth***	Youth	Age
Family or School***	School	Family
Swahili spoken by***	Neutral word	Pejorative word
Arabic spoken by***	Neutral word	Praise word
Land here is ____ ***	allude to poverty	allude to beauty
People here are ____ ***	Neutral word	Praise word
Favorite radio station	Kenyan station	Somali station

Exhibit 6	Listening: Passage Read

EAA's First African Jet Commander

A pilot with East African Airways Corporation has become the first African to qualify as a jet aircraft commander in East Africa. He is 37 year old Captain James Kiwanuka.

Born in Kampala, Uganda, where he obtained his primary and high school education, in 1960 he trained with Ethiopian Airlines at the national airlines training project in Addis Ababa on an Ethiopian Government scholarship and earned his commercial pilot's license and instrument rating in 1961. He was immediately employed as a first officer by Ethiopian Airlines on DC3 aircraft. He returned to Uganda in 1964 and worked as a pilot with the Uganda Police Air Wing with the rank of Assistant Superintendent of Police.

He has approximately 6,500 hours airline flying experience of which slightly less than 1,000 hours is on jet equipment.

His first flight as commander of a DC9 jet aircraft took place on May 5, when he operated flight EC911/912 from Nairobi to Entebbe and back.

(*Daily Nation*, Nairobi, May 15, 1973)

Exhibit 7 Listening: Answer Sheet and Hypotheses

Y=yes; ?=don't know;
N=no.   Age _____; Class _____.

Characteristic	Person 1	Person 2	Person 3	Person 4
Tall	Y ? N	Y ? N	Y ? N	Y ? N
Intelligent	Y ? N	Y ? N	Y ? N	Y ? N
Dependable	Y ? N	Y ? N	Y ? N	Y ? N
Kind	Y ? N	Y ? N	Y ? N	Y ? N
Having Character	Y ? N	Y ? N	Y ? N	Y ? N
Ambitious	Y ? N	Y ? N	Y ? N	Y ? N
Religious	Y ? N	Y ? N	Y ? N	Y ? N
Sincere	Y ? N	Y ? N	Y ? N	Y ? N
He is from	_____	_____	_____	_____
He works as a	_____	_____	_____	_____

Person 1 and 3 was the same voice, reading in Somali and English respectively

Person 2 and 4 was the same voice, reading in English and Somali respectively.

Hypotheses: (1) That even though English is the language of the colonizer and the language of jobs and education, speakers in Somali would be rated equally high as speakers in English, other factors being equal.

(2) On "religion," the Somali speakers would be rated more highly than the English speakers.

(3) That geographical distinctions about the speakers could be made when Somali was being spoken, but not when English was being spoken.***

(4) That job distinctions about the speakers could be made when English was being spoken, but not when Somali was being spoken.***

confident that the technique would work in the Somali context. Because my questions were culturally specific, based on differences I perceived between Somali and English, I did not consider pretesting necessary before returning to the field. I was able to get two Somalis living in America to participate in both the role playing and the interview, and some kinks were worked out. I planned to do extensive pretesting in one school in the Somali Republic before settling on what questions would be asked and how they would be asked, envisaging considerable experimentation with the questioning technique. Unfortunately that became impossible when I could work only in the Northeastern Province of Kenya. Spontaneity of response seemed of primary importance, so that any pretesting done among some of the students would seriously impair the actual testing. Many ill-conceived questions, ones which failed to address the issue I wished to address, were therefore asked.

The subjects. For the interview and the role playing, I decided to have sixty-four subjects—sixteen students from each of the four grades (forms I to IV) in the secondary school. I asked my informants to request volunteers, telling the students that I was doing a study of bilingualism and education. My informants listed sixteen students in each grade, assigning them numbers randomly. Thirty-two students would participate in the interview in English, and thirty-two in Somali. The thirty-two that were interviewed in English would constitute sixteen role-playing pairs in Somali; and the thirty-two subjects that were interviewed in Somali constituted the role-playing pairs in English. Because I wanted spontaneity of response, I decided not to have each subject act as his own control by participating in both exercises in both languages, but rather to have each subject speak in different languages for the two different exercises.

In most respects the two groups were remarkably alike. Group A (interview in English, role playing in Somali) had a mean age of 16.7 with the median at 16.25, while group B (interviewed in Somali, role playing in English) had a mean age of 17.3 with the median at 16.75. The differences, needless to say, are not statistically significant. There were two female subjects in each group, who did the role playing with each other. One hundred percent in both groups claimed that Somali was their mother tongue. The two groups were also alike in terms of clan membership. In group A there were sixteen Ogaadeen, ten Dagodiya, four Gurry, one Isxaaq, and one trans Jubba Harti. In group B there were fifteen Ogaadeen, ten Dagodiya, two Gurry, two Isxaaq, two trans Jubba Harti, and one Murale. While I set up the role-playing groups randomly, both groups A and B had both partners in eight out of the sixteen pairs from the same clan, and partners in the other eight from different clans.

Group A was, however, slightly more "Westernized" than group B. While group B only had two participants who claimed that their fathers could speak English, group A had seven. While only one student in group B was born outside of the Somali national boundaries, five in group A were. And while twenty-five students in group A claimed to have traveled outside of the Somali populated areas, only twelve in group B made that claim. These data need to be put into a proper context. For a Somali to be born outside of the national boundaries (say in Nairobi) does not mean that he is born outside of a Somali community. For a Somali, to travel extensively in East Africa is quite often to travel from one kin group to another.

The subjects for the composition exercise and the listening exercise were chosen differently. Since both of those exercises were of the "closed" question type, I could get many more subjects without being overencumbered by transcripts. I decided to use standard V of the local primary school and forms I and II of the secondary school That decision was based on some of Lambert's findings that, somewhere between the ages of thirteen and eighteen, attitudes about languages and their speakers begin to take on a new form. My subjects here were thus under thirteen years of age or older than sixteen. The subjects in the primary school were not volunteers; I was invited to their classrooms during school hours. There were two sections of standard V, and while one informant administered the composition to one section, the other informant administered the listening exercise in the other section. Then they switched rooms. The secondary students, however, who were volunteers, gave up study time to participate in these two tests. There were no significant differences in age or background between these two groups.

Testing schedule. The interview and the role playing were done in four straight days—one day to a form. In forms I and III the interviews were administered before the role playing, and in forms II and IV the reverse was done. We also alternated in each form the language that was used first. Participating students gave up time during their rest period after lunch and their evening study period. The composition and listening exercises were done on one day for the primary school and on the following day for the secondary school.

What the subjects thought they were doing. My first thought was that each participant should be told right before the test the nature and the purposes of the test. I thought it would be harmful to the test if I told them I was looking for differential responses depending on their language; so I planned to tell them that we were doing the interview and the role playing in order to understand attitudes and also to see how well they have maintained bilingualism. My problem was that whenever I wrote out an explanation of this sort, and got it translated, when it was retranslated by another informant back into English I could hardly recognize it. Deciding that explanation of that nature would bring more confusion than enlightenment, I let all participants know that I was studying the Somali language and wanted to know how well Somalis spoke both Somali and English in spontaneous settings. They seemed fully satisfied. When the testing period was over, I gave all interested participants a full explanation of my purposes.

Seriousness of participation. Although there was a certain level of giddiness among the role-playing participants, and one participant walked out of the room saying *been badan*, "a pack of lies," I think the general level of earnestness was quite high. The giddiness usually appeared after fifteen minutes or so of role-playing activity when there was no resolution in sight, and it rarely marred the general performance. The *been badan* came from a person who did not grasp any of the complex Somali concepts and therefore made her answers up. Most students "got into" their roles and played them as they thought they should be played. I feared the results of a first form role-playing session where a twelve-year-old boy who was under five feet in height happened to be matched with a seventeen-year-old boy well over six feet tall. Yet when the youngster was assigned to the role of headmaster, he suddenly took on stature that I would not have believed possible, and his voice got deeper and stronger. He was able to order his compatriot around as he never would have considered doing before.

In one sense I was playing up to Somali vanity—a characteristic quite apparent throughout the Somalilands, and no less so in Waajeer. A British anthropologist I had met in southern Somalia in 1969 told the villagers she was working among that she was writing a book about their customs and traditions. To that, she told me, most of the Somalis expressed assent. They thought so highly of their customs and traditions that it was no surprise to them that someone would travel thousands of miles to spend well over a year living with them. I found the same attitude. Most of the students told me that their language was so great that they had an obligation to help me with my studies. One of my informants told me that it was very good what I was doing because I would become wise if I learned Somali correctly. Most of the subjects believed that they were contributing to my knowledge, and to the knowledge of those who would read what I wrote, if they told me what they thought.

Problems. Innumerable small problems marred the research. After form I had performed the interview and role-playing, some of the questions began circulating through the dormitory, and prepared answers were being discussed. At least one of the students thought he was taking an examination; in the middle of the interview he blurted out that he had "failed." In some instances, my informants attempted to explain a question further to the subject if it was not understood. I had to discard a number of answers because the reformulation was different from the intent of the question. I would hear the tapes of each form every evening, and I could only catch errors of this sort after they had been made to a whole form. One of the informants would occasionally take "Let me think for a few moments," as an answer, and go on to the next question. For one student, I accidentally put the cassette in on the wrong side, and erased the last few answers of another student's interview. In the role-playing sessions, one informant forgot to have person A remain the same throughout all three situations, so that I was unable to compare systematically the same people in different roles. In the listening exercise we were unable to make it clear to the students that the speaker was neither the radio announcer reporting on the East African Airways pilot, nor the pilot himself. Most of the answers to the question asking, "He works as a ———" were either "broadcasting" or "airlines"; and most of the answer to, "He is from ———" were "Uganda." I had to discard those two questions. The lack of understanding of those questions casts some doubt on the data (presented in chapter 2) about evaluation of speakers.

In both the composition and the listening exercises for the primary school students, although I tried vigorously to control it, the level of "shared" answers was probably high. With three students to a desk, and some forty-five students in a twelve-by-fifteen-foot classroom—a situation quite common in African primary education—most instructors recognize that the answers to their tests will reflect the collective consciousness of a particular desk. I may therefore have counted one independent observation (response from the desk) as three (response from three students). I could not collect a "desk" answer, because the relevant group was not always the desk, and because many students had answers that were different from those of other students at their desk or the neighboring desk.

General evaluation of test administration. Put into perspective, the problems were relatively inconsequential. When I arrived in Waajeer, the headmaster of the secondary school informed me that the school's checks were bouncing and that if money were not sent by the Ministry of Education in a matter of days, he would have to send all the boys home because he could not provide food for them. The closure of school, he told me, was imminent. I was therefore in somewhat of a rush to train informants, because if they were sent home, it would have been six months before they returned. A day before the testing was to begin, some of the students came down with cerebral malaria, including one student who was my first choice as an informant. As more and more students were being hospitalized, I recognized how precarious my situation was, and the consequences for my research if one of my informants contracted malaria. I was therefore quite pleased when I got the number of students I had wanted as participants, and that technically the machinery ran without any problems. The tapes of all the interviews and role-playing sessions were reasonably clear.

After I completed all my testing, I spent a whole day quietly watching the local blacksmith making a knife out of a Land Rover spring and the horn of a cow. I had met him him shortly after my arrival, and had told him I was working at the school. When a man walked in and asked the proprietor who I was, the proprietor answered that I was a student of languages, working in the local secondary school, giving tests to the students in both Somali and in English, and planning to compare the answers to see if there were any differences. I was startled, not only because the metal workers were considered of low caste and therefore somewhat outside the society, but that anyone in the village would have such a clear idea about what I was doing. I had already told the subjects this purpose, but I rather suspect that my real intentions were more transparent than I had hoped. Insensitivity to the testing environment on the part of the experimenter, which this anecdote documents, is a serious problem.

Data analysis. For the interview and the role playing, all the tapes were transcribed. The Somali transcriptions were also translated and retranslated before being coded. I had three Somali students doing the translations, with two different translators working on any one transcription. Where there were differences, I tried to get from the translators the sense of the message, and we all suggested translations until the two translators were satisfied. The topics were purposely banal, and the conversation reflected this. So translation was relatively easy compared with translations of Somali poetry or philosophy. Because I set the criteria for coding responses and did the coding myself, I was, in a sense, both judge and jury.

The question of objectivity in coding deserves further elaboration. In the role-playing sessions, for example, the conversations in English were fraught with direct confrontations of opinion and approach. The students would attempt to find the weakness of their partner's position and then attack it directly. In contrast, the Somali dialogues seemed to leave room for exchange of opinions, with students often asking in a diplomatic way how their partner might handle the issue. With seemingly endless pages of transcripts, how can one code for approaches such as "direct confrontation" or "diplomatic exchange"? In the case of confrontation, I had the excellent suggestion from other experimenters to code for the word "but," as "but" is a signal for "disjunctive thought."[5] But why just "but"? Why not "although," "however," "on the other hand," or "despite"? I think these near synonyms lack the force of the word "but" in their ability to contrast one person's opinion with another's. I find that the differential impact between "but" and the other suggestions is a sufficient reason to limit my coding to "but." But then I want to see the null hypothesis rejected, and it is questionable whether it should be my decision. There is an additional problem. Often "but" is used without any confrontational intent, as, for instance, in "But you're right!". Aren't some "buts" to be factored out of the coding? The problem with doing that is that it would force me to judge each "but" for its "confrontational quality," a judgment that would further weaken the objectivity of the research design. I therefore counted all "buts," whatever their intent. Incidentally, I faced the same problem in coding for "diplomatic exchange," but in this case I ended up without significant findings. To have created coding directions for "diplomatic exchange" which would have yielded significant results would have required me to judge whether the role player was "seriously" asking for his adversary's opinion on the issue. I resisted that strong temptation. To overcome some of these problems, I coded all the open-question data twice and at an interval of about six months. Only in those cases where the coding decisions were the same did I accept the original codings. In this way I avoided some gross misrepresentations of my data, but I did not overcome an important structural problem for social scientific research.

About two hundred pages of transcripts in each language emanated from about fifteen hours of tape. The amount of talk generated by the questions and role-playing situations in each language was about equal.

Methodological Issues

Individual controls. Although in the interview, role playing, and composition exercises, each individual did not act as his own control, the two tested groups were closely related on all other factors, including age, sex, clan membership, and language abilities. But even if the groups had been unalike, there was a built-in control, as each subject participated in one exercise in English and the other in Somali, and some hypotheses in both the interview and the role playing were confirmed in the predicted direction. In the listening exercise, since each subject judged all the voices and I compared each subject's ratings of the Somali speaker with his ratings of the English speaker, each judge was acting as his own control.

Societal controls. Because most aspects of what we consider to be Western culture did not permeate the Somali lands, for a Somali in Waajeer to speak English is not really to be reminded of Western culture in general. I can therefore confidently say that it is something about language itself which is bringing about the perceived changed values and commitments. If this argument should not be accepted, the evaluation of the findings would be the same; but the attribution of the cause for the differential answers would be different.

Uncontrolled
Variables

The nature of open-ended questions. Open-ended questions and role playing almost never elicit a set of responses that differ in only one respect, thereby allowing one changed variable for each question with every other variable held constant. Several different processes were varying simultaneously within each open-ended question and within each role-playing situation. Therefore few of the findings were the only varying element in the answer.[6]

Language domain. It is possible that it is not language itself that causes different attitudes, but rather the domain in which a speaker uses a particular language. Perhaps Somalis feel comfortable lying to Europeans in English, or perhaps they are regularly obscure in Somali because they generally use it in personal rather than academic settings. The results I obtained may therefore be the result of factors quite different from those hypothesized.

A more serious objection along these lines is that since English is the language of the school and Somali the language of the home, it is the structural differences of the domain proper to the language that can explain any perceived differences. That is to say, students may demonstrate "schoollike" behavior when speaking English and "homelike" behavior when speaking Somali. This objection has special merit in the hypothesis concerning "authority" (and will be discussed more fully in chapter 8). However, the objection assumes that since the students have learned English in a relatively formal atmosphere, they are only attuned to the more formal uses of English, and will thus use that formal style in all milieus in which they speak English, however inappropriate from a native speaker's point of view. But the students did not use "formal" English in what were to me "informal" situations. The level and scope of informal English—"I'm in hot soup," "for heaven's sake," "I'm broke," "by hook or by crook," "I'm dead serious," and "it's all Greek to them"—among these students from the Somali desert was high. That they were able to speak English so informally suggests that the school atmosphere did not have that significant effect on limiting their language range. Furthermore, some of the perceived differences, such as "political style" and "self-conception," have little to do with the school atmosphere. Nonetheless I consider this structural problem to be an important objection, one which suggests a different independent variable to explain at least one of the differences I found.

Nonverbal behavior. A major question not dealt with in this study is whether nonverbal "language" changes with a change in spoken language. Students of anthropology and linguistics are well aware of how much meaning is transmitted through nonverbal signals; the meaning so transmitted may well have overriding importance for understanding of a message.[7] I attempted to observe some of the role-playing sessions for differences of this sort (the sessions were in a lighted room in the evening, and I was outside a screen window; I could thereby observe the evening sessions without being "present"), but the differences were either not relevant or too subtle for my eyes. I questioned my informants about this several times, but they detected no nonverbal differences.

Changes over time. It has been pointed out to me by a few scholars, particularly those involved in Hindi studies, that it is merely a matter of time and diffusion for the English language to be molded by the Somali culture. That is to say, as the English language diffuses throughout the society, the society will make of the language what it wants and needs, and not be subject to any abstract requirements of the language. There are indeed some examples which suggest that this is already occurring in Waajeer. Some students used "yesterday" to mean "recently," as the word for "yesterday" implies in Somali. Some students called an easy examination "cheap," for "cheap" and "easy" are expressed by the same word in Somali. I therefore think this point has merit and deserves further scrutiny and testing.

Without denying that a "Somalization" of Somali English may occur, and increasingly so as the foreign language diffuses to the masses, I can still defend the type of study I have designed. Perhaps it would be useful to compare the diffusion of a foreign language with the diffusion of one of the great religions. It is certainly true that to some extent Christianity and Islam have molded and changed the societies that adopted them, even though it is also true that those religions were modified and reinterpreted by each of those same societies. If there is mutual reformulation occurring—between religion and society or between language and society—it is sociologically relevant to isolate the effect of one on the other in one particular time span. Only by choosing (in this case) language to see its independent effect on society can we ultimately understand how and in what ways culture and society interact.[8]

Post Hoc Hypotheses

Some of my "findings" were not expected or predicted. The results were, so to speak, gratuitous. I think findings of this nature should not be ignored but should be put under greater critical scrutiny. I stress this because when I was explicit about my hypothesis beforehand, I attempted to build in controls for that hypothesis to reduce the chances of getting findings that were spurious. For these post hoc hypotheses, no such controls were built in. In my listing of hypotheses (see exhibits) the double asterisk (**) is the signal for a hypothesis developed after examining the transcripts.

Statistical Tests

Once the data were coded, I employed a battery of different statistical significance tests. I relied completely on nonparametric statistical tests, because my data could not meet the more stringent conditions of the parametric tests (assumption of normal distribution of population, and necessity of measuring data in intervals, to name just two). The nonparametric tests, that is to say, the set of tests that do not "specify conditions about the parameters of the population from which the sample was drawn" were more suitable to my data. I relied on Sidney Siegel's *Nonparametric Statistics*[9] for the choice of a proper test for each of my hypotheses. After making the choice, I checked for suitability with a statistical consultant, and then I fed in my data. I have written up my findings in such a way that the layman can understand them, and the professional will be aware of the critical choices.

Null Findings

If the null hypothesis (the hypothesis that there is no statistically significant difference between the answers in the two languages) cannot be rejected on a certain item, one of two things may be operating: either there may be no difference between the languages on that factor; or there may be a difference but my test was insufficiently sensitive to get results. Since it is always possible to demonstrate why one's test was insensitive, even for those tests where the null hypothesis can be rejected, there is no prima facie reason for accepting the latter assumption.

But the question arises whether I should report the cases where the null hypothesis cannot be rejected. As a practical consideration it seemed an unnecessary encumbrance to discuss a hypothesis at length, to give reasons for it, and then to state that I have no reason to believe it to be so. Yet since I am rejecting the null hypothesis at the $p < .05$ level (which means that the probability is less than 5 percent that the null hypothesis is true, though my sample was sufficiently skewed to show it to be false), it might be argued that with one hundred hypotheses, even if language has no effect, there is the random chance that "significant" results would be found for five of those hypotheses. It would therefore be useful to report all findings, whether the null hypothesis is accepted or rejected.

I have resolved the dilemma by listing all the hypotheses (see exhibits). For all hypotheses where I cannot reject the null hypothesis, I have put a triple asterisk (***). For most of those, no more will be said, It will be clear that the percentage of significant findings is greater than 5 percent, and that my findings are not randomly significant. For some hypotheses, I have asked more than one question, and only some of the response patterns were significantly different. In cases of that sort, I will discuss the questions where the null hypothesis cannot be rejected in the main text.

A final point on null findings: since my general hypothesis is that language relativity is manifest in Somali-English bilinguals in some areas, it is not incumbent on me to show that it is manifest in all areas. Nor am I obligated to show that relativity of response occurs more often than similarity of response. I do not consider the question of how much relativity does operate, or, if you will, what extent of the variance in thought and action it can explain. I have only attempted to show that in some areas it does operate.

Relation to
Politics
Two important qualifications ought to be made about the relationship of my findings to politics.

Two steps removed. In the role-playing situations, I am not asking people involved in politics about their attitudes; rather, I am asking secondary school students to play out roles. Role playing is a step removed from real life because nothing is at stake and the subjects are free to say anything. These sessions are therefore two steps removed from the rough and tumble of political life, and any assumption that the findings in the role playing sessions have any relevance to real political life would be heroic.

Nonpolitical context. Although I do deal with concepts such as "authority," "nationality," and "political bargaining," I do so in everyday contexts, generally that of the school. It could be argued that these relationships are substantively different in the political realm from the school realm, and that the role-playing sessions are not sensitive to political concepts at all.

If I had dealt with people who were politically active, or if I had chosen patently political themes, I do not believe I would have elicited the spontaneous talk and the freshness of conversation that I did. Since the subjects never considered that there were political issues at stake, they were not in a position to give me packaged ideas about their political positions.

Also, I was interested in eliciting something different from the political attitudes that would have emerged from the talk about patently political themes by political actors. I was concerned about the very assumptions behind interpersonal behavior in Somali society. I wanted to see what was taken for granted and what was not questioned. While this kind of information is unlikely to reveal a Somali's political posture concerning the burning political issues of the day, it does reveal the boundaries of political discourse in an emerging Somali political theory. The questions often asked by intellectuals interested in politics are in part influenced by the societal norms. Societal norms concerning authority—to use but one example—will, I assume, spill over into the political realm.

8 Linguistic Relativity

The Somali Experience

> What did we learn from the (sensitivity training) experience...? I learned that we—the African participants—had imbibed uncritically so much of Whiteman's concepts of social and political organizations that we spend all our time parroting outdated and mischievous nineteenth-century European fictions, like sovereignty, without being original or even intelligent about them.... It is a European-educated group that extends the original African concept of one's land to all the political entity which is described as "Ethiopia." An African would approach the problem from the point of traditional occupation and use of land, and not from the unprincipled principle of state sovereignty.
>
> Yuusuf Jaamac Cali Dhuxul,
> Somali advocate and journalist.[1]

To what extent have Africans "imbibed ... Whiteman's concepts of social and political organizations"? Why have they not excreted them after having attained political independence? What can explain the persistence of those concepts in postcolonial Africa? Although I am more equivocal about the answers than Yuusuf is, the questions he raises are some of the ones that delineated my research in Somali country; the concern about the persistence of colonial values in "independent" Africa is one of the sources of the rather elaborate research design described in the previous chapter. In terms of that design, I am suggesting that a language change can explain some of the variance in responses to direct questions and to role-playing situations. I have been able to factor out four areas in my research where a change in language did evoke differential responses: (1) self-conception and nationality, (2) the understanding of and deference to authority, (3) the acceptability of different bargaining or political styles, and (4) the relevance of religious values.

**Language and
Self-Conception**

Students of nationalism know well that a person's conception of who he is is rarely unambiguous and is usually complex and highly dependent on context. A person whose home region is Nyanza Province might consider himself a Luo when he meets a Kikuyu, a Kenyan when he meets a Muganda, and an African when he meets an Mzungu. And if he met a Martian, he might consider himself a citizen of Earth. This phenomenon is of course true in every continent. If a person's self-conception (or at least the reporting of it) changes according to circumstances, it may be politically relevant to know what those circumstances are and what the consequences of changing circumstances might be. It is politically relevant to ask under what circumstances a French speaker in Montreal will consider himself a Canadian or a citizen of free Quebec; or under what circumstances a Belfast Catholic will consider himself British or Irish.

The Somali-speaking population of Waajeer, Kenya, is in a particularly ambiguous political situation. A long, unsuccessful war has been fought in the Northeastern Province by Somali nationalists who demanded that the territory in Kenya which was Somali-speaking should join the Somali Republic. At the time of Kenyan independence, a British survey team reported an overwhelming majority of residents favoring that union. Nonetheless, this area has been part of independent Kenya for more than a decade now, and Kenyan flags fly over the district offices. The government-appointed chiefs loyally get out the Somali population for Kenyan national holidays, and go through the national rituals with only a touch of irony.

Yet the influence of the Somali Republic is great. Radio Muqdisho blares the news, the Qur'an, and the incomparable Somali music through the town of Waajeer. Many of the residents have relatives in the Somali Republic to the northeast, and many cross the border to visit. Camel herders usually ignore the border. New Somali styles of dress and verbal expression seem immediately to permeate the town. Under conditions of this sort, most young Somalis are not clear in their own minds who in fact they are. An important political question is, however, as I have suggested, in what contexts they might consider themselves "Kenyans" and in what contexts "Somalis."

The data that I have generated suggest that some of the variance in self-conception can be explained by the language in which conversation is conducted. The language being spoken is in part the political context which influences a person's self-conception. The most striking manifestation, in my research, of the linkage between language and self-conception was in the composition exercise, where we asked both primary and secondary school students to complete this sentence: "We were colonized by the English; I am not English, I am ———." Significant differences ($x^2 = 15$; $df = 2$; $p < .01$) in response can only be explained by the difference in the language of presentation. The most interesting difference in this pattern of responses was that a greater percentage of the students considered themselves to be Kenyan when asked in English than when asked in Somali. Only one student in the Somali writing group answered "Kenyan." Also significant was that a much higher percentage of the students answered "Somali" when asked in Somali than when asked in English. These differences can be examined from the data presented in table 6. To be sure,

Table 6 Question: We were colonized by the English; I am not English, I am ____

Question	Answer		
	"Somali"	"Kenyan"	"African"
Asked in English (N = 64)	48%	19%	32%
Asked in Somali (N = 69)	75%	1%	23%

Due to rounding off, percentages in this and the following tables will not always add up to 100.

language is not the only aspect of the political context that had influence. The high percentage of "African" responses probably reflects the facts that the students knew that an American was administering the exercise even though I was not present at the time, and that "the English" were the contrasting group. I would guess that if a Somali had been asking that question, or that if I had set a question where, say, a subbranch of the Galla people were the contrasting group, they might well have mentioned their clan memberships. But this test did not vary who it was that was asking the questions, or to whom it was that the Somalis were being compared; it only varied the language in which those questions were asked. And, to a significant extent, the language in which the nationality question was asked influenced the way the subjects reported their answers.

Other questions attempted to elicit the subjects' understanding of their nationality in different ways. Who you are is largely a function of what you perceive yourself doing. Might then a question inquiring what language the young bilingual elite chooses to use when more than one language is available to them indicate to some extent who they think they are? Or might a question asking which radio station respondents prefer to listen to when they have free time indicate something about their self-conception? I found that the answers to these relatively straightforward "factual" question also varied according to the language employed.

In the interviews I tried to elicit from the students their language preferences in various situations. In asking the first question, "What language do you speak with your friends in the dormitory?" I was fully cognizant that the students lived dual lives in the dormitory: they were in school, and the school was clearly an English language domain area; yet in the dormitories they were living out one of the more informal aspects of their school life, which would favor their speaking Somali. In fact, most of the talk was in Somali, with some in English and some Swahili among the students from other regions. As can be seen in table 7, however, a significant difference ($x^2 = 6.22$; $df = 1$; Swahili answers omitted: $p < .05$) in reported responses occurred depending on the language of presentation. When asked in Somali, considerably

Table 7   Question: What language do you speak with your friends in the dormitory?

Question	Answer		
	"Somali"	"English"	"Swahili"
Asked in English (N = 32)	46%	46%	8%
Asked in Somali (N = 31)	81%	16%	3%

fewer students reported that they spoke English in the dormitory; and considerably more reported that they spoke Somali. It ought to be mentioned that, due to dialect problems between the Somali language interviewer and some of the subjects, it was possible to interpret this question as "What language do you speak with your friends (female suffix) in the dormitory?" No more than two students interpreted the question that way, and even though both of them answered "Somali," omitting those two would not have spoiled this finding.

In the second question of this series, we asked the students, "What language do you use when playing football?" Again this is an ambiguous situation, as it represents an informal language domain (where Somali would be favored) yet in a European activity (where English would be favored). The results here, reported in table 8, are equally striking ($x^2 = 6.91$; $df = 1$; Swahili answers omitted; $p < .05$), with more students who were asked in Somali reporting that they used Somali than students who were asked in English. I had hypothesized in

Table 8 — Question: What language do you use when playing football?

Question	Answer		
	"Somali"	"English"	"Swahili"
Asked in English (N = 31)	28%	67%	5%
Asked in Somali (N = 32)	55%	36%	9%

general that, when reporting about ambiguous situations, the students who were thinking in and speaking Somali would be more likely to perceive themselves as using Somali when a choice was involved; and that the converse would hold for those students questioned in English. The answers to these two questions confirm this view.

But the third question of this series yielded a surprise. We asked the students, "What language did you use with Mr. Xasan Guleed outside of class?" The person in question was the only Somali-speaking teacher on the secondary level in the entire country, and he happened to be on leave, furthering his education, when I was there. The answers, while not significant ($x^2 = .99$; $df = 1$; Swahili answers omitted) at the $p < .05$ level, go strongly *against* what I would have predicted. I have no adequate explanation for this result, and so it forces me to be more cautious in interpreting the answers to the first two questions in the series. The answers to this series of questions imply that in certain (as yet unspecified) areas, the students' conception of who they are, as indicated by the language they believe they use when a choice is involved, varies according to the language in which this aspect of their lives is explored.

In the composition exercise, I asked some questions concerning preferences. I attempted to force choices between what might be considered Somali national culture and what might be considered Kenyan or English culture. I hypothesized that, all other things being equal, students would more readily identify themselves with Somali national culture when they were thinking in Somali than when they were writing English. The most straightforward of these questions was:

"Between the English language and the Somali language, I prefer ———." The results, presented in table 9, confirm the hypothesis that the students would identify more with the Somali culture when speaking Somali. A significant difference ($x^2 = 12.63; df = 1; p < .01$) in response emerged. Although more than half of the students (55 percent), when asked in English, write that they preferred the Somali language, a much greater percentage (81), when asked in Somali, reported that they preferred the Somali language.

Table 9 Question: Between the English language and the Somali language, I prefer ———

	Answer	
Question	"Somali"	"English"
Asked in English (N = 66)	55%	45%
Asked in Somali (N = 70)	81%	19%

More striking, perhaps, were the results when I asked the students to indicate their favorite radio station. The ambiguity involved in this question is quite interesting. As I mentioned earlier, the Somali Republic's radio stations can be heard nearly all day in the town of Waajeer, and most of the students sing and hum the latest songs. Yet, as primary students, many of them regularly listen to the Voice of Kenya, from which they get their daily Swahili language instruction. And in the dormitories, many of the non-Somali students have organized to get the Voice of Kenya played more often. Which radio station should be listened to thus had rich political overtones among the students tested. The results (see table 10) show that a majority of the Somali students, when asked in English, reported that the Kenyan station was their favorite; and when asked in Somali, a majority reported that the Somali station was their favorite. The differences are

Table 10 My favorite radio station is ———

	Answer		
Question	"Voice of Kenya"	"Somali Radio"	"BBC"
Asked in English (N = 56)	54%	43%	4%
Asked in Somali (N = 70)	24%	51%	24%

significant: ($x^2 = 16.7; df = 2; p < .01$). The high number of responses in the Somali group in favor of the British Broadcasting Corporation is difficult to analyze. Two of the respondents mentioned gratuitously that they listened to the Somali Service on the BBC, which would suggest that for the students the BBC is a counter to the Kenya radio station. But the other fifteen who said they favored the BBC (and were writing in Somali) gave no further explication. I cannot be sure of the political meaning of choosing the BBC for those students. It is nonetheless apparent that the language in which this preference question was asked was influential on the response pattern. When asked in Somali, these Kenyan Somalis were more partial to the radio station of the Somali Republic; and when asked in English, a majority showed a preference for the Kenyan station.

Two of the other forced preference questions yielded significant differences between the group asked in Somali and the group asked in English, but these results cannot be properly analyzed. I asked the students, "Between history and geography, I prefer ——"; and "Between my home and my school, I prefer ——." Both of these questions, suggested by the work of Leonard Doob in the South Tyrol, might be indicators of patriotism. A preference for "history" and for "family," it was hypothesized, could signal predispositions toward patriotism. I included these question even though I was unsure whether a high patriotism score would be reflecting loyalty to Kenya or to Somalia. I was somewhat amazed that the pattern of responses would be so different based on the different languages of presentation.

On the question concerning "home" (*reer* in Somali) and "school" (*dugsi* in Somali) those who performed the exercise in English overwhelmingly (68 percent) stated that they preferred their homes; and those who performed the exercise in Somali even more overwhelmingly (75 percent) stated that they preferred their school. The results of these data (see table 11) show statistically significant differences ($x^2 = 23.33$; $df = 1$; $p < .01$).

Table 11 Question: Between home (*reer*) and school (*dugsi*), I prefer ——

Question	Answer	
	"Home"	"School"
Asked in English (N = 68)	68%	32%
Asked in Somali (N = 71)	25%	75%

Similarly, but not so strikingly ($x^2 = 4.185$; $df = 1$; $p < .05$), there were significant differences in response to the forced preference between history and geography. Where 51 percent of the group which responded in Somali favored history, 70 percent of the English group favored history. These results (see table 12) along with the results previously mentioned, might suggest that the Somali students are greater

Table 12 Question: Between history and geography, I prefer ____

Question	Answer	
	"History"	"Geography"
Asked in English (N =67)	70%	30%
Asked in Somali (N =68)	51%	49%

patriots when they are thinking in English. But to which country their patriotism is directed is unclear. In the history-geography choice, one could argue that since history in Waajeer schools is Kenyan and British history, the higher response pattern for history in the English-speaking group suggests greater assimilation of Kenyan values. But that does not explain students' highly negative reaction, when speaking Somali, to their homes, which have no affiliation with the Kenyan state. One explanation might be that in outlawing tribalism in the Somali Republic, the Supreme Revolutionary Council has proscribed the use of the word *reer*, which has rich clan overtones. Furthermore, the word I chose for school, *dugsi*, was once primarily used to denote Qur'anic schools, so is not an exact translation of "school."

Only on one forced choice (old age versus youth) were there no significant differences in response between the group which did the exercise in Somali and the group which did the exercise in English. The level and the scope of the differences on the other questions suggest that a different mental map, a different cognitive framework, exists for the same person when he is speaking in a different language. Political movements for the assertion of nationality have been common in this century; and although many observers have noticed that language is associated with perceptions of national identity, it is less often suggested that language helps draw the map of personal identity.

I can illustrate this point with one more example. In the interviews, we asked the students to state their career aspirations. After asking them what job they wished to have at the age of thirty, we asked them why they preferred that job. Twenty-nine students in each group answered that question. I had hypothesized that, when speaking in Somali, the respondents would demonstrate less personal ambition than when they were speaking English. One Somali intellectual had pointed out to me that Somalis rarely begin their sentences with the first person singular, and rarely use the word comparable to the English "I." He told me that he always felt "ego aware" when conversing in English, almost unnaturally so. While a greater percentage of those students who participated in English stated personal ambition or emoluments or fringe benefits as their reason than those in the Somali group, the differences were not significant, so that the original hypothesis was not confirmed. But something else emerged from a closer examination of the two groups of students who stated some desire to be useful or helpful to others. Only one student in the English language group implied that it was the Somali people that he wished to help. He did not state any job, but commented that "I would prefer to help my people in any way I can, solving their problems, helping them, and giving them all what I can give them" (IV-2).[2] Not one student in the English group made any explicit mention of the Somali people, or the people of the particular region. In the Somali language group, eight students suggested that they wished to help the Somali people in particular:

> *Soldier*: I would like to defend my country Somalia because it is my mother country (III-3).
>
> *Medicine:* Our people, I mean the Somalis, they need me to do something good for them (III-8).
>
> *Teacher*: Our country which is called the Northeastern Province is backward and they haven't any teachers now. I want when I finish to enter teacher's course. Then I am with my brothers to teach them something (III-4).
>
> *Teacher*: Because teachers teach the people the culture and the traditions (I-5).

While the number of respondents is too small for a statistical significance test to be reliable here, in conjunction with the other responses analyzed in this section these answers fit into a general pattern. Somali consciousness, or awareness of Somali identity, is more salient for the bilingual students when they are speaking or writing in Somali than when they are engaging in the same activities in English. Conversely, these Somali students were more amenable to a Kenyan identity when they were in an English language framework.

What all the data in this section suggest is that "language," at least in the Somali case, is more than an *indicator* of nationality; it is a *shaper* of nationality. To converse in Somali is, for these Somali students, to see themselves unambiguously as Somalis; and to converse in English is to begin to introduce ambiguities and to allow for wider notions of national membership. This conclusion has wide implications for any strategy of national integration, and for any understanding of nationality.

**Language
and Authority**

Traditional Somali social structure is, as we saw in Chapter 2, highly fluid and egalitarian. In the political council of the nomadic group (*shir*), there are no defined roles which give a person special authority. While it is certainly true that some members of the *shir* have greater influence due to religious knowledge (the wadaads), and that respect is given to age (*oday*) and to recognized leaders (*ugaas*), in practice any member of the clan can participate actively in matters of common concern. In clan politics, no person has the special right to articulate and formulate clan policy.

The lack of defined authority roles in Somali social structure is reflected in the language. Except for the word *sheekh*, employed to indicate religious deference, or a weaker *adeer* (uncle) or *inadeer* (cousin), to denote friendship, hardly ever in Somali conversation is a person addressed with a title. In fact, titles preceding names are perceived by most Somalis to be an affectation. Luling, in her studies of the more settled Geledi Somalis, noted that they used the word *Aw* (literally, "father") for "Mr." and the word *Ai* (literally, "mother") for "Mrs.," and that these terms were used "scrupulously" in interactions between the nobles and the half-castes (*xabash*). The continual use of these titles, Luling relates, "strikes people from northern Somalia as comic."[3] That most Somalis find titles to be comic is, incidentally, one of the ironies of the use of the word *jaalle*, "comrade" (literally, "friend" or "playmate"), in modern revolutionary Somalia. The word "comrade" had the political function in the Russian revolution of doing away with titles, and in the Somali revolution of instituting titles. While at first everyone was jaalle, increasingly the term is used to lend prestige to the ardent supporters of the revolution.

The traditional social structure spills over into the modern sector. When I taught at the National Teachers' College in the Somali Republic, the janitor and bus driver could walk into staff meetings, listen carefully to the arguments, and participate, without their right to do so being questioned. I was also struck by the fact that the head of my department, at least in critical discussions, attempted to switch discourse to the English language, where I felt he could more easily exert his authority by saying, "Since I am the chairman, I think I should decide." This particular dynamic suggested to me that perhaps the introduction of role-specific criteria in the Somali language would sound odd, and probably would not be resorted to.

With this in mind, I structured a role-playing situation in which one student was assigned the role of teacher in a secondary school, and the other that of headmaster. The headmaster, according to my plan, has written the final examination for the English language, which he has made very difficult for the students because he feels that the students are being treated too leniently by the teacher. The teacher enters the headmaster's office to protest the difficulty of the examination, and to attempt to get him to change it. As I specified in chapter 7, sixteen pairs of secondary school students performed this role-playing session in the English language and sixteen pairs in Somali. I had hypothesized that the fact of the headmaster's authority in the school would have more bearing in the English sessions than in the Somali sessions.

That both the headmaster and the teacher called each other "Mr." in English in most of the sessions, and simply by their first names (or with *jaalle*) in Somali, is interesting but, by itself, of little import. It should, however, lead one to make further investigations. It soon became apparent that the conflict was defined differently in many of the Somali sessions from the way it was defined in the English situations, and along the lines I had predicted. The major question in most of the English sessions was who had the right to make up the test, and who had the right to decide what test would be given when there were differences in opinion. I found that statements of this kind: "I am the teacher, so———"; "Since you are the headmaster, you———"; and "You are not the teacher, so you should not ———," were quite prevalent in the English dialogues but rarely used in the Somali dialogues. What is particularly poignant is that the structural position of the speaker was used to justify statements. Who he was became significant for the correctness of the argument. By virtue of making statements of this type, one is implicitly justifying the rights and privileges of certain authority roles.

In a content analysis of the dialogues I found that statements of the kind I have been discussing appeared sixty-nine times in nine of the sixteen English language sessions. In the Somali dialogues, such statements appeared only fourteen times, and in eight of the sixteen sessions. I used the Kolmogorov-Smirnov two-sample test for this data because of its sensitivity to differences in location or central tendency in distributions. As can be seen from figure 3, the significant difference ($K_d = 7$; one-tailed; $p < .05$) appears at the point of four and five uses of authority statements. Seven Somali pairs made at least five such statements while no English speaking pairs used as many as five. Eight Somali pairs used at least four such statements, while only one English pair did so.

And there is evidence that those Somalis who did use statements of this sort felt odd in doing so. Even though we used a Somali word for teacher, *bare*, and for headmaster, *maamule*, very few times did I encounter *waxaan ahay baraha*, "I am the teacher." Most of the fourteen statements of this type were more like *waxaan ahay teacher*, using the English word to signify the role. When the Somali-speaking participant did use role differentiating arguments, he almost was forced to switch temporarily to English. It was out of character for statements of this kind to be made in Somali.

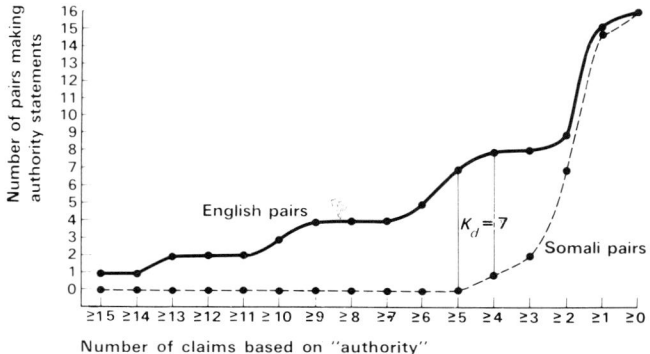

Figure 3 From the Role-playing Session between Headmaster and Teacher

The examples from the English transcripts that follow show that in the English dialogues the person's structural position in the school was used as a weapon in a policy debate, and therefore that considerations of authority contributed substantively to the debate. These illustrations should not be considered typical; rather, they exemplify what was occurring at one extreme of the distribution (where authority mentions were great). A common mode of exchange in the English dialogue involved the careful delineation of one's own authority or of one's partner's authority. Three examples of this follow.

(II-10, 12) 10. *The fact that I'm the headmaster doesn't mean* that I don't teach. I know how to teach and I know what is good: I know what is bad. I know the standard of Cambridge papers that they will...
12. It seems you haven't learned what to do.
10. Wait!
12. You haven't learned what kinds of, you know, course to follow, the procedure to follow.
10. You claim to know a lot, but you seem to be, you know, not knowing what you are doing. Actually, have you ever gone through those Cambridge

papers? Those papers which will test them later on? Well it doesn't seem to do. The second thing, *since you are the English teacher*, as you claim to be . . .

12. *Am I not?*
10. Well . . .
12. *So my claim is right!*

(II-9, 10)

9. You just want to show that they can get very high marks.
10. No, please, it's not like that. I teach them as much as I can teach and the result, we shall be looking in on the result after they do their Cambridge, but now, *since I am the English master*, you leave the English to me. *You are the headmaster* of the school, but you are not supposed to interfere with my subjects.
9. Well, *although you are the English master here,* and you can be anything you want, but then you should teach it well. Because in this school, *I am the one who is supposed to know what is going on*; and then if you are not teaching well, the sooner you leave this school the better.

(III-2, 8)

8. But let me remind you of one thing. *Are you the English teacher or am I the one?* You answer me that.
2. First of all, do you know me?
8. *You are the headmaster.*
2. Then . . .
8. *I, as the English teacher*, am asking you that, why did you set such a tough test?
2. *Being an English teacher* doesn't mean that you have to mislead the children.

Interestingly, each of these three sessions—sessions in which authority roles were most clearly delineated of all the groups—ended in disaster. In the first illustration, the headmaster called the teacher an "idiot," and the teacher left with no resolution to his problem. In the second one, the English teacher resigned from teaching, and the headmaster took over his English class. And in the final one, the headmaster reassigned the English master to geography, and the teacher left saying, "to hell with geography."

A second mode of role assertion involves not the power inherent in the position, but rather the competence or the knowledge that ought to be assumed for the person who is in that position. Two English language dialogues of this type follow.

(II-9, 10) 9. *Since you know I am the headmaster* and I know what I'm doing. What you did is not also good. You see, since this class is so high, and they have been learning for about ten years, you see they have to use their common sense to do hard things and instead of doing these things, I have seen the test you wrote for them was too easy for even standard 7. Even standard 7 could do it. So I decided to write a tough English so that I may see how they do their test.

10. Uh. *In fact I am the English teacher* of this class and I know what they were learning and what they are in this class. And *you are the headmaster* of this school. I think *although you are the headmaster*, I know more than you. Because *you are only the headmaster*, and I know I'm the one who teaches them. In that case, you gave them a test which was beyond their standard. Why have you done that?

(III-1, 3) 3. Now, the question I am trying to raise to you is that how can you do that. I have already got the syllabus, the English language syllabus, and I followed the syllabus to bring this examination...

1. I've done that *as a headmaster.*

3. Now well you can't do that *as a headmaster*; you do that *as a headmaster*, you also do it *as an English master.*

1. What are you going to do?

3. Well ... *as an English master*, I just came to say what were my difficulties, and what I saw was right and wrong for my pupils, having known their abilities for a long period. Now, again, this comes again the idea again you say, *"as a headmaster"* ... a Headmaster, I can just call you that any portfolio, if you just continue like that. What's wrong? Not to consider what the staff members are saying, anyway.

1. The *fact that you are the English master* does not mean you know all of them.

In the first of these two dialogues, while there is no evidence that the teacher acquiesced, the headmaster did present a compromise which would have allowed the teacher to save face. In the second example, the teacher became so angered that he even suggested fisticuffs as he stormed out shouting, rather appropriately, "To hell your office, your damn office."

A final mode in which a person's role was used as a justification for the validity of his position was one in which the headmaster asserted his authority in order to foreclose all further discussion. I will give two examples, again from the English dialogues.

(II-11, 12) 12. I don't think that is fair; so you better write again a test.

11. I, *I'm the headmaster of the school*, and I know what is fair and I know by giving them a tough exam, they are going to think ahead and next time (prepare) for a tough test.

(III-6, 7) 6. Well, Mr. Yuusuf, *as the headmaster*, you have to agree with me what I do, because I never told you to just leave your exam aside and you do mine, for the time being; but I told you we do the same tests and you'll see the . . . and by looking for the average you do that, and now we disperse because it is time for me to do some other business. There's another officers who are coming from another place; and there are some other parents, other students' fathers, who are coming to tell me about problems of their children, so I don't have more time...

7. Wait...

But the headmaster in this case, as officious as a headmaster can get, used his prerogative and ordered the teacher out of his office. The teacher in this case, and the previous one, bowed to the headmaster's authority. In all these examples of claims to authority, the person's position, with its structured rights and obligations, was a relevant and often deciding point in a policy debate.

If significantly more English dialogues turned on the question of who had the right to formulate the test, or who had the right to decide in a policy debate, the Somali dialogues were marked by a concern for substance. The basis of many of the Somali dialogues was which test— the easy one of the teacher, or the difficult one of the headmaster—was better pedagogically. In my content analysis of the dialogues, I counted the number of arguments used that claim one test was better because, by having to take it, the children would either learn more, or advance more smoothly through the educational system. Again, using the

Kolmogorov-Smirnov test, I found that there were significantly ($K_d = 8$; one-tailed; $p < .05$) more justifications based on pedagogical arguments in the Somali dialogues than in the English dialogues. As can be seen from figure 4, eight of the Somali pairs used at least four such arguments while none of the English pairs used as many as four.

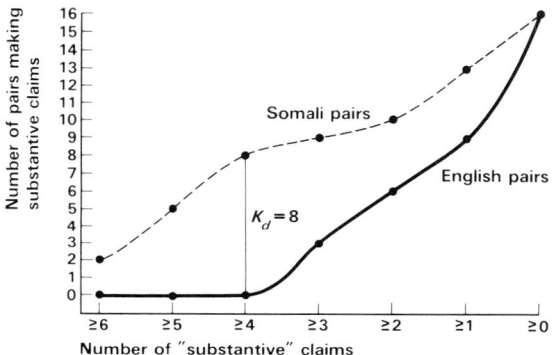

Figure 4   From the Role-playing Session between Headmaster and Teacher

Again, I will illustrate from a few of the dialogues to give some feeling for the point of difference. One pedagogical question that arose was whether education should proceed step by step, carefully programmed, or whether it should continually challenge the students by making educational leaps. The following Somali dialogue explores this question.

(I-12, 13)   13.   *Progress is through understanding bit by bit*, and even though they are a bit behind, they can say it by heart, starting where I began for them till where they are now. It is not my plan to go forward without knowing what we have studied. I'm teaching in a measure, and even though the situation became so, I want to mix your easy questions and the ones which I put, those similar to your difficult questions, and my easy questions, then devise an exam for the children.

                12.   I prefer to cancel yours, and expose mine, because *we are pushing the children forward*, and all of them understood, but I'm letting them understand, and push them forward, and they all

will understand. But now which is better for you: to make them understand and advance them, I mean, than understand as a whole, and they are not faster than their class.

13. *Now if they get confused*, for instance, if you were told to carry more than your intelligence, what will happen? What would you do if you were told to sleep and work at night? You are talking about imaginary things, and surely that is not possible.

The participants in the Somali dialogues were very concerned about their students' psyches. An important consideration was whether a difficult examination would discourage them to such an extent that they would give up; or whether an easy examination would make them so overconfident about their abilities that they would no longer invest so much effort in their studies. The following two Somali dialogues show the importance of this consideration.

(II-1, 2)

1. The reason I gave the hard test to the children is, I mean, is that it is possible, when the big test comes, that *the children will be accustomed to easy tests, and will not understand the hard one.* It will be hard for them. Now if I do not tell the children how to do the hard one, later on their minds will get hard, and they will not be able to manage the hard one. Then that is the reason I have given them the hardest one.
2. That cannot be a reason, for an easy test is good for the children. It is not possible to know something one has not learned, and so the simple test should be given. That would be good, and to give them a big test as if they were sitting for an exam that the whole world was taking, *that would not be good for their minds.*
1. It cannot be so, because if they took the test *their minds would be destroyed.* Then they would not be able to take the hard one; they know the easy material and do that work. For that reason it is not something we accept.
2. The easy one is good for them, because if they see the hard one, *their minds will become confused*, and they will become discouraged [literally, "with broken thoughts"] and say that we gave them a hard test. Now they get discouraged all the time. That is not good. What is good is to give them easy tests all the time.

	1.	They won't become discouraged because if we teach them now, they will be as we taught them; *if we teach them easy things, later on they will become nothing.* Then when the hard one comes, they won't be able to do it however much they try. So now we have to teach them and talk to each other. We have to teach the hard things because if they come to know the simple material only, their minds will not be good.
(II-5, 6)	6.	Now I come to you to stop that test you wrote for the students, because it is too hard; not even a single one can pass, I think. What do you think about what I'm saying?
	5.	Yes, very good, God knows, I was expecting you, and if you hadn't come, I would have gone to you. Then first, these things we ask of them, like that, I mean, if we do like you did—everything for the children is made easy and the work they would do we made easy—later on, you, know, *they think,* and you see, they *are not challenged.* Then if I look at what the paper you set tests, this is not the kind of test that children on their level take. Then what would be of the use of their knowledge, so many years getting knowledge, that they should be getting tests which are on their level. It is not something, you see, that can be made easier. Because, as you know, there are many children who will take that test. *If all the children pass the test, then at a later time, problems will come from it.* And it is easy like that, but we want to see each person use his wisdom, and get difficult problems, and you see; if we make it easy now, if they get tests lower than their level, *then later they will not do anything.* It will seem to them, you see, to be food cooked for them and put in their mouths. Now what is wanted is only that they be given the food. I am not talking as a higher person than you, but we are talking of knowledge itself. So it is not to be made easy. If I look and follow the work, I think these people, the level they are on, the children where they are, there is no way they can get that kind of test, how easy you made it...
	6.	....*If I made the test hard* and gave it to them, then no one could pass. Then I am afraid that *the students would get shaken and say, "What has happened to this English?* so for that reason, I did not make the test so hard. You didn't do

wrong, as you wanted the students to make use of their minds. And although the test is hard, it will make them use their minds. As for me, I looked at one thing, that if I make the test hard now, the students may say afterward that "we don't know English." You know, the English [test], when they sit [for it], if they say, "this English, I failed a few days ago, then why should I be making myself tired. [studying it any more]" Then they just look at the papers and do not write anything. "I failed a few days ago in this test, so that is why I am like this."

Occasionally, these discussions reached higher levels of abstraction and made more than a pedagogical point, as demonstrated in the following extract.

(IV-4, 8)   4.   ... The reason I shall take back this test is that the English language has no end. It is not like history and geography, where you can say, read that part. Language is very wide. I took only a part of it. If you thought that the test was hard, is it possible to give them the simple one and have them do it? ...

                 8.   Let it be this time. Do not return that one to the children. What did I teach the children? I taught them all that I know. The paper you brought is something I did not teach them. It is something higher than their level. So if we say let them have the test although it is hard, I think that is not showing great wisdom. *Everything goes to its own level.* A baby who was born last in the family cannot be taught how to talk at the same time as the others. First he has to start crawling. When he learns crawling, he starts standing beside walls. Then when he learns how to stand beside walls and stretches himself for a while, then he starts to walk. But the way they are, we can't start with running. I can say to you that your test is higher than the children, so let us drop it.

In the first Somali dialogue cited (I-12, 13), a judicious compromise, one which involved mixing the two tests, was reached. In the other three, the teacher gave in to the arguments of the headmaster. In none of these dialogues, which were chosen because they illustrate the presence of substantive pedagogical arguments in the Somali dialogues, was any ill will demonstrated. In all four the teacher left the office on good terms with the headmaster.

When I coded these role-playing sessions to determine modes of conflict resolution, I counted the number of cases where there was some "satisfactory" resolution—"satisfactory" defined as acceptance by both sides, however reluctant, on some procedure to give the examination, with both participants staying on their original jobs. I ought to note now that coding for "successful resolution" was a very subjective judgment. I had to decide by context, or by the statements after my informant asked why someone had given in, whether silence meant acquiescence or refusal. In the English sessions there were five successful resolutions (31 percent), and in the Somali sessions twelve (75 percent). But those figures do not accurately relate the presence or absence of justifications based on "authority" or "substance" to success in achieving a resolution.

To do that, I rearranged the groups. I took all those pairs that used substantive arguments more than the median. I did the same for those who used authority arguments more than the median. I then eliminated three pairs which used more than the median on both dimensions. I was then left with two groups: those who used substantive arguments more than the median but used authority arguments less than the median; and those who used authority arguments more than the median but used substantive arguments less than the median. I then compared these two groups in terms of whether there was a successful resolution of the conflict. As can be seen from table 13, the differences (Fisher Exact Probability Test; $p < .01$) are rather substantial. The

Table 13	Type of Claim and Conflict Resolution		
	Predominant claim	Successful resolution	No successful resolution
	Substantive (N = 13)	85%	15%
	Authority (N = 9)	22%	78%

point to be made here is that argument in terms of substantive issues was more likely when Somali participants were speaking Somali than when there were speaking English; and that when these substantive arguments were more prevalent than arguments concerning authority, peaceful conflict resolution was also more likely.

It could well be argued, however, that, although these differences have been correctly perceived, the explanation for them is wrong. Although I have argued that the only important influence from the Western world on these students is the English language, it is quite apparent that the school system itself, with its values, has been at least as influential on these people's lives as has the English language. It could be further argued that if I had chosen subjects who had learned English aboard ship, for example, and not in formal education, there would be less consciousness of authority roles when they spoke in English.[4] That the school system inculcates a respect for authority in Africa was poignantly brought out by one of Wilfred Whiteley's observations in East Africa: "I have myself been present in Gusii homesteads," he has written, "when a father has switched from Gusii to English in order to quiet his children, and then immediately justified this by reference to the classroom situation, commenting that nowadays children take much more notice of their teachers than they do of their parents. A number of interviewees reported the use of English to give added authority to the user, who in every case is cited as the father."[5] The objection, then, is that it is not the English language which is giving these students a sense of authority, but rather, it is the school system itself, with its highly stratified roles.

I think there is merit to this objection; and it is clear that my experimental controls were not sufficient to counter the effects of the school system. Nowhere else could I have gotten such a controlled group of Somali-English bilinguals than in the school system. But the data I have presented demonstrate that the school system itself cannot explain the use of role-specific arguments among the students, or else they would have used those arguments in the Somali dialogues as well. Speaking the English language at minimum put these students in a mental framework where authority arguments suddenly became more relevant. Second, and in contrast to the observations made by Whiteley, I am not suggesting that using English gives the speaker authority by virtue of his speaking it, but rather that speaking English makes authority considerations more relevant. Only in some instances in my tests was authority "exerted"; more often it was used to delineate rights and obligations. This use of authority is less easily tied to the school system. Finally, these data ought to be examined in conjunction with the findings concerning self-conception, religion, and political style, which are less clearly related to the values of the school system. These considerations suggest to me that, in this case, "language spoken" is a better explanation than "influence of the school system" for the perceived differences. But I cannot rule out the other explanation as a complementary one.

The data presented here do not demonstrate that Somalis will never accept authority roles. Functional role specificity usually develops along with modern society, and one can surely predict that if areas in the Somali desert do modernize, more specific authority roles will develop, no matter which language is used in education, politics, or administration. Yet my results do suggest that if the language of discourse is Somali, the rigidifying aspects of role assumption could well be softened. This is not to say that in the English-speaking West we are doomed to rigidified roles, but only that in the Somali cultural setting the use of the Somali language in modern institutions might force those institutions to respond more to reason than to authority.

In the Somali dialogues, to return to the linguistic relativity theory, the "teachers" and the "headmasters" saw each other as equals, with equal claims to rightness on an educational issue. In the English dialogues, on the other hand, the "teachers" and the "headmasters" saw each other as having certain rights and obligations which would have bearing on the educational claims being made. To an important degree, then, both the "teachers" and the "headmasters" were seeing different people and making different claims depending on what language they were speaking. The language these Somali bilinguals were speaking did, then, influence the way they perceived and acted in the world.

Language and Political Style

In traditional Somali political culture, as we saw in chapter 2, debate is usually in poetic prose, and arguments are couched in metaphor (*guudmar*). Long, seemingly irrelevant exigeses are often made as a prelude (*arar*) to the point to be made. Guudmar and arar serve a very important function in Somali politics; they allow for sufficient public ambiguity concerning the issue at hand as to allow the person who cannot get his way to leave without losing face. In a small-scale society, this is most important, because it is very difficult for a clansman to avoid seeing members of his political contract group all the time. In my dealings in Somalia, I thought that bilingual Somalis used guudmar and arar when speaking Somali, but did not when speaking English.

As I examined the transcripts of the three role-playing sessions, I attempted to categorize political bargaining styles, and to see whether these styles were at all related to the language of the speaker. I found in the English dialogues what might be called the politics of confrontation, where one laid his views right out on the table and tackled the opponent directly. One indicator of this was in the word "but." Osgood and Richards, in "From Yang and Yin to *and* or *but*," have suggested that "but" is an indicator of "disjunctive thought" and that the level of its usage might vary interculturally. I had also read Roger Brown's *Words and Things,*[6] where research was cited that suggested that the length of a word is negatively correlated with use; so "shorter names... are nearer the top of the cognitive deck—more likely to be used in ordinary perception, more available for expectancies and inventions."

In Somali, the word for "but," *laakiin*, has two syllables, and one might hypothesize that it would be less used than its English counterpart. Also, it is a loan word from Arabic. Quite often Somali borrows technical or religious words or words for ritual greetings from the Arabic language but it is rare for everyday conversational words to be borrowed. Is it possible that direct confrontation is less common in Somali society? And, if so, would the absence of confrontation be reinforced by language? These questions led me to hypothesize that there would be less direct confrontation of opinions in the Somali dialogues than in the English dialogues, and this would be reflected by fewer uses of the word "but."

I therefore counted the number of "buts" in the English dialogues and *laakiin*s in the Somali. The difference was overwhelmingly significant, with about four times as many "buts" as *laakiin*s. In the Kolmogorov-Smirnov test, as can be seen from figure 5 ($K_d = 11$; one-tailed; $p < .01$), fifteen out of sixteen pairs of Somali students used "but" at least eight times in their English dialogues, while only four out of sixteen used as many as eight in the Somali dialogues. This point can be seen and understood better by a few examples from the English dialogues.

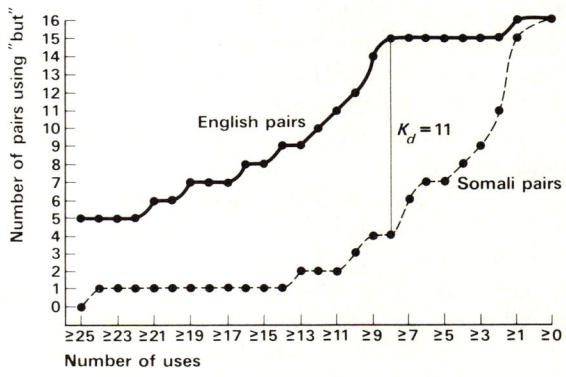

Figure 5   Confrontational Political Style in the Three Role-playing Sessions

Most of the "buts" appeared in the second role-playing situation, in which a student, who has promised to return a book he had borrowed, forgets it, and is approached by the friend who lent him the book as he gets to school. Since the student who lent the book was preparing to study from it before an examination, a confrontation is inevitable.

Following are three examples of how that confrontation was handled in the English sessions.

(II-13, 14)

14. *But* we are having the examination today, and what is the use of my having it tomorrow?
13. Now I am going to the school and you too are going, how can I go back home and bring the book again?
14. *But* you did wrong first, you forgot it.
13. Since I was thinking about the exam itself so I haven't.
14. *But* isn't it your fault you left the book?
13. Yes, it's my fault.
14. Now you refuse to do that?
13. Although I couldn't do that I forgot it ... I should bring it tomorrow.
14. Now about that book, what shall we do about the examination and that's just once the book, and I am also in need of your book, of my book?
13. When you do an exam you don't have need for a book so what is the use of that?
14. *But* I want to study the book before the examination.

(IV-11, 16)

11. *But* you know the exams are beginning. What could you have read within just the remaining hour? It's just an hour before the exam begins. What could you do then? Just get another book and read it.
16. It is never too late to learn my friend.
11. *But* you know there are very many books in the school; this is not the only book. Just ... a friend of yours; you want me to go back to my home now?
16. Do it, and come back before the exam.
11. Actually, I can't do it. My home is five miles away.
16. There's very important notes; suppose I find the same notes I wrote in the exam?
11. *But* you know you can't know what you never knew before. What you couldn't learn within one year's time you can't learn within an hour.
16. *But* still, suppose I be lucky and I find one of the questions...
11. *But* you know always luck is there. Even now you

		may be lucky and get questions which were already there; which you knew.
	16.	Abas, listen! If I see, if I fail this exam, really if I do not do well, I'm going to fix you.
(IV-13, 14)	14.	*But* how can you forget the book when I told you I needed the book tomorrow morning?
	13.	Because I was very excited when I knew the exam was tomorrow, and I left all my things at home.
	14.	*But* it is very difficult for me to enter the examination without going through that book.
	13.	*But* how can I come back to home now? I left all my things at home and I can't go back home.
	14.	You must try to go back home within these fifteen minutes.
	13.	*But* how can I go?
	14.	You must go!
	13.	My home is very far from school, and I can't go back until I walk some distance.
	14.	*But* you should also know that exams are very difficult for me without using that book.

What is involved in these dialogues is something more than the attachment of some ritual word in front of their English sentences, as would be the case with phrases like "you know" or "you see." The "buts," as I think these examples demonstrate, set the tone, the style, for the dialogues. Following each "but" is a statement which directly confronts the partner's position, with no attempt to soften the blow.

Additional evidence that in speaking English these Somali bilinguals adapted to a different bargaining style is found in one colloquy where the English role felt uncomfortable to the Somali actor.

(III-2, 8)	8.	*But* that's what the students are complaining about, it's not me. I'm speaking on behalf of them, you know.
	2.	You are speaking on behalf ... so you want to ... you want them to observe what you say and what I say.
	8.	No, *but, but, but* ...
	2.	Don't misuse the word *but, but, but* throughout.

In contrast to a bargaining style of *confrontation* in the English dialogues, I perceived a style of *diplomatic exchange* in the Somali language dialogues. But whereas it had been possible to test for "confrontation," I was unable to develop a coding technique appropriate for capturing the diplomatic style. To be sure, the Somali dialogues had longer greeting rituals and other conversational mechanisms (*arar*) before the issue at hand was proposed, but these reflect the use of the Somali language in informal milieus and not necessarily a difference between Somali and English bargaining styles. Also, the Somali dialogues involved more seemingly irrelevant but allegorical talk (*guudmar*) than the English dialogues, but I was unable to develop adequate criteria for a "relevant" statement to make coding possible. Finally I attempted to code the number of questions asked in the style, "What do you think we ought to do?" This style seemed more prevalent in the Somali dialogues, and because it tended to ask for compromise, or for adjustment of position, these questions seemed to mark what might be considered a diplomatic style. Indeed, there were many more questions asked in the Somali dialogues, but not significantly so, by the Kolmogorov-Smirnov test. As I explained in chapter 7, I was unable to ferret out rhetorical questions and "confronting questions" (But didn't you promise?), which were quite common in the English dialogues, because what sounds like a rhetorical question might well be answered, and then I could not be sure if it was rhetorical or not. I therefore was unable to set even moderately objective coding rules to capture the quality of diplomatic exchange. I will give three examples of what I think are paradigmatic Somali language interchanges, but they ought to be taken more tentatively than my other examples. All come from the dialogue concerning the forgotten book.

(III-9, 11)
- 9. Yes Xasan, how are you?
- 11. Peace.
- 9. How's everything?
- 11. Peace.
- 9. The book I lent you, did you tear it or how was it?
- 11. The book was good last night, but I forgot it now.
- 9. Oh God, did you say, "I forgot it"?
- 11. Yes.
- 9. Have you forgotten the book? In the name of God, how did you forget it?
- 11. It happened, I forgot the book because I was thinking about the examination.
- 9. "I was thinking about the test"—don't I think about the test?
- 11. It just happened. I forgot it and I left.
- 9. Oh God, what shall I read now?

	11.	It was wrong. The book was left behind, so how can you read now, as no one can go back to fetch it?
	9.	Now, I left all my books for the sake of that one. Again there is a test and there is no book at all, what shall I do in the test?
	11.	Now what shall we do? It happened by the will of God.
(IV-2, 6)	6.	Hello, Saciid, what's your news?
	2.	Hello, peace.
	6.	Then?
	2.	I am fine.
	6.	Is that right?
	2.	I woke up in peace.
	6.	Now, where is my book? The test is tomorrow.
	2.	I forgot the book.
	6.	What was that you said?
	2.	I forgot the book.
	6.	Did you say, "I forgot it"?
	2.	I am very sorry, yes.
	6.	Now, you forgot the book, it that it?
	2.	I forgot the book.
	6.	How did you forget it, didn't you know today that tomorrow we have a test?
		. . .
	6.	Now what do you want me to do? The test is tomorrow, and the family is very far, so what do you want me to do? I want to take the test and cannot do without my book at all.
	2.	What shall we do now?
(III-13, 14)	13.	. . . I left it at home and I shall bring it.
	14.	Why don't you bring it now? If I miss this test, there is no other test which follows. I have not read it, and before reading it I gave it to you. Why did you do this to me?
	13.	The reason I did it to you, although the test hasn't begun, I do not have time to go back to the house. You can't bring back the dead. This time, what shall I do? Just forgive me.
	14.	Although this forgiveness is something else, forgiveness with a purpose can be good. Now what shall I do?

If the examples from the English dialogues could be described as a series of quick jabs to the chin, then these Somali dialogues might be described as a series of artful parries. Rarely was an attempt made in the Somali dialogues to knock one's partner out; more often an attempt was made to wear him down. I have no evidence that conflict is more easily resolved through the Somali diplomatic style than the English confronting style. Strong differences of opinion are just as possible and occur just as often in the Somali sessions as in the English, although hardened positions were more subtly disguised in the Somali dialogues. Where the differences in style might have an effect would be in future dealings, especially in a small community.

In the small nomadic reer where the Somali language developed, every member of the community saw every other member every day. Direct confrontation when there were differences was a bad strategy for communal living, and that is one explanation for the existence of guudmar, or allegorical speech, which enables Somalis to circle around their point for a considerable time, feeling out their partners, until both fully know what is being requested, without it ever having been explicitly stated. If no agreement is going to be reached, either partner can terminate the conversation without having lost face; because the issue is never brought out in the open. This type of diplomatic "feeling out" is characteristic, I believe, of the Somali conversations among my subjects. Bargaining by confrontation is more characteristic of more urbanized Western societies, where time does not allow for guudmar, and where the scale of society is so much larger that one can avoid someone with whom one has just had a particularly nasty encounter. That the Somali desert will long remain a small-scale society makes me think that the full introduction of English, if the Somali language had remained unwritten, would have brought unnecessary societal friction.

The results presented here have, I think, even broader resonance. Language styles, as I have suggested in chapter 6, can have important implications for political substance. Murray Edelman has gone so far as to say "that style does convey meaning and that the meaning is a central explanation of political stability or polarization."[7] In characterizing different language styles, he suggests that different styles may have consequences for the political system, and that political actors may be unaware of this. I believe that the diplomatic bargaining style is more consistent with the development of "community"; and that the confronting style is more consistent with the development of a manifestly polarized political "society," a society perhaps polarized along right-versus-left lines, and one in which two-party politics could emerge. And the language of political discourse could have some bearing on these developments.

In terms of the linguistic relativity hypothesis, each participant in my tests seemed to perceive and relate to his role-playing partner differently depending on the language of discourse. In Somali the participants seemed to relate to their partners as human beings with whom they would have regular and continued future contacts, while in English the students saw their partners as adversaries with whom future dealings were unimportant. The students therefore acted differently in the two (linguistic) worlds which they perceived so differently.

A related question to political bargaining style is how political bargaining itself is regarded. If politics is quintessentially talk, then it is important to know if the evaluation of talk is interculturally relative. Hannah Arendt has argued that pre-Socratic Greek thought was characterized by the notion that speech and action are "coeval and coequal, of the same rank and the same kind." She claims that the "stature of the Homeric Achilles can be understood only if one sees him as 'the doer of great deeds and the speaker of great words.'" She differentiates this conceptualization from the modern one in which speech is seen merely as a conveyer of thought, and as distinct from, and less important than, action. And so, for the ancient Greeks, speech was in itself political action. "Only sheer violence is mute, and for this reason violence alone can never be great."[8] Arendt's point is, I believe, that the modern distinction between speech and action, with speech subordinate to action, cheapens politics. Only in a society where speech and action are "coeval" can politics be considered ennobling.

In traditional Somali culture, the boundaries between speech and action overlap. The importance of poetic style in the traditional council is but one indication of this. A Somali proverb accords with Arendt's explication of pre-Socratic thought: "Rag waa raggii horay; hadalna waa waxay yireen," "The great men were the men of before, and speech is what they said." The greatness of the men of the past was attributed to their words and not to their actions.

The proverb seemed odd—at least to my English understanding, and I used it to make further investigations. In the interviews, we asked each of the participating students to explicate the meaning of the proverb, to state whether they agreed with it or not, and to justify their agreement or disagreement. I had my informants prepared to offer counterarguments to either position, in order to draw the subjects out and to justify their positions more fully. (In the English sessions, the proverb was said in the Somali language but all other discourse was in English). In both the English and Somali interviews, "speech" was taken to mean proverbs, customs, and religion; but in Somali a significant number of students saw the proverb as meaning that the men of the past took great actions. There seemed to be no consideration of "speech" as distinct from "action" in the Somali answers. In Somali, twelve of the twenty-four codable responses made some reference to the great actions of the men of the past; whereas in the English interviews only three of the codable nineteen responses made any such reference. This is a significant difference ($x^2 = 7.07$; $df = 1$; $p < .01$), but again it is best told through illustrative examples.

The most common answer for those students who agreed with the proverb was that all the great proverbs came from the men of the past. Some excerpts from both sets of interviews follow.

> I agree because they had something on us; this generation of today hasn't proverbs; but before they narrated proverbs. (In English, I-12)

> Of course I can't say they are the only people who introduced proverbs; even to this day someone can just introduce proverbs, but then we can say they were the first people, because from the generation, even ourselves, if they were not there, we could not be here; even myself today, if I produce a proverb, how could I produce that proverb if they were not there, because they were my parents? (In English, II-6)

> What they said no one can say more than that, because the Somali words are very many, the proverbs that were handed down and the poems are what we have in hand. (In Somali, I-8)

> If I come to you now and speak to you in Somali, and say proverbs, you can understand the topic, you see, when I say a proverb, isn't that so? Then the proverb is, you see, a complete wisdom, which is filled with pithy and cogent truths. If I have something to tell you without a proverb, it will be like crossing the words left to right all day long. (In Somali, IV-10)

Some of the answers reflected the idea that the origins of the Somali customs, traditions, and religions came from the people of before. More excerpts from the English:

> Well, what they have said actually helps us a lot; you know, without what they have said, suppose what they have said were not recorded or heard, today some of us could not remember our traditions, and tradition is important in life. (II-3)

> Those men who used to live in previous generations are men in the real sense, they used to stick to their customs, their religion, their traditions and they were men. (IV-2)

And from a Somali interview:
> This one that we have now in this world, the Mohammedan religion is not accepted. The early people had both the religion and the traditions. That is what I accept. (II-10)

None of the cited answers points to great actions of the former men. Either they emphasize "speech" or the correct following of what is customary and right. A substantial number of Somali responses, however, did point to great actions of men in the past to justify a proverb claiming that the man of the past said great words. This was not nearly so prevalent in the English responses. Some examples of Somali responses follow:

> The reason is that those men, what they said was not just talk, because what they said they finished. (II-9)

> I agree with them of the early days, everything they said was true and existent and the people followed them.... The early people were mediators and they were agreeing in a good way. The land they wanted they got with agreement, however they could find it. But the people of now are a people who want war and war is not good for Africa.

> You can take it to mean we are not brave; we are cowards. Where the bravery is and where the cowardliness is, I am not saying. We are the cowards. But I am saying our forefathers were better than we. (III-3)

> The reason even myself, I saw some early people are of the old generation and old and who at the same time solved all arguments and other such things. If you saw them, you would be surprised.
> (IV-11)

> Speech is the speech of the early people means that too much talk is no good. The early men were men, not like the men of today who are like women, like the clitoris, hanging in the middle. (IV-15)

> If we look at the proverbs and the ways they used to take care of their animals, and the world which is now, they are not the same. Today everybody follows what the whites do. (IV-16)

Although I have no lexical or syntactic explanation for this phenomenon, students, when asked in Somali to explicate a proverb which exalts the "speech" of the men of before, took that proverb to claim that the "actions" of the men of before are being exalted. When the interview was in English, however, the students restricted themselves more to the great words of the past. The English language it seems, has introduced the notion of the dichotomy between speech and action to these Somali students. This, according to Arendt's thesis, would indicate greater respect for politics when politics is in Somali than when it is in English; and less reliance on (mute) violence. It would seem to me that in Somali society, the political process might well be taken more seriously, less hypocritically, now that the language of politics is Somali, a language in which speech is on the same plane, "coequal and coeval," with action.[9]

Language and Religious Values

Somalia is an Islamic society of long standing, and at least some Islamic values must be assumed to have been adopted by Somalis. One important aspect of Islamic community is the inseparability of religious and secular values. Islamic values are relevant for all domains of life. Although this is theoretically the same in the Judeo-Christian societies of the Western world, in the modern world a distinction between the religious and the secular aspects of our lives is usually made and sometimes upheld as a matter of faith.

To what extent is the relevance of religious values in what seems to me to be secular domains tied to language? Or, in the case study at hand, to what extent are Islamic values upheld or heralded in English conversation among Somali students? It is important to note first that Somali is not the language of religion in Somali society, and that the sacred books are recited in Arabic. The question here is to what extent those values are relevant in areas which, in my view at least, are secular in Somali and English.

In the role-playing sessions, reference to God and religion were far more prevalent in Somali (forty-seven) than in English (six). This difference is significant ($K_d = 8$; one-tailed; $p < .05$) and is illustrated in figure 6. Eight pairs in the Somali dialogues referred to religious

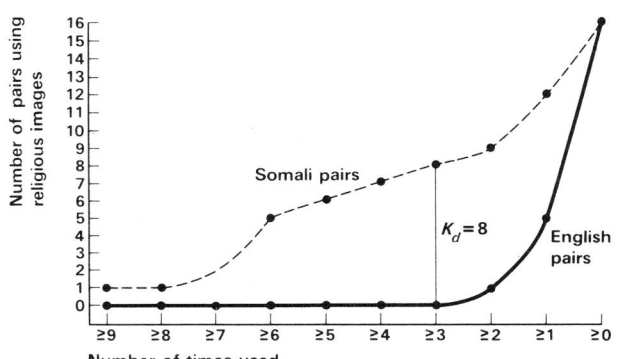

Figure 6 Religious Values Expressed in the Three Role-playing Sessions

themes at least three times, while no English speaking pairs made reference to religious themes more than twice. Although many of the Somali references merely invoked the name of God, many expressed religious values. Two Somali examples of the latter type follow:

(I-9, 10) 10. First of all, I have forgotten the book, that's first; even though I have forgotten, I had not done so with my knowing it, *it happened because of the order of God.* Then, you say, the name of God, and *he will help you go and do the examination* as I have forgotten the book.

9. There is a proverb that says, *"Trust in God and ask his help, though do not risk your neck."* Don't say God will bring it to where he likes and I will be where he decided.... God said, "Trust in me and be careful." Therefore to ask help from God is right, but there must be care, and the care is to get the book and read it. You made a promise, and you broke it, how did this happen to a man?

10. I don't know what to say, first everything has happened by the order of God, and nothing we can bring back and *what God has written for you you will never lack*, therefore if God has written it so, then it must take place.

9. Then listen if it is true what you have said to me that I shall see what God has written for the examination of tomorrow, then I shall never read anything.... *It is impossible to say, "Trust God for the test tomorrow."* ... Have your personal affairs become more important than the promise?

10. No, *it happened by the order of God.*

(IV-4, 8) 4. Brother. Do not say that to me. Kindly do not say to me that I took your book. Now since I took it because of your kindness, I had to do the same way that was right. Things used to be forgotten, and *everyone forgets except the Almighty God...*

8. Just be quiet, I shall be quiet, but I will trust you. I shall trust you and all the people. What I shall do is, since no one will bring back what you will not do what you know and at the same time makes it wrong, then that shows you in this world *there is no one you can trust. Even with God as your best friend....*

4. Yes, enough. *God will bring back the test* since you missed your chance to read for it.

The Islamic ideas that mere humans cannot overcome the will of God, and that we must learn to become subservient to his will, are felt to be relevant to discourse concerning a forgotten book in these Somali dialogues. Reference to religious values was exceedingly rare in the English dialogues.

A similar relation between language and religious notions in a secular setting was perceptible in the Somali interviews. In one question we suggested that perhaps it would be better for the Somali nomads to consider the needs of future generations by reducing the number of their camels so that there would be less erosion of the grazing land. We asked, "Do you think our view of the future should change our customs or traditions?" Of the twenty-four students in the Somali group who understood the question, four rejected the notion of this kind of planning, basing that rejection on religious values. None of the twenty-one students in the English group based their rejection of planning on religious grounds. While the numbers here are too small for any test of significance, I mention them because the group which took the interviews in English is the same group which participated in the role-playing sessions in Somali. So the significant difference in religious imagery in the role-playing sessions, in conjunction with the answers here in the interview, suggest that it is language, and not differences between the two groups, which can explain the use of religious justifications in nontheological conversations. Two of the justifications from the Somali interviews are:

> If we did not follow the past ways, now there would be nothing, that we can follow, and at the end we will say there is not God, and thus I prefer the past practices. (I-7)

> Everything is in the hands of God. Then for the sake of that we cannot foretell something we did not attain, and to consider it. I think in the religious part it is not our right. (III-8)

The point here, as it has been in the earlier sections, is not that Somali students could not invoke religious values in the English language, but that they did not, and to have done so probably would have felt odd. Islamic values seemed to have more relevance, more poignance, when these students were speaking Somali. Indeed, the world these students perceived was different in the two languages. The dichotomy between religious and secular values, so natural when they were speaking in English, did not emerge when they were speaking Somali.

This observation has some bearing on one of the major arguments of the "alphabet war" discussed in chapters 4 and 5. Adherents of Islam fought gallantly against the use of the Latin script for the Somali language, arguing that the Latin script would destroy religious values. The consequence of religious objection to the Latin script for the Somali language was the continued use and the expansion of the

English language in Somali public life. My data suggest that the spread of the English language would pose a far greater threat to religious values in Somali-speaking areas than would the introduction of the Latic script for writing the Somali language. The data further suggest that by intimidating the religious lobby and instituting the Latin script, General Siyaad has even helped preserve religious values.

Conclusion

Language change, and its implications for political equality, participation, and culture, has been the central focus of this study. In the African context, the political ramifications of the implantation of European political institutions has been widely studied; but the political ramifications of the spread of European cultural institutions have not been clearly delineated. To what extent can the continued presence of one cultural institution —language—explain changes in values and stratification in African societies? To what extent can the continued use of European languages as the official languages of new African states explain the seeming complicity of many African elites in the establishment of neocolonial relations between former colony and metropole? These were the initial questions which guided my research in Somali language politics.

In part 1, "The Politics of Language," I examine what proves to be a very limited colonial impact on Somali society. The colonial period yielded very little urbanization, industrialization, or, in a wider sense, modernization. European parliamentary institutions were not introduced until a few years before independence, and had markedly little influence in bringing about social change. But the English, Italian and Arabic languages were imparted during this period, and many of the most influential Somalis in the nationalist movement spoke at least one of these languages.

Although linguistically homogeneous when it received its independence, Somalia took English, Italian, and Arabic as its official languages. Because of a controversy involving technical, religious and political questions, no orthography could be agreed upon, either in the trusteeship period of 1950-60 when the Italians provided a forum for national debate, or in the parliamentary years, 1960-69, when there were a number of forums for debate on questions of a national script.

The consequences of a nondecision in regard to script were great for the Somali polity and society. With English becoming the principal language of education and the civil service, new bases of social stratification, supplanted on a fundamentally egalitarian society, were forming. Social and economic divisions between north and south, city and bush, religious men and laymen began to grow wider. Also, those exposed to the English language were better able to participate in the newly adopted democratic institutions.

Those democratic institutions—the parliament and free press especially—were unsuited to deal effectively with the question of national script, a question which lent itself to no compromise and evoked such deep emotions. Nondecision on the part of the democratic institutions is in large part responsible for the erosion of the social basis for democracy. It took an authoritarian regime, one which was fundamentally opposed to liberal democratic institutions, to make a decision in regard to script and thereby to decree that Somali was to be the language of political and administrative discourse in the Somali Republic. From this act, the restoration of the social basis for democracy in Somalia has begun.

In part 2, "The Language of Politics," I have attempted to give evidence in support of a modified linguistic relativity hypothesis—a hypothesis which suggests that the language a person speaks influences the way he perceives and acts in the world. I have also suggested what I thought to be the consequences of this hypothesis, if it is shown to be valid. If the language you speak influences the way you act in the world, then to change a people's language is to change a way of life. European languages penetrated extensively throughout Africa in its first decade of independence, but few scholars have examined the cultural implications of the spread of a foreign language. It is possible that the persistence of colonial values even after the attainment of political independence can be partly explained by the persistence and growing use of the colonial languages. The acceptance of foreign languages in Somalia after the Somalis received political independence may have been more threatening to the maintenance and development of Somali social structure and values than a century of direct colonial rule.

In my Somali case study I found that, in certain realms, the language Somali students spoke did influence the way they acted and the way they perceived themselves. While these findings were statistically significant and congruent with expectations based on a study of Somali social structure, I have expressed some reservations about both the quality and the interpretation of the data. Nonetheless, the data support at minimum this conclusion: language change can explain some of the variance in responses to direct questions and in discussions between Somali bilinguals.

I have discussed four areas where a Somali political culture in the Somali language might be different from a Somali political culture in the English language. These areas are distinct, and I am wary of making general statements concerning modal political cultures. For concluding purposes, however, I stress the differences between the Somali language responses and the English language responses, and assume that my data—collected from a limited segment of the Somali population and in a limited time period—represent a more general reality. Somali political actors in a Somali language political culture would be more conscious of the uniqueness of Somali cultural institutions and have a clearer sense of the meaning of a Somali identity. They would attempt to eradicate any new basis of social stratification and see it as unnatural and odd. Arguments based on a person's structured position in the society would carry little weight; and if any citizen attempted to gain political influence, he would find that appeals to the substance of the issues would carry more weight. Political life would gain respect, I would suggest, if it were carried on in the Somali language, and it would take the form of diplomatic repartee rather than that of direct confrontation. Finally, Somalis acting in a Somali language political culture would make a lesser distinction between secular and religious values, and the claims of the religious leaders would have greater political relevance.

Somali political actors in an English language Somali political culture, on the other hand, would be less conscious of Somali cultural identity, and would be more likely to accept "integration" with other African peoples. It is probable that they would accept role specification and see nothing odd about decisions made by people who had the "authority" to do so. Structured inequalities would seem less outrageous. Politics would be more confrontational, more polarized, with less concern for the maintenance of good will among citizens and for the community fabric. And religious values would seem out of place in a more clearly defined secular realm.

Parts 1 and 2 conjoined paint a wider picture. In Somalia and, I suspect, elsewhere in the newly independent states, political independence and democratic institutions could not assure cultural and political autonomy. As the imperial powers took down their flags, they did not repatriate the cultural institutions which were transferred during the colonial process. The language of the imperial power remained in most newly independent states the official language of politics. Those people who were most successful in resisting colonial rule found themselves least able in the postindependence period to participate in independence politics. New systems of stratification were often weighted so that those who gained from them were those who had the greatest interest in maintaining the cultural institutions of the former imperial power. The very language of the imperial society influenced the way the Somali speakers of the language thought and acted politically. If Somalia had continued to rely extensively on English as an official language, its neocolonial relationship with its former imperial rulers would have met less internal resistance, and its traditional participatory and egalitarian political culture would have been more deeply challenged. Indeed the results of this study suggest that the decision to make Somali the national and official language of the Somali Democratic Republic was a key to the maintenance and development of Somali cultural and political autonomy.

Notes

Chapter 1

1. I do not intend to discuss all the issues relating language policy in the new states to social and political concerns. A good overview of this newly developed subdiscipline is in Joshua A. Fishman et al., *Language Problems of Developing Areas* (New York: John Wiley, 1968). Fishman's introductory essay, "Sociolinguistics and the Language Problems of Developing Countries," has a good bibliography on language politics. Jyotirindra Das Gupta's contribution, "Language Diversity and National Development," is the best introduction to concerns of language policy for political scientists. See Selig S. Harrison, ed., *The Most Dangerous Decades: An Introduction to the Comparative Study of Language Policy in Multi-Lingual States* (New York: Language and Communication Research Center, Columbia University, 1957), for a discussion of many of the problems facing the new states in regard to language.

2. I am referring to the Sapir-Whorf literature. A general review of the theory and the findings of the "linguistic relativists" is presented in chapter 6.

3. David Apter, *Ghana in Transition* (New York: Atheneum, 1963), p. 20.

4. See, for example, Lucian W. Pye's "Democracy and Political Development" in his *Aspects of Political Development* (Boston: Little, Brown, 1966).

5. Barrington Moore, Jr., *Social Origins of Dictatorship and Democracy* (Boston: Beacon, 1966), p. 410. My reference to John Kautsky is to his introductory essay in Kautsky, ed., *Political Change in Underdeveloped Countries* (New York: John Wiley, 1964).

6. See, for example, Aristide R. Zolberg, *Creating*

Political Order (Chicago: Rand McNally, 1966); or his "The Structure of Political Conflict in the New States of Tropical Africa," *American Political Science Review* 62, no. 1 (March 1968).

7. Jyotirindra Das Gupta, *Language Conflict and National Development* (Berkeley: University of California Press, 1970), p. 260.

8. Ibid., p. 268.

9. This argument is put into terms of democracy more explicitly in Das Gupta and John Gumperz, "Language, Communication, and Control in North India," in Fishman (n. 1 above).

10. I am quoting from S. I. Benn and R. S. Peters, *The Principles of Political Thought* (New York: Free Press, 1959), p. 420. For Tocqueville, of course, social equality was the defining characteristic of democracy. Even Robert A. Dahl, who centered his statement of democratic theory on institutions, still considered that all citizens need to have "identical information about the alternatives." By this criterion of "polyarchy," Dahl would have to rule out any state in which the language of government were different from the language of the people as a polyarchy. One must assume that citizens who do not speak the language of the state will have greater difficulty in getting access to political information. See *A Preface to Democratic Theory* (Chicago: University of Chicago Press, 1956), p. 84. In a later work, *Polyarchy* (New Haven: Yale University Press, 1971), Dahl concedes that it is possible for states which have "subcultural pluralism" to be polyarchies, but suggests that they are unlikely to remain so (pp. 111ff). See Apter, p. 328, n. 6, which was written in the less optimistic postindependence years. Here Apter attempts to deal with this criticism.

11. Pierre Alexandre, *Languages and Language in Black Africa,* trans. F. A. Leavy, (Evanston: Northwestern University Press, 1972), p. 86.

12. In John Spencer, "Language and Independence," in Spencer, ed., *Language in Africa,* Leverhulme Conference (Cambridge: Cambridge University Press, 1963), p. 31.

13. The French derided the African vernaculars as uncivilized; but they had no more intention than the British to spread their language beyond a small African elite. See Georges Hardy, *Une conquête morale: L'enseignement en A.O.F.* (Paris: Librairie Armand Colin, 1917).

14. Joseph Stalin, *Marxism and the National Question* (New York: International Publishers, 1942). The quoted passage was from a statement in 1923.

15. Das Gupta, *Language Conflict,* pp. 162, 237-39.

16. Quoted in Einar Haugen, *Language Conflict and Language Planning: The Case of Modern Norwegian* (Cambridge, Mass.: Harvard University Press, 1966), p. 103.

17. Ibid. This study merits careful scrutiny by anyone interested in language politics.

18. Alexandre, p. 81.

19. Carol M. M. Scotton, *Choosing a Lingua Franca in an African Capital* (Edmonton: Linguistic Research, Inc., 1971), p. 27.

20. Ibid., pp. 88-92.

21. Thomas Gorman, "A Survey of Educational Language Policy; And An Enquiry Into Patterns of Language Use and Levels of Language Attainment among Secondary School Entrants in Kenya" (University of Nairobi, Ph.D. diss. 1971), p. 201.

22. Carol M. M. Scotton, "Language in East Africa: Linguistic Patterns and Political Ideologies." In Joshua Fishman, *Advances in the Study of Societal Multilingualism* (The Hague: Mouton, forthcoming), vol. 2.

23. Karl Deutsch, *Nationalism and Social Communication* (Cambridge: M.I.T. Press, 1953), pp. 130ff.

24. Quoted in Claude Wauthier, *The Literature and Thought of Modern Africa,* trans. Shirley Kay (New York: Praeger, 1967), p. 31.

25. Ibid., p. 31.

26. Frantz Fanon, *Black Skin, White Masks,* trans. Charles Markmann (New York: Grove Press, 1967), pp. 38, 17-18.

27. Quoted and translated by Thomas Gorman, in "Language Policy in Kenya," paper presented at the 1970 meeting of the Language Association of Eastern Africa, Nairobi (mimeo).

28. V. S. Naipaul, interview in *Transition* 8, no. 40 (December 1971).

29. Gabriel Almond, "Comparative Political Systems," *Journal of Politics* 18 (1956).

30. "Conclusion: Comparative Political Culture" (by Verba), in Lucian W. Pye and Sidney Verba, eds., *Political Culture and Political Development* (Princeton: Princeton University Press, 1965), p. 513.

31. Verba, ibid., p. 516, footnote. The reader may want to refer to Rodney Needham, *Belief, Language, and Experience* (Oxford: Basil Blackwell, 1972), for an explanation of why any attempt to study beliefs comparatively is fraught with dangers.

32. Verba, "Germany: The Remaking of Political Culture," in Pye and Verba (n 30 above), p. 132. Emphases added.

33. Ibid., p. 162. Emphases added.

34. Ibid., p. 133. Emphases added.

35. Ibid., p. 168. Emphases added.

36. That is the number Joseph H. Greenberg catalogues in *The Languages of Africa* (The Hague: Mouton, 1966), pp. 164-71. William E. Welmers has provided a "Checklist of African Language and Dialect Names" in Thomas A. Sebeok, *Current Trends in Linguistics,* vol. 7: *Linguistics in Sub-Saharan Africa* (The Hague: Mouton, 1971), in which he presents 142 pages of names, with about 35 names per page. While many languages are listed more than once under different names, and many mutually intelligible dialects are listed separately, the list is still overwhelming.

Chapter 2

1. Quoted in Somali Republic, Information Services, *The Somali Peninsula:*

A New Light on Imperial Motives (Muqdisho: Somali Government Information Services, 1962).

2. For those readers interested in exploring Somali ethnography, the two leading ethnographers are I. M. Lewis and Enrico Cerulli. The leading ethnolinguists are B. W. Andrzejewski and Muuse X. I. Galaal. Their works are cited in the notes that follow and in the bibliography.

3. William Travis, *The Voice of the Turtle* (London: Allen and Unwin, 1967), pp. 153-54.

4. Ibid., p. 154.

5. I. M. Lewis, *Peoples of the Horn of Africa* (London: International African Institute, 1955; reprinted with supplementary bibliography, 1969); The oversimplification which I presented was suggested by Lewis's useful summary in James L. Gibbs, ed., *Peoples of Africa* (New York: Holt, Rinehart and Winston, 1966).

6. See Xuseen M. Adam, "A Nation in Search of a Script" (M.A. thesis, University of East Africa, 1968); W. H. Whiteley, "Notes on the Ci-Miini Dialect of Swahili," *African Language Studies* 6, (1965); and I. M. Lewis, *A Pastoral Democracy* (London: Oxford University Press, 1961), p. 13.

7. A. N. Tucker and M. A. Bryan, *The Non-Bantu Languages of Northeastern Africa* (London: Oxford University Press, 1956); and Greenberg (chap. 1, n. 36, above), p. 49.

8. Richard Burton, *First Footsteps in East Africa* (New York: Praeger, 1966), p. 93.

9. B. W. Andrzejewski and I. M. Lewis, *Somali Poetry* (Oxford: Clarendon Press, 1964), p. 2.

10. Lewis, *Pastoral Democracy*, pp. 161-95.

11. Ibid., p. 198.

12. Ibid., p. 228.

13. Virginia Luling, "The Social Structure of Southern Somali Tribes" (Ph.D. diss., University of London, 1971), pp. 180-91; on the councils, see pp. 131-32.

14. Lewis, *Pastoral Democracy*, p. 241.

15. Luling, p. 357.

16. Douglas Jardine, *The Mad Mullah of Somaliland* (London: Herbert Jenkins, 1923), pp. 235, 213-14.

17. Recorded and translated for me by Axmed Faarax Cali "Idijaa."

18. This theme will be picked up in chapter 3. I will be referring to A. M. Brockett, "The British Somaliland Protectorate to 1905" (Ph.D. diss., Lincoln College, Oxford, 1969); John Drysdale, *The Somali Dispute* (London: Pall Mall Press, 1964); and Saadia Touval, *Somali Nationalism* (Cambridge, Mass.: Harvard University Press, 1963).

19. Luling, pp. 51-52.

20. Isak Dinesen, *Shadows on the Grass* (New York: Random House, 1961), pp. 8, 12, 14.

21. E. R. Turton, "Somali Resistance to Colonial Rule and the Development of Somali Political Activity in Kenya, 1893-1960," *Journal of African History* 13, no. 1 (1972): 128-29. Turton doesn't mention that to be classified as an Asian conferred certain business rights.

22. Ralph E. Drake-Brockman, *British Somaliland* (London: Hurst and Blackett, 1912), p. 102. I commend this volume to students of the British colonial service.

23. Burton, pp. 25, 32.

24. Margaret Laurence, *New Wind in a Dry Land* (New York: Alfred Knopf, 1964), p. 19.

25. Leonard W. Doob, ed., *Resolving Conflict in Africa* (New Haven: Yale University Press, 1970), p. 45.

26. Andrzejewski and Lewis, p. 144.

27. See Wallace Lambert, *Language, Psychology, and Culture* (Stanford: Stanford University Press, 1972), chap. 13, "A Social Psychology of Bilingualism," for a general overview. See also Lambert's original contribution on this theme in *Journal of Communication* 16 (1966).

28. Details of the experiment are provided in chapter 7.

29. Burton, p. 90.

30. Jardine, p. 249.

31. General Siyaad is being paraphrased by David W. Shenk, "A Study of Mennonite Presence and Church Development in Somalia from 1950 through 1970" (Ph.D. diss., New York University, 1972), p. 323. Siyaad, I am sure, was being hyperbolic here, as he has not persecuted any Somali Christians.

32. Lewis, *Pastoral Democracy*, p. 256.

33. Burton, p. 25.

34. Somali Republic, *New Light*, p. 3.

35. Brockett, p. 1.

36. Recorded and translated in Andrzejewski and Lewis, pp. 86-93.

37. Sylvia Pankhurst, *Ethiopia: A Cultural History* (Woodford Green, Essex: Lalibela House, 1955), pp. 435-38.

38. Burton, p. 31.

39. Ibid., p. 60.

40. Somalia, Statistical Department, Ministry of Planning and Coordination, "Multi-purpose Survey of Baidoa District, February-April 1968," p. 14.

41. Edourd Duchenet, *Histoires Somalies* (Paris: Larose, 1936), p. 73.

42. Translated in W. H. Whiteley, ed., *A Selection of African Prose* (Oxford: Clarendon Press, 1964), pp. 149ff. It is available in Somali in B. W. Andrzejewski and Muuse X. I. Galaal, *Hikmad Soomaali* (London: Oxford University Press, 1956).

43. B. W. Andrzejewski and Muuse X. I. Galaal, "The Art of the Verbal Message in Somali Society," *Neue Afrikanistische Studien* (Deutsches Institut für Afrika-Forschung, Hamburg), 1966, p. 29.

44. I. M. Lewis, *The Modern History of Somaliland* (New York: Praeger, 1965), p. 5.

45. F. M. Hunter, quoted by B. W. Andrzejewski and Muuse X. I. Galaal in "A Somali Poetic Combat," *Journal of African Languages* 2 (1963): 15-16.

46. B. W. Andrzejewski, quoted by Colin Legum in "Somali Liberation Songs," *Journal of Modern African Studies* 1, no. 4 (1963): 503-4.

47. Andrzejewski and Galaal, "Somali Poetic Combat," p. 22.

48. Ibid., p. 190.

49. Ibid., p. 191.

50. Andrzejewski and Lewis, p. 122, in a poem called "Ingratitude."

51. Ibid., p. 128.

52. Andrzejewski and Galaal, "Somali Poetic Combat," p. 24.

53. Ibid., p. 95.

54. B. W. Andrzejewski, "Reflections on the Nature and Social Function of Somali Proverbs," *African Language Review* 7 (1968): 74-85.

55. Andrzejewski and Galaal, "Art of Verbal Message."

56. Hannah Arendt, *The Human Condition*, (Chicago: University of Chicago Press, 1959), pp. 25, 307.

57. Paolo Contini, *The Somali Republic: An Experiment in Legal Integration* (London: Frank Cass, 1969), pp. 50-52.

58. Legum, p. 505.

Chapter 3

1. Recorded and translated by Andrzejewski and Lewis (chap. 2, n. 9, above), p. 57.

2. Quoted in Tareq Y. Ismael, *The UAR in Africa: Egypt's Policy Under Nasser* (Evanston: Northwestern University Press, 1971), p. 117.

3. Ibid., pp. 4-12. See also the elementary Somali Government textbook *Buugga Taariikhda*, (Muqdisho: Guddiga Af Somaaliga, 1972), pp. 6-8.

4. J. Spencer Trimingham, *Islam in East Africa* (Oxford: Clarendon Press, 1964), p. 3.

5. Lewis, *Modern History* (chap. 2, n. 44, above), p. 22.

6. Trimingham, pp. 5, 6.

7. Lewis, *Modern History*, pp. 36-37. See also Robert L. Hess, *Italian Colonialism in Somalia* (Chicago: University of Chicago Press, 1966), p. 7.

8. Brockett (chap. 2, n. 18, above), p. 9.

9. Ibid., pp. 16-30.

10. Jalal Yahya, *Egyptian Somali Relations* (Cairo: 1960) translated for me from the Arabic by Assad Busool, pp. 34-47.

11. Brockett, p. 55.

12. Yahya, pp. 48-69.

13. See two conflicting approaches to the Egyptian evacuation: Yahya, pp. 180ff., and Brockett, pp. 77ff.
14. Yahya, p. 183.
15. Ismael, pp. 36-37.
16. From Nasser's *The Philosophy of the Revolution,* 1954; quoted in Ismael, pp. 99-100.
17. Ismael, pp. 103-4.
18. Ibid., pp. 120, 127. Egyptian exports to Somalia peaked in 1964, and never formed a significant proportion of either Egypt's or Somalia's total trade. See figures presented in chapter 5.
19. Legum (chap. 2, n. 46, above), p. 506.
20. Lewis, *Modern History,* p. 199.
21. A good example of this species is Talaat Saleh, *The Independence of Somalia* (Cairo [?]: Middle East Publications, c. 1959), available in the Hoover Library at Stanford University.
22. Travis (chap. 2, n. 3, above), pp. 194-195.
23. Burton (chap. 2, n. 8, above), p. 87.
24. Lewis, *Modern History,* pp. 4-5.
25. From a poem in Arabic by Cabdillaahi Xaashi; recorded and translated by Andrzejewski and Lewis, p. 153.
26. J. Spencer Trimingham, *Islam in Ethiopia* (London: Oxford University Press, 1952), p. 211.
27. Luling, (chap. 2, n. 13, above), p. 39.
28. Muuse Galaal, talk to Peace Corps volunteers, Afgoy, Somali Republic, May 1969.
29. Lewis, *Pastoral Democracy* (chap. 2, n. 6, above), p. 11.
30. B. W. Andrzejewski and Muuse X. I. Galaal, "A Somali Poetic Combat" *Journal of African Languages,* 2, (1963), p. 94.
31. Burton, p. 115.
32. Xuseen Adam, "A Nation in Search of a Script" (unpublished master's thesis, University of East Africa at Makerere, 1968), p. 81.
33. Anwar G. Chejne, *The Arabic Language: Its Role in History,* (Minneapolis: University of Minnesota Press, 1969), p. 11.
34. Adam, p. 75.
35. Luling, pp. 161-162.
36. Trimingham, *Ethiopia,* p. 215.
37. Ismael, p. 139.
38. Somali Republic, Ministry of Education, *Annual Report, 1967* (Muqdisho, 1968), pp. 11, 16.
39. Ismael, p. 330.
40. Somali Republic, Ministry of Education, *Annual Report, 1967,* p. 16.
41. Ibid., p. 47.

42. Ibid., p. 17.
43. Lewis, *Modern History*, p. 5.
44. Andrzejewski and Lewis, pp. 52-53; and for Arabic poems by Somalis in translation, ibid., pp. 150-67.
45. I. M. Lewis, "Literacy in a Nomadic Society: The Somali Case" in Jack Goody, ed., *Literacy in Traditional Societies* (Cambridge: Cambridge University Press, 1968) p. 266.
46. Somali Republic, Ministry of Education, *Annual Report, 1968* (Muqdisho, 1969), p. 36.
47. Somali Democratic Republic, Ministry of Education, *Annual Report, 1971* (Muqdisho, 1972), p. 35.
48. Quoted in Denis Mack Smith, *Italy: A Modern History* (Ann Arbor: University of Michigan Press, 1959), p. 253.
49. Ibid., p. 128.
50. Hess, pp. 11-16.
51. I owe this interpretation of Crispi, and indeed much of my understanding of Italian imperialist motivation, to the lectures of Richard A. Webster on modern Italian history at the University of California, Berkeley.
52. 15 January 1889; Hess, p. 25.
53. Ibid., pp. 37-38.
54. Mack Smith, p. 265.
55. Ibid., p. 186.
56. E. Sylvia Pankhurst, *Ex-Italian Somaliland* (New York: Philosophical Library, 1951), p. 29.
57. Hess, p. 89.
58. Luling, pp. 199-200.
59. Hess, p. 108.
60. Mack Smith, p. 448.
61. Ibid., p. 476.
62. Hess, p. 177.
63. Ibid., p. 196.
64. Mark Karp, *The Economics of Trusteeship in Somalia* (Boston: Boston University Press, 1960).
65. Hess, p. 186.
66. Luling, p. 218.
67. Ibid., p. 229.
68. Hess, p. 150.
69. Ibid., pp. 167-70, 187.
70. The entire agreement is available in George Henry Becker, Jr., *The Disposition of the Italian Colonies 1941-1951* (Université de Genève, Thèse No. 87, 1952), pp. 246-59. The article cited is on p. 249.

71. Donald R. Scott, "Education in Italian Somalia: A Preliminary Report," mimeo. (Muqdisho), n.d. [1960?].

72. UNESCO, Report of the Educational Planning Group On Their First Mission to Somalia, March 6—May 26, 1962 (Paris: August 1962), pp. 91, 114, 120.

73. Ibid., p. 16.

74. Lewis, *Modern History,* p. 112.

75. Luling, p. 249.

76. *Corriere della Somalia,* 14 August 1952; my translation.

77. I. M. Lewis, *"Nationalism and Particularism in Somalia,"* in P. H. Gulliver, ed., *Tradition and Transition in East Africa* (Berkeley: University of California Press, 1969), p. 350.

78. Luling, pp. 205-6, and 228, footnote.

79. Andrzejewski and Lewis, pp. 78-79 (my emphasis).

80. Travis, p. 22.

81. Salisbury's remark, made in a private communication (1887) to Sir Evelyn Baring, consul-general in Egypt, is quoted in Brockett, p. 134.

82. Brockett, p. 14.

83. Ibid., p. 15.

84. Burton, p. 18.

85. Brockett, p. 51.

86. Ibid., p. 80.

87. Ibid., p. 90.

88. Ibid., p. 102.

90. Ibid., pp. 146-47.

91. Ibid., p. 243.

92. Ibid., p. 280.

93. H. F. Prevost Battersby, *Richard Corfield of Somaliland* (London: Edward Arnold, 1914), p. viii. It should be mentioned that Battersby attributed these deaths to the Sayid.

94. The poem is recorded and translated in Andrzejewski and Lewis, pp. 70-75.

95. For various treatments of the Dervish movement, see Jardine (chap. 2, n. 16, above); Lewis, *Modern History*; Battersby, *Richard Corfield*; Brockett; and Saadia Touval (chap. 2, n. 18, above). It will be years before Somali historians can deal correctly with the Sayid, even though their perspective would be most important. The Sayid constantly engaged in Somali clan politics, playing one clan off against the other, and built coalitions around clans. Most of his poetry reflects this. Today, since the Supreme Revolutionary Council deems it important not only to ban all clan obligations but to assert that clans do not and never did exist, it is impossible for Somalis to write about the Sayid in terms other than that he fought gallantly against the heathen imperialists. This

is why the newly written elementary text of Somali History, *Buugga Taariikhda*, gives only limited treatment to the Dervish movement.

96. Drysdale (chap. 2, n. 18, above). See also Touval; and Somalia, *New Light* (chap. 2, n. 40, above).

97. Battersby, p. viii.

98. [Dame] Margery Perham, *Major Dane's Garden* (1926; reprinted London: Rex Collings, 1970), p. 5.

99. Ibid., pp. 8-9.

100. Alys Reece, *To My Wife—50 Camels* (London: Harvil Press, 1963), p. 105.

101. Douglas Collins, *A Tear for Somalia* (London: Harrolds, 1960).

102. Brockett, pp. 148-54.

103. Lewis, *Modern History*, p. 104.

104. Reece, *To My Wife*.

105. Turton, (chap. 2, n. 21, above), p. 126, footnote.

106. Becker, p. 38.

107. Luling, p. 250.

108. Brockett, p. 155.

109. Ibid., p. 293.

110. UNESCO, Report, pp. 55-56.

111. Lewis, *Modern History*, pp. 132-33.

112. UNESCO, Report, p. 57.

113. Ibid., p. 74-75.

114. Pankhurst, *Ex-Italian Somaliland*, pp. 168-169.

115. Donald Rothchild, "Ethnic Inequalities in Kenya," *Journal of Modern African Studies* 7, no. 4 (1969): 694.

116. Somali Republic, Ministry of Education, *Annual Report, 1968*, p. 47.

117. Touval, p. 107.

118. Lewis, *Modern History*, p. 171.

119. Andrzejewski and Lewis, pp. 116-19.

120. Lewis, *Pastoral Democracy*, p. 271.

121. Somali party politics and its relationship to traditional clan structure is a topic too wide to explore here. The clan basis of interest in the SYL will be discussed in chapter 4. For a fuller treatment, see A. A. Castagno, "The Political Party System in the Somali Republic," in James S. Coleman and Carl G. Rosberg, Jr., eds., *Political Parties and National Integration in Tropical Africa* (Berkeley: University of California Press, 1964). Lewis, *Pastoral Democracy*, pp. 266-295; and Touval, pp. 85-108.

122. Lewis, *Pastoral Democracy*, p. 282.

Chapter 4

1. Quoted in Drysdale (chap. 2, n. 18, above), pp. 21-22.
2. See I. M. Lewis, "The Gudabiirsi Somali Script," *Bulletin of the School of Oriental and African Studies* 21, no. 1 (1958): 135; and Somali Democratic Republic, Ministry of Information and National Guidance, *Somalia Today* (1970), pp. 65-66.
3. Capt. J. S. King, "Somali as a Written Language," part 1, *The Indian Antiquary*, August 1887; part 2, ibid., October 1887.
4. Muuse X. I. Galaal, "Arabic Script for Somali," *Islamic Quarterly* 1, no. 2 (July 1954).
5. From Mario Maino, *Lingua Somala, strumento d'insegnamento professionale* (1953), pp. 23-24. Reprinted in *Somaliya*, Antologia Storico-Culturale, 7-8 (June 1969), pp. 93-95.
6. Lewis, "Gudabiirsi," p. 134.
7. Evangeliste de Larajasse and Cyprien de Sampont, *Practical Grammar of the Somali Language*, (London: Kegan Paul, 1897), p. viii.
8. J. W. C. Kirk, *A Grammar of the Somali Language* (Cambridge: Cambridge University Press, 1905. Reprinted Westmead, England: Gregg International Publishers, 1969).
9. Galaal and Andrzejewski, *Hikmad Somaali* (chap. 2, n. 42, above).
10. R. C. Abraham, *The Somali-English Dictionary* (London: University of London Press, 1962); *The English-Somali Dictionary* (London: University of London Press, 1967).
11. Martino Moreno, *Il Somalo della Somalia* (Rome: Istituto Poligrafico dello Stato, 1955), p. 290.
12. A. N. Tucker, relying on Andrzejewski in "Orthographic Systems and Conventions," in Sebeok (chap. 1, n. 36, above), p. 639.
13. Lewis, *Modern History* (chap. 2, n. 44, above), p. 115.
14. Adam (chap. 2, n. 6, above), p. 51. Without Professor Adam's kind help, this chapter could not have been written.
15. Ibid., p. 90.
16. Castagno (chap. 3, n. 121, above), p. 552.
17. Adam, pp. 100, 101, 141.
18. See, for example Yaasiin Cismaan, "La Nostra Lingua Madre," *Corriere della Somalia*, 7 March 1952; reprinted in *Somaliya*, 1969, pp. 69-73.
19. B. W. Andrzejewski, "The Problem of Vowel Representation in the Isaaq District of Somali," *Bulletin of the School of Oriental and African Studies* 17, no. 3 (1955): 568.
20. Most of them are cited in John William Johnson's "A Bibliography of the Somali Language and Literature," *African Language Review*, November 1969.
21. Lewis, *Modern History*, p. 158, n. 16.
22. Adam, p. 62.

23. Galaal, p. 115.
24. Adam, p. 59.
25. Ibid., p. 95.
26. Ibid., pp. 100, 96.
27. Maxamuud Axmed Cali, quoted in ibid., pp. 64-65.
28. Interview with Axmed Faarax Cali "Idijaa," 8 March 1973.
29. *Somalia: The Writing of Somali* (Paris: UNESCO, 1966), p. 15.
30. Anwar G. Chejne, *The Arabic Language: Its Role in History* (Minneapolis: University of Minnesota Press, 1969), pp. 9, 158.
31. Charles F. Gallagher, "Language Rationalization and Scientific Progress," in K. Silvert, ed., *The Social Reality of Scientific Myth* (New York: American University Field Staff, 1969), p. 68.
32. Galaal, p. 115.
33. Adam, p. 81.
34. Ibid., p. 66.
35. Ibid., pp. 101, 100, 141.
36. Ibid., p. 17.
37. From articles 3 and 20; reprinted in Becker (chap. 3, n. 70, above), pp. 248, 255.
38. Xasan Cali Mirreh, "Il riconoscimento della lingua somala come lingua madre," *Corriere della Somalia,* 8 May 1950; reprinted in *Somaliya,* 1969, pp. 27-28.
39. "Il problema della Lingua somala," reprinted in *Somaliya,* p. 8.
40. Moreno, "Problemi culturali della Somalia" (1952); reprinted in *Somaliya,* p. 58.
41. Lewis, *Modern History,* p. 123.
42. Yaasiin, reprinted in *Somaliya,* pp.6-7.
43. SYL, memorandum, reprinted in *Somaliya,* pp. 24-25.
44. *Corriere della Somalia,* 20 June 1952; reprinted in *Somaliya,* pp. 77-78. To Xaaji's clan, reer Xamar, Somali was sometimes considered a foreign language. I, who speak Somali poorly, have twice been identified as reer Xamar when the person listening could not see me.
45. *Corriere della Somalia,* 24 July 1952; reprinted in *Somaliya,* p. 87.
46. See "Copia del verbale di Riunione No. 8 del 2 Febbraio 1951 del Consiglio Territoriale della Somalia," reprinted in *Somaliya,* pp. 47-50.
47. *Corriere della Somalia,* 1 September 1950; reprinted in *Somaliya,* p. 34.
48. Castagno, pp. 523-25, explains the change in the power balance by suggesting that the British Military Administration favored the Daarood clan family, while the Italian administration favored the Hawiya.
49. Party statute, reprinted in *Somaliya,* p. 115.
50. "La nostra lingua madre," *Corriere della Somalia,* 7 March 1952; reprinted in *Somaliya,* pp. 69-73.

51. Yaasiin Cismaan, "La Nostra Lingua Madre."
52. Yaasiin Cismaan, "La funzione sociale del linguaggio," *Somalia d'Oggi* 1, no. 1 (October 1956); reprinted in *Somaliya,* pp. 105-13.
53. Ibid., pp. 109-10.
54. See, for example, Sido Roble Cismaan Simba, in *Corriere della Somalia,* 28 January 1957; reprinted in *Somaliya,* pp. 127-29.
55. All in *Corriere della Somalia.* Axmed Atto, 21 January 1957; Xuseen Cabdi "Farmacia," 23 January 1957; Cabdi Aaden Aptidon "Huhle," 5 February 1957; and Cabdillaahi Sultan Axmed, 5 February 1957. All reprinted in *Somaliya* pp. 122-24.
56. *Corriere della Somalia,* 6 March 1957; reprinted in *Somaliya,* pp. 144-45.
57. Abokor Sheekh Maxamad "Fod-Adde," *Corriere della Somalia,* 20 March 1957; reprinted in *Somaliya,* pp. 153-55.
58. Adam, pp. 52-53.
59. *Corriere della Somalia,* 16 March 1957; reprinted in *Somaliya,* pp. 150-52.
60. Adam, p. 37.
61. 1961 Linguistic Commission, *Report,* p. 2.
62. Ibid., p. 4.
63. Ibid., pp. 72-73; see Adam, p. 37.
64. Somali Republic, Ministry of Education, "Our Educational Policy in the Light of Deliberations, Conclusions, and Recommendation of the Conference of African States on the Development of Education in Africa, Held Jointly by UNESCO and E.C.A. at Addis Ababa, 15-26 May, 1961," pp. 1, 4.
65. *Somali News,* 11 October 1963.
66. Ibid., April 10, 1964.
67. The Somalis' feelings of resentment toward the Latin script should not lead the reader to believe that they had no sense of humor or of proportion about the issue. The army trucks had *hoga* written on them, the Somali word, the army sign painters thought, for "army." Depending on what version of Latin script you chose, the word should have been written as *xoogga* or *hhoga.* The word, as written, was closer to *hoogga,* the word for "calamity" or "disaster." The army trucks were laughed at far more for that irony than the fact that they were using "unholy" letters for the national language.
68. I have been relying on the weekly English and Italian newspapers. They differed considerably in content. I have no access to the Arabic weekly, and this should be considered an important gap.
69. *Somali News,* 31 August 1962.
70. Ibid., 15 November 1963.
71. Ibid., 2 April 1965.
72. Ibid., 3 July 1964.
73. Ibid., 30 April 1965.

74. Ibid., 22 May 1964.
75. Adam, p. 95.
76. Muuse Galaal, "The Problem of Written Somali: A Plan on the Possible Introduction of Written Somali," printed in *Somaliya*, p. 190. Muuse was a student and remains a friend of Andrzejewski's, one of the technical experts. In this memorandum he therefore wishes to do more than communicate his thoughts to the UNESCO commission.
77. Ibid., pp. 193-94.
78. *Corriere della Somalia,* 23 March 1966; reprinted in *Somaliya,* p. 207.
79. Maxamuud Xaaji Axmed Cali, memorandum, printed in *Somaliya*, pp. 202-6.
80. M. Jaamac Maxamad "Afballaar," public statement, 25 March 1966; printed in *Somaliya,* pp. 208-9.
81. *Corriere della Somalia,* 26 March 1966; reprinted in *Somaliya,* pp. 210-14.
82. *Somalia: The Writing of Somali,* p. 6.
83. Ibid., p. 12.
84. Adam, p. 37, from an interview with Muuse Galaal.
85. Adam, p. 48.
86. Hersi Magan Ciise, November 1967; printed in *Somaliya,* pp. 243-51.
87. *Somaliya,* pp. 252-55.
88. *Somali News,* 17 May 1969.
89. Ibid., 20 June 1969.
90. Adam, p. 146, from an interview with Cabdirisaaq Xaaji Xuseen.
91. *Somali News,* 8 September 1969.
92. Ibid., 16 September 1966.

Chapter 5
1. Reported in Somali Democratic Republic, Ministry of Information and National Guidance, *Beautiful Somalia,* (Paris: Jeune Afrique, 1971), p. 73.
2. Somali Democratic Republic, National Language Commission, *Report on Somali Text Books* (Muqdisho, 1972), letter dated 6 January 1971.
3. National Language Commission, *Report,* p. 2.
4. Ibid., p. 9.
5. Ibid. (no page).
6. Ibid., p. 10.
7. *Dawn,* 7 April 1972; 14 April 1972.
8. Ibid., 22 October 1972.
9. Ibid.
10. Ibid., 3 November 1972.
11. Ibid., 27 October 1972.
12. The verve with which the game of party politics was played in Somalia is

ably described by Touval (chap. 2, n. 18, above); and Castagno (chap. 3, n. 121, above). The Hoover Library at Stanford University has a good collection of the independent journal *Dalka,* which demonstrates the wide latitudes of criticism permitted by the government.

13. I owe this point to Jyotirinda Das Gupta. Indeed, it is a subsidiary theme in his *Language Conflict* (chap. 1, n. 7, above).
14. Adam (chap. 2, n. 6, above), p. 122.
15. Adam, p. 121.
16. Camillo Bonanni, "Literacy for Nomads in Somalia," *Overseas Education* 33, no. 2 (July 1961).
17. Reported in *Somali News,* 6 January 1967.
18. Adam, p. 115.
19. Somali Republic, Ministry of Education, *Annual Report 1967* (Muqdisho, 1968), p. 17.
20. *Annual Report 1968* (Muqdisho, 1969).
21. *National Review,* no. 3 (July 1964).
22. Economic Commission for Africa, Summaries of Economic Data, Somalia, compiled January 1975, M75-168, 6th year, no. 9.
23. *La Tribuna* 2, no. 2, (1 July 1968), p. 17.
24. *Nuovi Ovuzzonti* 1, no. 1, (October 1969).
25. *Annual Report 1971* (Muqdisho, 1972), p. 32.
26. That the era of party politics was a continuation of the Somali tradition is a theme in chapter 9 of Lewis's *Pastoral Democracy* (chap. 2, no. 6, above).
27. See Jack Goody and Ian Watt, "The Consequences of Literacy," in Jack Goody, ed., *Literacy in Traditional Societies* (Cambridge: Cambridge University Press, 1968), esp. p. 55, where the consequences of literacy for democracy are discussed.
28. Thomas A. Johnson, "Somali Schools to Close a Year So Students Can Teach Nomads," *New York Times,* 23 June 1974.
29. Barrington Moore, Jr., *Social Origins.*
30. Verba (chap. 1, n. 30, above).
31. On interdependence, see Kenneth N. Waltz, "The Myth of National Interdependence," in Charles P. Kindelberger, ed., *The International Corporation,* (Cambridge: M.I.T. Press, 1970); and Ernst B. Haas, "Is There a Hole in the Whole?" *International Organization,* summer 1975. My thoughts relating this issue to concerns of cultural dependency were clarified by an unpublished paper by Harry Kreisler, "Cosmopolitanism: The Problem of Cultural Autonomy and Cultural Dependence" (Berkeley, 1973).
32. *Annual Report 1969* (Muqdisho, 1970), p. 20.
33. Adam, p. 112.
34. *Dawn,* 13 August 1971.
35. Maxamad Ismaaciil, quoted in Adam, pp. 106-7.
36. D. M. Preece and H. R. B. Wood, *Foundations of Geography* (London:

University Tutorial Press, *1972*). I was asked to use this text when I taught "O" level (i.e., preparatory for the General Certificate of Education, Ordinary Level) geography in the West Indies. What I found most distressing was that it was I who had to convince the students that their book was wrong. I saw students purchasing this book in Nairobi, Kenya.

37. See Xasan Sheekh Mumin, *Shabeelnaagood* (*Leopard Among the Women*), tr. B. W. Andrzejewski, (London: Oxford University Press, 1974), with texts in both Somali and in English. See as well the extensive bibliography of written Somali in B. W. Andrzejewski, "The Rise of Written Somali Literature" *African Research and Documentation*, No. 89 (1975).

38. It is thought that capital flow data might be more reliable than trade flow data. I am presently working on a study which shows that capital movements do correlate with language policy in Somalia and in other African states.

Chapter 6

1. Translated by Andrzejewski and Lewis, in *Somali Poetry* (chap. 2, n. 9, above), p. 142.
2. For linguistic traditions that have attempted to see language as an independent agent in maintaining cultural values, see, for example, Hans Kohn on Herder in his "Language as a Political Issue," in Harrison (chap. 1, n. 1, above); and Harold Basilius, "Neo-Humboldtian Ethno-Linguistics," in Joshua A. Fishman, *Readings in the Sociology of Language* (The Hague: Mouton, 1968).
3. Boas, quoted in Dell Hymes, "Linguistic Method in Ethnography: Its Development in the United States," in Paul L. Garvin, *Method and Theory in Linguistics* (The Hague: Mouton, 1970), p. 255.
4. Hymes, p. 259.
5. Edward Sapir, *Language* (New York: Harcourt Brace and World, 1921), pp. 217-18.
6. Ibid., p. 127.
7. Ibid., p. 120.
8. Ibid., p. 127.
9. Ibid., p. 218.
10. Ibid., p. 219.
11. Sapir, quoted in Dan I. Slobin, *Psycholinguistics* (Glenview: Scott, Foresman, 1971), p. 120.
12. Sapir, "Conceptual Categories in Primitive Languages," *Science* 74:578.
13. Benjamin Lee Whorf, *Language, Thought and Reality,* ed. John Carroll (Cambridge, Mass.: M.I.T. Press, 1956), pp. 134-36. The essay was written in 1939.
14. Whorf, pp. 214, 221; my emphasis.
15. In Whorf's essay, "Science and Linguistics," ibid., pp. 213, 217.
16. Ibid., pp. 217-18.

17. Ibid., pp. 233-35. This example, and similar ones, have been the subject of much review. See Hanna Pitkin, *Wittgenstein and Justice* (Berkeley: University of California Press, 1972), p. 105; E. Adamson Hoebel, *Anthropology: The Study of Man* (New York: McGraw-Hill, 1958), pp. 45-46; and John B. Carroll, *Language and Thought* (Englewood Cliffs, N.J.: Prentice-Hall, 1964), pp. 107-8.

18. Dell Hymes, in *Language in Culture and Society* (New York: Harper and Row, 1964), p. 117, insists that Whorf made a distinction between "habitual" and "potential" behavior, and felt that while the potential range of perception is probably the same in all languages, linguistic relativity operates on the habitual level. But Whorf sometimes does imply the "potential" aspect, which is consistent with linguistic determinism. My analysis here is a formal attempt to discredit the determinist argument, whether or not it was seriously and consistently upheld by Whorf.

19. Carroll, p. 107.

20. Whorf, p. 216.

21. See Pitkin, p. 108, who is relying on Stanley Cavell, "The Claim to Rationality" (Ph.D. diss., Harvard University, 1961-62).

22. Thomas S. Kuhn, *The Structure of Scientific Revolutions* (Chicago: University of Chicago Press, 1962), p. 110. Kuhn is not fully prepared to accept the implications of the quoted statement. He feels that in a sense the world does change. But in another sense, it's still the same world. He suggests a new philosophical paradigm is required in order to reconcile these two "senses." See, esp., pp. 119-20.

23. Eric H. Lenneberg, *Biological Foundations of Language* (New York: John Wiley, 1967), p. 365.

24. Max Black, "Linguistic Relativity: The Views of Benjamin Lee Whorf," *Philosophical Review* 68 (1959), p. 238.

25. Joshua Fishman, "A Systematization of the Whorfian Hypothesis," *Behavioral Science* 5, no. 4 (October 1960).

26. Slobin, p. 124.

27. Lenneberg, pp. 354-55, summarizing Lantz and Stefflre, and p. 355, his conclusion.

28. Leonard W. Doob, *Communication in Africa* (New Haven: Yale University Press, 1961), p. 199.

29. Carol Scotton, "Some Swahili Political Words," *Journal of Modern African Studies* 3, no. 4 (1965).

30. In Fishman, "Systematization," p. 332.

31. In Slobin, pp. 131-32.

32. Fishman, "Systematization," p. 337.

33. Carroll, p. 110.

34. For example, see Eugene F. Miller, "Positivism, Historicism, and Political Inquiry," *American Political Science Review* 66, no. 3 (September

1972), p. 803. The quote is from Wittgenstein's *Philosophical Investigations,* 3d ed. (New York: Macmillan, 1968), paragraph 19.

35. Wittgenstein, *The Blue and Brown Books* (New York: Harper Torchbooks, 1965), pp. 102-3.
36. Wittgenstein, *Investigations,* p. 175.
37. Ibid., paragraph 577, slightly altered.
38. Ibid., p. 224.
39. Ibid., p. 225.
40. Discussed in Pitkin, p. 83.
41. In V. C. Chappell, ed., *Ordinary Language* (Englewood Cliffs, N.J.: Prentice-Hall, 1964), p. 46, emphasis deleted.
42. J. L. Austin, in ibid., p. 56.
43. John Gumperz and Dell Hymes, eds., *Directions in Sociolinguistics: The Ethnography of Communication* (New York: Holt, Rinehart, and Winston, 1972), is the latest volume focusing on this theme.
44. See Ethel M. Albert, "Culture Patterning of Speech Behavior in Burundi," in Gumperz and Hymes, *Directions,* for a particularly good discussion of the nature of field research. See also David J. Parkin, "Language choice in Two Kampala Housing Estates," in W. Whiteley, ed., *Language Use and Social Change* (London: Oxford University Press, 1970).
45. See Hymes, "Two Types of Linguistic Relativity," in Bright, *Sociolinguistics* (The Hague: Mouton, 1966). While Hymes calls for studies of "language in use" to test for relativity, his evidence is within language communities.
46. Jean Piaget, *The Moral Judgment of the Child,* trans. Marjorie Gabain (Glencoe: Free Press, 1948).
47. Lev Vygotsky, *Thought and Language,* ed. and trans. Eugenia Hanfmann and Gertrude Vakar (Cambridge, Mass.: M.I.T. Press, 1962), pp. 16-17.
48. Wittgenstein, *Investigations,* paragraph 570.
49. Whorf was not unaware of this point. See his "The Relation of Habitual Thought to Language," in *Language* (n. 13 above), footnote on p. 151. Other social scientific research has taken language "in gear" with fruitful results. See Leonard Shatzman and Anselm Strauss, "Social Class and Modes of Communication," *American Journal of Sociology* 60 (1955), for a comparison between the way lower- and middle-class respondents perceived the same event. And see B. J. Chandler and Frederick D. Erickson, "Sounds of Society" (mimeo, U.S. Department of Health, Education, and Welfare, 1966), for a comparison between inner-city black language/culture and suburban White language/culture. In both of these studies, the investigators analyzed tape recordings of extended talk by different individuals and groups all in the same context of events.
50. Wittgenstein, *Investigations,* paragraphs 23, 546. See, also, Pitkin, pp. 36-43.

51. Wittgenstein, *Investigations,* paragraph 27.
52. J. L. Austin, *Philosophic Papers* (Oxford: Clarendon Press, 1961), pp. 66-67.
53. Pitkin, p. 39.
54. See John Searle, *Speech Acts* (Cambridge: Cambridge University Press, 1969), and "Chomsky's Revolution in Linguistics," *New York Review of Books* 18, no. 12 (29 June 1972). Searle criticizes linguists for ignoring the fact that to speak is to communicate.
55. Pitkin, p. 115.
56. Lenneberg, p. 362.
57. Murray Edelman, *The Symbolic Uses of Politics* (Urbana: University of Illinois Press, 1964), p. 114.
58. Arendt (chap. 2, n. 56, above), pp. 26-27.
59. Ibid., p. 3.
60. Thucydides, *The Peloponnesian War,* trans. John H. Finley (New York: Modern Library, 1951), book 3, paragraph 82.
61. George Orwell, "Politics and the English Language," in Denis Val Baker, *Modern British Writing* (New York: Vanguard, 1957), pp. 205-6.
62. See R. Cranford Pratt, "The Cabinet and Presidential Leadership in Tanzania: 1960-1966," in Michael F. Lofchie, *The State of Nations* (Berkeley: University of California Press, 1971), p. 104.
63. Anthony Nutting, *Nasser* (New York: E. P. Dutton, 1972), p. 37.
64. Trimingham, *Islam in East Africa* (chap. 3, n. 4, above), p. 187.
65. Ali A. Mazrui, "The English language and Political Consciousness in British Colonial Africa, "*Journal of Modern African Studies* 4, no. 3 (1966): 295-97.
66. I have self-consciously limited myself to an examination of the literature which (a) looks at language as an independent variable; and (b) consciously looks at those elements in language which might be relative. I fully recognize that there is much excellent research which sees language as a dependent variable, adjusting itself to other cultural or technological changes. See, for example, Marshall McLuhan, *The Gutenberg Galaxy* (New York: Signet, 1969), and Paul Friedrich, "The Linguistic Reflex of Social Change: From Tsarist to Soviet Russian Kinship," *Sociological Inquiry* 36, no. 2 (spring 1966). The research tradition that attempts to discover universals in language is also substantial. See, for example, Charles E. Osgood, *et. al., The Measurement of Meaning* (Urbana: University of Illinois Press, 1961). That language can be a dependent variable and that there are linguistic universals do not detract from my general point that language can also affect culture, and that in certain areas languages may induce their speakers to see the world in different ways.

Chapter 7

1. See Lewis, *Peoples of the Horn of Africa* (chap. 2, n. 5, above), for a

discussion of the relationship of these penumbral clans to Somali social structure. B. W. Andrzejewski has done an informal study of language use in Kenya's Northeastern Province, W. H. Whiteley, ed., *Language in Kenya* (Nairobi: Oxford University Press, 1974), pp. 65-68.

2. Tom Okelo-Odongo, public lecture at the University of Nairobi, 10 May 1973.

3. International Labor Organization, *Employment, Incomes, and Equality: A Strategy for Increasing Productive Employment in Kenya* (Geneva, 1972), p. 78. See also, Kenya, Ministry of Education, *Annual Report, 1971.*

4. Leonard Doob, *Patriotism and Nationalism* (New Haven: Yale University Press, 1964). Doob in fact provided for linguistically differential answers, but it did not seem to be the main purpose of the study.

5. Suggested in an inventive paper by Charles Osgood and M. Richards, "From Yang and Yin to *and* or *but*," *Language* 49, no. 2 (1973).

6. See Lenneberg, *Biological Foundations* (chap. 6, n. 23, above), p. 346, on this very important point.

7. This topic merits scrutiny. Some seminal work on nonverbal communication has been done. See Ray L. Birdwhistell, *Introduction to Kinesics* (Louisville: University of Louisville Press, 1952); Edward T. Hall, *The Silent Language* (New York: Fawcett, 1959); and Erving Goffman, *Relations in Public* (New York: Harper and Row, 1971).

8. I grappled with this same problem in chapter 3, in an attempt to assess the level of independent effect of the Islamic religion on Somali society. I would suggest that an approach similar to the one I am using to assess the independent effect of language on society might be helpful in the case of religion. I hope to do research on the relationship of religion and politics.

9. Sidney Siegel, *Nonparametric Statistics* (New York: McGraw-Hill, 1956). The quote is from p. 31.

Chapter 8

1. Yuusuf Jaamac Cali Dhuxul is writing his impressions of a sensitivity-training project among Ethiopian, Kenyan, and Somali intellectuals, designed to reduce tensions and increase understanding among the participants concerning the areas claimed by the Somalis but which are now under Ethiopian and Kenyan jurisdiction. See Doob et al., *Resolving Conflict in Africa* (chap. 2, n. 25, above), pp. 54-55.

2. The Roman numerals signify the form (grade) of the participant, and the Arabic numerals refer to the number arbitrarily assigned him.

3. Luling (chap. 2, n. 13, above), p. 79.

4. I would like to thank Norman Uphoff, who pushed me further on this point than I really wanted to go.

5. Wilfred Whiteley, *Language in Kenya* (chap. 7, n. 1, above), tentatively, p. 320.

6. Roger Brown, *Words and Things* (New York: Free Press, 1958), pp. 235-36.
7. Edelman (chap. 6, n. 57, above), p. 133.
8. Arendt (chap. 2, n. 56, above), pp. 25-26.
9. I. M. Lewis, in a personal communication, has noted that "Somali patriotism and nationalism have *increased* since the adoption of written Somali."

Selected Bibliography

In this study, I have relied on three separate research traditions: (1) Somali studies; (2) language and linguistic relativity; and (3) comparative language politics. This bibliography is categorized according to these traditions. Somalis are alphabetized according to their first names. Spellings have been changed to accord with the modern Somali script.

Somali Studies

Abraham, R. C. (Major). *Somali-English Dictionary, English-Somali Dictionary.* London: University of London Press, 1962, 1967.

Andrzejewski, B. W. "The Problem of Vowel Representation in the Isaaq Dialect of Somali." *Bulletin of the School of Oriental and African Studies* (University of London) 17, no. 3 (1955).

———. "Reflections on the Nature and Social Function of Somali Proverbs." *African Language Review* 7 (1968).

———. "The Roobdoon of Sheikh Aquib Abdullahi Jama: A Somali Prayer for Rain." *African Language Studies* 11 (1970).

Andrzejewski, B. W., and Galaal, Muuse X. I. "The Art of the Verbal Message in Somali Society." In *Neue Afrikanistische Studien* (Hamburg), 1966.

———. "A Somali Poetic Combat," parts 1, 2, and 3. *Journal of African Languages* (1963).

Andrzejewski, B. W., and Lewis, I. M. *Somali Poetry.* Oxford: Clarendon Press, 1964.

Battersby, H. F. Prevost. *Richard Corfield of Somaliland.* London: Edward Arnold, 1914.

Becker, George Henry, Jr. *The Disposition of the Italian Colonies 1941–1951.* Doctoral dissertation, Université de Genève, 1952.
Bell, C. R. V. *The Somali Language.* London: Longmans, 1953.
Bonanni, Camillo. "Literacy for Nomads in Somalia." *Overseas Education* 33, no. 2 (July 1961).
Brockett, A. M. "The British Somaliland Protectorate to 1905." Ph.D. Doctoral dissertation, Lincoln College, Oxford, 1969.
Burton, Sir Richard. *First Footsteps in East Africa,* ed. Gordon Waterfield. New York: Praeger, 1966.
Castagno, A. A. "The Political Party System in the Somali Republic." In James C. Coleman and Carl G. Rosberg, Jr., eds., *Political Parties and National Integration in Tropical Africa.* Berkeley: University of California Press, 1964.
Cerulli, Enrico. *Somalia,* 3 vols. Rome: Ministero Degli Affari Esteri, 1964.
Chejne, Anwar G. *The Arabic Language: Its Role in History.* Minneapolis: University of Minnesota Press, 1969.
Contini, Paolo. *The Somali Republic: An Experiment in Legal Integration.* London: Frank Cass, 1969.
Dalka. An independent English language journal published in Muqdisho; Yuusuf Dhuxul, editor. Ceased publication in 1969. Available at Hoover Library, Stanford University.
Dinesen, Isak. *Shadows on the Grass.* New York: Random House, 1961.
Doob, Leonard W., ed. *Resolving Conflict in Africa.* New Haven: Yale University Press, 1970.
Drake-Brockman, Ralph E. *British Somaliland.* London: Hurst and Blackett, 1912.
Drysdale, John. *The Somali Dispute.* London: Pall Mall Press, 1964.
Duchenet, Eduard. *Histoires somalies.* Paris: Larose, 1936.
Greenberg, Joseph H. *The Languages of Africa.* The Hague: Mouton, 1966.
Grottanelli, Vinigi L. "Asiatic Influences on Somali Culture." *Ethnos* 12, no. 4 (October–December, 1947).
Hess, Robert L. *Italian Colonialism in Somalia.* Chicago: University of Chicago Press, 1966.
International Labor Organization. *Employment, Incomes, and Equality: A Strategy for Increasing Productive Employment in Kenya.* Geneva: 1972.
Ismael, Tareq Y. *The UAR in Africa: Egypt's Policy Under Nasser.* Evanston: Northwestern University Press, 1971.
Jardine, Douglas. *The Mad Mullah of Somaliland.* London: Herbert Jenkins, 1923.
Johnson, John William. "A Bibliography of the Somali Language and Literature." *African Language Review,* 8 November 1969.
———. "The Family of Miniature Genres in Somali Oral Poetry." *Folklore Forum* 5, no. 3 (July 1972).
Karp, Mark. *The Economics of Trusteeship in Somalia.* Boston: Boston University Press, 1960.

King, J. S. (Captain). "Somali as a Written Language." *The Indian Antiquary* (Bombay). Part 1, August 1887; part 2, October 1887.

Kirk, J. W. C. *A Grammar of the Somali Language with Examples of Prose and Verse and an Account of the Yibir and Midgan Dialects.* Cambridge: Cambridge University Press, 1905. Reprint, Westmead (U.K.): Gregg International Publishers, 1969.

Laurence, Margaret. *New Wind in a Dry Land.* New York: Alfred Knopf, 1964.

Legum, Colin. "Somali Liberation Songs." *Journal of Modern African Studies* 1, no. 4 (1963).

Lewis, I. M. "The Gudabiirsi Somali Script." *Bulletin of the School of Oriental and African Studies* (University of London) 21, no. 1 (1958).

———. "Literacy in a Nomadic Society: The Somali Case." In Jack Goody, ed. *Literacy in Traditional Societies.* Cambridge: Cambridge University Press, 1968.

———. *The Modern History of Somaliland.* New York: Praeger, 1965.

———. "Nationalism and Particularism in Somalia." In P. H. Gulliver, ed., *Tradition and Transition in East Africa.* Berkeley: University of California Press, 1969.

———. "The Northern Pastoral Somali of the Horn." In James L. Gibbs, Jr., ed., *Peoples of Africa.* New York: Holt, Rinehart and Winston, 1966.

———. *A Pastoral Democracy.* London: Oxford University Press, 1961.

———. *Peoples of the Horn of Africa.* London: International African Institute, 1955.

Luling, Virginia. "The Social Structure of Southern Somali Tribes." Doctoral dissertation, University of London, 1971.

Muuse X. I. Galaal. "Arabic Script for Somali." *Islamic Quarterly* 1, no. 2 (July 1954).

Muuse X. I. Galaal, and Andrzejewski, B. W. *Hikmad Soomaali.* London: Oxford University Press, 1956.

———. "Seeskah Hiddadaa Soomaalida." Mimeo. Muqdisho, 1969.

———. "Written Somali." *National Review* (Muqdisho) 3 (July 1964).

Nuovi Ovuzzonti. Independent Italian language journal, Muqdisho.

Nuruddin Faarax. *From a Crooked Rib.* London: Heinemann, 1970.

Pankhurst, Sylvia. *Ethiopia: A Cultural History.* Woodford Green, Essex: Lalibela House, 1955.

———. *Ex-Italian Somaliland.* New York: Philosophical Library, 1951.

Perham, Margery. *Major Dane's Garden.* 1926. Reprint, London: Rex Collings, 1970.

Reece, Alys. *To My Wife—Fifty Camels.* London: Harvill Press, 1963.

Rothchild, Donald. "Ethnic Inequalities in Kenya." *Journal of Modern African Studies* 7, no. 4 (1969).

Saleh, Talaat. *The Independence of Somalia.* pamphlet. Cairo (?): Middle East Publications, c. 1959. Available at Hoover Library, Stanford University.

Scott, Donald R. "Education in Italian Somalia: A Preliminary Report." Mimeo (Muqdisho).

Shenk, David W. "A Study of Mennonite Presence and Church Development in Somalia from 1950 through 1970." Doctoral dissertation, New York University, 1972.
Shire Jaamac Axmed. *Iftiinka-Aqoonta.* Occasional journal in Somali, Muqdisho.
Thompson, Virginia, and Adloff, Richard. *Djibouti and the Horn of Africa.* Stanford: Stanford University Press, 1968.
Touval, Saadia. *Somali Nationalism* (Cambridge, Mass.: Harvard University Press, 1963).
La Tribuna, independent Italian journal in Somalia, published until 1969.
Trimingham, J. Spencer. *Islam in East Africa.* Oxford: Clarendon Press, 1964.
———. *Islam in Ethiopia.* London: Oxford University Press, 1952.
Tucker, A. N., and Bryan, M. A. *The Non-Bantu Languages of North-Eastern Africa.* London: Oxford University Press, 1956.
Turton, E. R. "Somali Resistance to Colonial Rule and the Development of Somali Political Activity in Kenya, 1893-1960." *Journal of African History* 13, no. 1 (1972).
UNESCO. "Report of the Educational Planning Group on their First Mission to Somalia, March 6-May 26, 1962." Paris, August 1966. WS/0862.300.
———. "Somalia: The Writing of Somali." Paris, August 1966. WS/0866.90 CLT.
Whiteley, W. H. "Notes on the Ci-Miini Dialect of Swahili." *African Language Studies* 6 (1965).
———. *A Selection of African Prose.* Oxford: Clarendon Press, 1964.
Xuseen M. Adam. "A Nation in Search of a Script: The Problem of Establishing a National Orthography for Somali." Master's thesis, University of East Africa, Makerere, 1969.
Yahya, Jalal. *Egyptian Somali Relations.* Cairo, 1960. In Arabic.

Somali (Democratic) Republic; Government Publications

Annual Reports of the Ministry of Education.
Beautiful Somalia. Prepared by the Ministry of Information (and National Guidance). Paris: Jeune Afrique, 1971.
Codka Macallinka ["Teachers' Voice"]. Journal of the Ministry of Education.
Corriere della Somalia. Weekly newspaper published at Muqdisho until 1969.
Current Statistical Trends in Somali Education. Prepared by the Ministry of Education. Muqdisho, 1961.
Dawn. Weekly newspaper published after 1969. Available at the Hoover Library, Stanford University.
Government Activities from Independence until Today. 1 July 1960 to 31 Secember 1963.
"Multipurpose Survey of Baidoa District." Prepared by the Ministry of Planning and Coordination. February-April 1968. Mimeographed.
The Nation. Journal published until 1969.

National Review. Journal published until 1969.
New Era. Journal published after 1969.
"Our Educational Policy in the Light of the Deliberations, Conclusions, and Recommendations of the Conference of African States on the Development of Education in Africa, Held Jointly by UNESCO and E.C.A. at Addis Ababa, 15-26 May, 1961." Mimeographed.
Somali News. English-language weekly published until 1969.
The Somali Peninsula: A New Light on Imperial Motives. Muqdisho: Somali Government Information Services, 1962.
Somalia Today. Prepared by the Ministry of Information (and National Guidance). Muqdisho, 1970.
Somaliya, Antologia Storico-Culturale. Occasional journal of the Cultural Department of the Ministry of Education. See especially "Il problema della lingua somala (I)," in June 1969 issue. Available at the Guddiga Af Somaaliga, Muqdisho.

**Language Politics:
A Comparative
Perspective**

Although many of the works cited here are not referred to in the text, my study was informed by them. These citations have an Africa focus, but excellent works in other areas are mentioned.

Alexandre, Pierre. *Language and Language in Black Africa.* Trans. F. A. Leary. Evanston: Northwestern University Press, 1972.
Anderson, Anders. "Multilingualism and Attitudes: An Explorative-Descriptive Study among Secondary School Students in Ethiopia and Tanzania." Doctoral dissertation, Institute of Education, University of Uppsala, 1967.
Barnouw, Adriaan J. *Language and Race Problems in South Africa.* The Hague: Martinus Nijhoff, 1934.
Das Gupta, Jyotirindra. *Language Conflict and National Development.* Berkeley: University of California Press, 1970.
Deutsch, Karl W. *Nationalism and Social Communication.* Cambridge, Mass.: M.I.T. Press, 1953.
Dickens, K. J. "Orthography in the Gold Coast." *Africa* 6, no. 3 (July 1933).
Doke, C. M., "European and Bantu Languages in South Africa." *Africa* 12, no. 3 (1939).
East African Conference on Language and Linguistics, Dar es Salaam, 18-21 December 1968. Mimeographed papers, available at the University of Nairobi Library. Papers on language policy in the Sudan by Sayed Hamid Hurreiz and C. N. Hawkes, on Burundi by M. Albert Verdoodt, and on Rwanda by Betty Tuska.
Ferguson, Charles A. *Language in Ethiopia.* London: Oxford University Press, forthcoming.
Fishman, Joshua A.; Ferguson, Charles A.; and Das Gupta, Jyotirindra, eds. *Language Problems of Developing Nations.* New York: John Wiley, 1968.

Many useful papers. See especially Das Gupta's introductory essay, which is designed to introduce political scientists to the plethora of issues that relate to language. See also Heinz Kloss's "Notes Concerning a Language-Nation Typology," and John J. Gumperz and Jyotirindra Das Gupta, "Language, Communication and Control in North India."

Gorman, Thomas Patrick, "A Survey of Educational Language Policy; and an Enquiry into Patterns of Language Use and Levels of Language Attainment among Secondary School Entrants in Kenya." Doctoral dissertation, University of Nairobi, 1971.

Halliday, M. A. K. "National Language and Language Planning in a Multilingual Society." *East Africa Journal* 9, no. 8 (August 1972).

Harrison, Selig S. *The Most Dangerous Decades: An Introduction to the Comparative Study of Language Policy in Multi-Lingual States.* New York: Language and Communication Research Center, Columbia University, 1957. See especially Hans Kohn, "Language as a Political Issue."

Haugen, Einar, *Language Conflict and Language Planning: The Case of Modern Norwegian.* Cambridge, Mass.: Harvard University Press, 1966.

Jones, W. R. *Bilingualism in Welsh Education.* Cardiff: University of Wales Press, 1966.

Kitchen, Helen, ed. *The Educated African.* New York: Praeger, 1962.

Labouret, Henri. "L'éducation des indigenes: Méthodes britanniques et françaises," *Bulletin du Comité de L'Afrique française* 38, no. 10 (October 1928).

———. "La situation linguistique en Afrique occidentale francaise." *Africa* 4, no. 1 (1931).

Ladefoged, Peter (with Ruth Glick and Clive Criper). *Language in Uganda.* Nairobi: Oxford University Press, 1971.

Language Association of Eastern Africa, Conference on Language for Development in Eastern Africa, 30 May-2 June 1970, Nairobi. Mimeographed papers available at the University of Nairobi Library. Papers are concerned with educational policy in Kenya, Uganda, Ethiopia, and Zambia.

Lepage, R. B. *The National Language Question.* London: Oxford University Press, 1964.

Malherbe, E. G. *The Bilingual Schools: A Study of Bilingualism in South Africa.* London: Longmans, Green and Co., 1946.

Mazrui, Ali A. "The English Language and Political Consciousness in British Colonial Africa." *Journal of Modern African Studies* 4, no. 5 (1966).

Mazrui, Ali A., and Mazrui, Molly. "The Impact of the English Language on African International Relations." *Political Quarterly* 38, 2, (April-June, 1967).

———. "Some Socio-political functions of English Literature in Africa." *European Journal of Sociology* 9 (1968).

Nsibambi, Apolo. "Language Policy in Uganda." *African Affairs* 70, no. 278 (January 1971).

Rubin, Joan and Jernudd, Bjorn H., eds. *Can Language be Planned?* Hawaii: University of Hawaii Press, 1971. This volume has a number of important papers in an emerging field. See especially H. Kelman, "Language as an Aid

and Barrier to Involvement in the National System," and J. Fishman, "The Impact of Nationalism on Language Planning."
Rustow, Dankwart A. *A World of Nations*. Washington, D.C.: Brookings, 1967.
Schmidt, P. W. "The Use of the Vernacular in Education in Africa." *Africa* 3, no. 2 (April 1930).
Scotton, Carol M. M. *Choosing a Lingua Franca in an African Capital*. Edmonton: Linguistic Research, 1971.
———. "Language in East Africa: Linguistic Patterns and Political Ideologies," in Joshua Fishman, *Advances in the Study of Societal Multilingualism*, vol. 2. The Hague: Mouton, forthcoming.
Seboek, Thomas A. *Current Trends in Linguistics*, vol. 7: *Linguistics in Sub-Saharan Africa*. The Hague: Mouton, 1971. A massive volume, with contributions by Desmond T. Cole, J. David Sapir, Marius F. Valkhoff, John Spencer, W. H. Whiteley, W. E. Welmers, Philip J. Foster, A. N. Tucker, Pierre Alexandre, and Gilbert Ansre, among others.
Spencer, John, ed. *The English Language in East Africa*. London: Longmans, 1971. Some important papers. See especially Anthony Kirk-Greene, "The Influence of West African Languages on English," and Gilbert Ansre, "The Influence of English on West African Languages."
———. ed., *Language in Africa*. Cambridge: Cambridge University Press, 1963. This volume emerged from the discussions at the Leverhulme Conference and has been influential among language planners.
Stalin, Joseph. *Marxism and the National Question*. New York: International Publishers, 1942.
UNESCO. *The Use of Vernacular Languages in Education*. Monographs on Fundamental Education, no. 8. Paris, 1953.
Whiteley, W. H. *Swahili: The Rise of a National Language*. London: Methuen, 1969.
———, ed. *Language in Kenya*. Nairobi: Oxford University Press, 1974.
———, ed. *Language Use and Social Change*. London: Oxford University Press, 1971. This volume contains some excellent contributions. See especially M. H. Abdulaziz, "Tanzania's National Language Policy and the Rise of Swahili Political Culture," and Aidan Southall, "Cross-Cultural Meanings and Multilingualism."

Language and Linguistic Relativity

Arendt, Hannah. *The Human Condition*. Chicago: University of Chicago Press, 1958.
Austin, J. L. *Philosophical Papers*. Oxford: Clarendon Press, 1961.
Black, Max. "Linguistic Relativity: "The Views of Benjamin Lee Whorf." *Philosophical Review* 68 (1959).
Bock, Philip K. "Social Structure and Language Structure." *Southwestern Journal of Anthropology* 20, no. 4 (Winter 1964).
Bright, William, ed. *Sociolinguistics*. The Hague: Mouton, 1966.

Brown, Roger. *Words and Things.* New York: Free Press, 1958.
Carroll, John B. *Language and Thought.* Englewood Cliffs, N.J.: Prentice-Hall, 1964.
Chafe, Wallace L. *Meaning and the Structure of Language.* Chicago: University of Chicago Press, 1970.
Chandler, B. J., and Erickson, Frederick D. "Sounds of Society: A Demonstration Program in Group Inquiry." Mimeo, U.S. Department of Health, Education, and Welfare, 1966.
Chomsky, Noam. *Syntactic Structures.* The Hague: Mouton, 1957.
Doneux, J. L. "Peut-on passer de la structure du langage à une compréhension des structures psychologiques et sociales?" *Psychopathologie africaine* 1, no. 2 (1965).
Doob, Leonard. *Commincation in Africa: A Search for Boundaries.* New Haven: Yale University Press, 1961.
Edelman, Murray. *Politics as Symbolic Action.* Chicago: Markham, 1971.
Fishman, Joshua A. *The Sociology of Language.* Rowley, Mass:, Newbury House, 1972.
―――. "A Systematization of the Whorfian Hypothesis." *Behavioral Science* 5, no. 4 (October 1960).
―――, ed. *Readings in the Sociology of Language.* The Hague: Mouton, 1968. Important articles by Clifford Geertz, "Linguistic Etiquette"; Harold Basilius, "Neo-Humboldtian Ethno-Linguistics"; Susan M. Ervin-Tripp, "Interaction of Language, Topic, and Listener"; Roger Brown and Albert Gilman, "The Pronouns of Power and Solidarity"; and William Labov, "The Reflection of Social Processes in Linguistic Structures."
Friedrich, Paul. "The Linguistic Reflex of Social Change: From Tsarist to Soviet Russian Kinship." *Sociological Inquiry* 36, no. 2 (spring 1966).
Gallagher, Charles F. "Language Rationalization and Scientific Progress." In Kelman H. Silvert, ed., *The Social Reality of Scientific Myth.* New York: American Universities Field Staff, 1969.
Garvin, Paul L. *Method and Theory in Linguistics.* The Hague: Mouton, 1970.
Gumperz, John J., and Hymes, Dell. *Directions in Sociolinguistics.* New York: Holt, Rinehart and Winston, 1972.
Hymes, Dell. *Language in Culture and Society.* New York: Harper and Row, 1964.
―――. "Linguistic Aspects of Comparative Political Research." In Robert Holt and John Turner, eds., *The Methodology of Comparative Research.* New York: Free Press, 1970.
Kaplan, Bert. *Studying Personality Cross-Culturally.* New York: Harper and Row, 1961. See especially Dell Hymes's "Linguistic Aspects of Cross-Cultural Personality Study."
Lambert, Wallace E. *Language, Psychology, and Culture.* Stanford: Stanford University Press, 1972.
Lenneberg, Eric H. *Biological Foundations of Language.* New York: John Wiley, 1967.
McLuhan, Marshall. *The Gutenberg Galaxy.* New York: Signet, 1969.

Mitchell, Claudia I. "Language Behavior in a Black Urban Community." Doctoral dissertation, University of California, Berkeley, 1969.
Needham, Rodney. *Belief, Language, and Experience*. Oxford: Basil Blackwell, 1972.
Osgood, Charles, and Richards, M. "From Yang and Yin to *and* or *but*." *Language* 49, no. 2 (1973): 380-412.
Osgood, Charles; Suci, George J.: and Tannenbaum, Percy H. *The Measurement of Meaning*. Urbana: University of Illinois Press, 1961.
Piaget, Jean. *The Moral Judgment of the Child*. Trans. Margorie Gabain. Glencoe: Free Press, 1948.
Pitkin, Hanna Fenichel. *Wittgenstein and Justice*. Berkeley: University of California Press, 1972.
Sapir, Edward. *Language*. New York: Harcourt Brace and World, 1921.
Schatzman, Leonard, and Strauss, Anselm. "Social Class and Modes of Communication." *American Journal of Sociology* 60 (1955).
Scotton, Carol M. M. "Some Swahili Political Words." *Journal of Modern African Studies* 3, no. 4 (1965).
Slobin, Dan I. *Psycholinguistics*. Glenview, Ill: Scott Foresman, 1971.
Trager, George L. "The Systematization of the Whorf Hypothesis." *Anthropological Linguistics* 1, no. 1 (1959).
Vygotsky, Lev Semenovich. *Thought and Language*. Ed. and trans. Eugenia Hanfmann and Gertrude Vakar. Cambridge, Mass.: M.I.T. Press, 1962.
Waismann, Friedrich. "Language Strata." In Anthony Flew, ed., *Logic and Language*. Garden City: Anchor Books, 1965.
Whorf, Benjamin Lee. *Language, Thought and Reality*. Ed. John Carroll. Cambridge, Mass.: M.I.T. Press, 1956. Carroll has compiled a useful bibliography of the research done in linguistic relativity. My bibliography is supplemental to Carroll's.
Wittgenstein, Ludwig. *The Blue and Brown Books*. New York: Harper, 1965.
———. *Philosophical Investigations*, 3d, ed. Trans. G. E. M. Anscombe. New York: Macmillan, 1968.

Index

Aadan Cabdulle Cisman, 84, 100, 108
Aaden Isxaaq Axmed, 113
'Abd al-'Aziz Fahmi, 94
Abdul Ghany Abdallah Khalaf Allah, 49
Abgaal, 87
Abgaal Youth Association, 81
Abraham, R. C., 88
Abyssinia. *See* Ethiopia
Aden: and Britain, 47, 60, 70-71, 78; and Somalia, 48, 72, 74
Adowa, Battle of, 58, 60, 73
Afgoy, 26, 51, 64-65, 91, 96
af-Rahanwiin (Somali dialect), 25, 91. *See also* Rahanwiin
Africa: colonial impact in, 44, 48-50, 57, 134, 221; democracy in, 11; language policy in, 17, 162-63; language situation in, 3, 5, 8, 10, 12-13, 18-19
Ahmad Ibn Hanibal, 53
Ahmadiyah (Sufi order), 73
Ajuraan, 165
Alexander, Pierre, 8-10
Algeria, 55
Almond, Gabriel, 17
Amharic language, 4
Andrzejewski, B. W.: as member of 1966 commission 108, 238 n.76; on Somali language and scripts, 37, 55, 88-89, 165; on Somali poetry, 25, 38, 41
Apter, David, 5, 7
'Aqil Abī Tālib, 20
Arab, 45-56, 80
Arabia, 52, 135-36
Arabic language: its penetration in Somalia, 4, 55-56, 83, 221; its support in Somali Republic as an official language, 85, 91, 99-101, 103, 222; its use in education, 54
Arabic script: development of, for Somali language, 85-87; evaluation of, for Somali language, 89, 93-97, 121; support for, in Somali Republic, 96, 108-9
arar (preface), 39, 207, 211

Arendt, Hannah, 42, 160, 214, 216
Assab, 57-58
assimilation, 12, 13, 128-29
Augustine, Saint, 156-57
Austin, J. L., 154, 157
authority: meaning of, 145, 159; testing for differential conception of, in Somali and English, 172, 181, 187, 194-207; understanding of, in traditional Somali cutlure, 29
Awal Yoonis, 72
Axmad Gran, 27, 53, 82
Axmed Cali Abokor, 117
Axmed Yuusuf Keenadiid, 108

Bajuni, 46
Bandung (Indonesia), 48, 50
Baydhabo, 62, 65
Benaadir: Coast, 45-46, 52, 59; Company, 60-61, 64; Italian Protectorate of, 60-61
Benn, S. I., 226 n.10
Berbera, 110; relations with Egypt, 47-48; schools in, 54, 79; trade with Europe, 70-71, 74
Berlin, Treaty of (1885), 61, 72
Bevin, Ernest, 63, 75
Biimaal, 62, 68
Black, Max, 146
Blank, Baron Alberto, 60
Blixen, Baroness Karen (pseud. Isak Dinesen), 30
Boas, Franz, 139-41
Bonanni, Camillo, 124
Borama, 86-87
Boran, 165
Bosaso, 74
Bòttego, Vittorio, 60
Brava, 25, 46, 59, 65, 86
Brin, Benedetto, 60
Britain: colonial policy of, in Somalia, 27, 59, 70, 73, 75, 130; economic and political influence of, in Somalia, 7, 69-81, 135-36; educational policy of, in Somalia, 55-56, 78-80, 134; language policy of, in Somalia, 8, 88; war by, against the Dervishes, 73-74
British Broadcasting Corporation, 21
British East India Company, 70-71
British Somaliland, 86; cultural situation of, 23, 166; political history of, 28, 63, 88, 126
Brockett, A. M., 35, 72-73, 78
Brown, Roger, 148, 207
Bullaxaar, 47, 72, 78
Bulo Burti, 62
Burco, 79, 88, 92
Burton, Richard, 25, 30, 33, 36, 50, 52, 71

Cabdillaahi Ciise, 50, 92, 98, 100
Cabdirisaaq Maxamuud Abobakar, 117

Cabdirisaaq Xaaji Xuseen, 82, 92, 108, 111, 121
Cabdurashiid Cali Sharma' arke, 20, 66, 111, 114, 121
Cabduuraxmaan Cabdishakuur, 106
Cairo, 54
Cali Dhuux, 38-40, 42
Cali Garaad Jaamac, 104-5
Cali Madoobe, 21
Cal Maxamad Hiraabe, 112
Camuud (Somali Secondary School), 80
Cape Guardafui, 71
Carletti (Italian governor), 61
Carroll, John, 144-45, 150-51
Casagrande, J. B., 150-51
Cavell, Stanley, 153
Cavour, Conte Camillo, 59
Cecci, Antonio, 58, 60
Cerulli, Enrico, 88
Chi Miini, 86
Ciise, 75
Cismaan Axmed Yuusuf, 62, 67
Cismaan Maxamad Jelle, 118
Cismaan Maxamuud: clan, 23, 90, 108, 112, 131; sultan of Majeerteen, 59-60, 62
Cismaan Yuusuf Keenadiid, 86, 108
Cismaaniya: development and use of, 86, 117; evaluation of, 89-91, 97; opposition to, 107, 112, 121, 131; support for, 96, 98-100, 103, 108, 116
Collins, Douglas, 76
colonial situation. *See* dependency
Corfield, Richard, 74-75
Corpo Zaptié, 65
Corriere della Somalia (Muqdisho), 68, 99, 101, 102-103, 110
Crispi, Francesco, 58-60
Cromer, Lord (British diplomat), 48
Cumar Maxamuud, 23, 108

Daarood: categorized as clan family, 23; foundation of, 50; members of, 28, 86, 90, 102, 104, 108, 121, 131, 165; political power of, 38, 98
Daarood Jabarti bin Isma'il, 50, 121
Dagodiya, 165
Dahl, Robert A., 226 n.10
D'Annunzio, Gabriele, 57, 61
Dante Alighieri Society, 65
Das Gupta, Jyotirindra, 6-7
Dawn (Muqdisho), 120
De Larajasse, Reverend Evangeliste, 87
De Martino (Italian governor), 61-62
democracy, 132, 222; institutional basis of, 5-7, 122, 129, 131; language policy and, 5-7; social basis for, 6-7, 11, 14, 123, 129
dependency, 15-16, 132-36, 164
Depretis, Agostino, 57-58

De Sampont, Venerable Cyprien, 87
Deutsch, Karl, 12, 13
Dhulbahante, 23, 38, 104
Digil, 23
Dinesen, Isak. *See* Blixen, Baroness Karen
Dir, 23
Dir Rudini, Antonio, 60
diya-paying group, 23, 25, 27, 82
Doob, Leonard, 149, 169, 192
Drake-Brockman, R. E., 30
Drysdale, John, 76
dubshid (Somali religious practice), 54
dugsi. *See* Qur'anic schools
Dul Madoobe, 74

Edelman, Murray, 160-61, 213
education: medium of instruction in, 14. *See also*, Arabic language, its use in education; Britain, education policy of, in Somalia; Egypt, cultural influence, in Somalia; English language, official role of, in Somalia; Italian language, official role of, in Somalia; Italy, influence of, in Somalia
Egypt, 45; colonial exploits of, in Somalia, 45-50, 70-71, 78; cultural influence of, in Somalia, 54-55, 99, 109-10; trade between, and Somalia, 52-53, 136
Eliot, Sir Charles, 77
English language: effects of, when relied on in Somalia, 129, 136, 224; official role of, in Somalia, 85, 88-89, 105, 163, 222; penetration of, in Somalia, 4, 80-81, 83, 128, 221
equality, 4, 7, 12-14, 129
Eritrea, 58, 60
Ethiopia: in Nasser's vision, 48; as perceived by Somalis, 95; relations of, with Britian, 48, 73-74; relations of, with Italy, 58-59, 62; Somali cultural areas in, 21, 28, 42, 49, 75-76, 102, 107, 129; use of wadaad's writing in, 85
European languages, 4, 14. *See also* English; French; Italian

Faarax Nuur, 43
Fakhr al-Dīn dynasty, 46
Fanon, Frantz, 15
Filonardi (Italian entrepreneur), 59, 60, 64
Fishman, Joshua, 146-47, 151, 156
France, 48, 59, 70-71, 73, 75
Franchetti, Leopoldo, 58
French language, 4
French Territory of Afars and Issas, 21, 28, 129. *See also* Jabuuti

Galla, 165
Garibaldi, Giuseppe, 57
Geledi, 26, 51, 53, 64-65, 68, 195
Genale, 64

General Certificate of Education, 56, 80, 134. *See also*
  Britain, educational policy of, in Somalia
Germany, 59, 71
Ghana, 5
Giolitti, Giovanni, 60
Gladstone, William, 72
Gorman, Thomas, 11
Great Britain. *See* Britain
Greater Somalia League, 81
Gudabiirsi (clan), 86-87
guudmar (allegory), 39, 41, 207, 211, 213
Gumperz, John, 155
Gurreh, 165

Habar Awal, 70-72, 78
Habar Garxajis, 72
Habar Toljaclo, 72
Hadramaut, 51
Hague Convention (1907), 77
Haile Selassie, 75
hantiwadaag (socialism), 171
Harar, 58, 71-72
Hargeysa, 79
Harti, 23, 121
Hawd. *See* Ethiopia, Somali cultural areas in
Hawiya: as a clan family, 23, 50, 87; political influence of, 46, 98, 100, 121, 131, 165
H. Cali Shiddo "Dighe," 107
H. Cismaan, 107
Hess, Robert, 63-65
Hisbia Digil Mirifle, 81
Hoijer, Harry, 150
Humboldt, Wilhelm von, 139
Hunter, F. M., 71, 72
Hymes, Dell, 155, 241 n.18

Ibn Battuta, 46
Ibn Sa'īd, 46
Ibraahiim Xaaji Cigaal, 111
Ibraahiim Xaashi Maxamuud, 92, 104, 116
Ibrahim al Rashidi, 73
Ilig, 74
Imperial British East Africa Company, 59-60
India, 70, 72-73, 76, 78
Isiolo, 77
Islam, 53-54; penetration of, in Somalia, 20, 37, 51, 56; political role of, in Somalia, 53-54, 82-83, 95, 111; relevance of, in the Somali and English languages, 217-20; role in, of sufi orders, 41; support for, by Cismaaniya supporters, 91
Ismaaciil Barood, 118

Ismaaciil Cali Abokor, 133
Ismaaciil Jimcaali Cosoble, 127-28
Ismaaciil Samatar, 23
Ismā'īl (Egyptian khedive), 47
Israel, 49
Istun (Somali festival), 54
Isxaaq: classification of, as a Somali clan family, 23; foundation of, as a Somali clan family, 51; members of, 38, 86; political role of, 30, 40, 131
Isxaaq bin Axmed, 51
Italian language: official role of, in Somalia, 85, 98-99, 105-106, 222; penetration of, in Somalia, 4, 67-68, 83, 221; political support for, in Somalia, 103, 128
Italian Somalia, 23, 80; independence of, 63, 88, 126; Trusteeship period in, 28, 84, 97-103
Italy: colonial administration of, in Somalia, 61-63, 79; colonial designs of, in East Africa, 48, 58-59, 71, 73, 74; influence of, in Somalia, 7, 57-69; receives and administers UN Trust, 63-67; relations between, and Somali Republic, 67, 130, 135-36

jaalle (comrade), 195-96
Jabuuti, 75. *See also* French Territory of Afars and Issas
Japan, 49
Jibriil Abokor, 72
Jilib, 65
Jordan, 55
Jowhar, 65

Kaddare script, 87
Kautsky, John, 6
Kenya: British colonial designs in, 59; importance of education in, for Somalia, 79-80; Somali cultural areas in, 21, 28, 42, 49-50, 52, 75-77, 79-80, 107, 129; Somali cultural areas in, as research site, 31, 165-67
Kenyatta, Jomo, 15, 16, 107
King, J. S., 85
Kirk, J. W. C., 34, 87
Kismaayo, 47, 59, 65
Kuhn, Thomas S., 145-46, 241 n.22

Lambert, Wallace, 31-33, 176
language: considered as capital, 8, 14; political implications of, 8-18; state policy toward 3-4, 6-11, 18
Latin script, 86; chosen as official, 119-20; effect of, on Somali culture and politics, 90, 110, 219-20; evaluation of, for Somali language, 89, 91-94, 97; political support for, 102-103, 116; use of, for Somali texts, 87-89, 117. *See also* Shire Jaamac Axmed
Laurence, Margaret, 30, 34
Lebanon, 55

Lenneberg, Eric, 146, 148, 159
Lewis, I. M.: on language in Somalia, 55, 67, 90; on Somali clanship, 23, 50, 165; on Somali poetry, 25, 37-38; on Somali politics, 26-27, 245 n.9
Libya, 59, 61-62
linguistic relativity: definition of, by Whorf, 141; distinguished from linguistic determinism, 143-44; experiments to test for, 146-51; findings on, in this study, 187, 223; findings on, relating to authority, 194-207 (*see also* authority); findings on, relating to political style, 207-16; findings on, relating to religious values, 217-20 (*see also* Islam); findings on, relating to self-conception, 187-94; theory of, 16-17, 139-46, 152-58, 162, 222; political terms and, 158-61; tests for, 167-85
literacy, 131
Luling, Virginia, 27, 51, 53-54, 64, 67, 77, 195
Luuq, 62

Macaulay, Thomas, 8
Mack Smith, Denis, 60
Maino, Mario, 88-89
Majeerteen: clan classification, 23; clan members of, 86, 90, 108; actions of, 59, 71, 121; region, 58, 60
Mancini, Pasquale, 57
Marka, 22, 46, 62, 65
Marreexaan, 23, 102, 121
Marreexaan Union, 81
Marsabit, 77
Massaia, Padre Guglielmo, 58-59
Massawa, 58
Maxamad Abshir, 53
Maxamad Axmed Sheff, 125
Maxamad Cabdille Xasan: clan bargaining of, 82; as Somali nationalist, 27-28, 33-34, 62, 67-68, 73-74, 87-88; as Muslim, 53, 82, 87-88; as poet, 35, 37, 95; as Somali historical figure, 233 n.95
Maxamad F. Jaamac "Shiine," 107
Maxamad Ismaaciil, 133
Maxamad Siyaad Barre, 77, 114; chooses Latin script, 117, 119-20, 131-32, 220; reflects on Somali culture, 34, 83, 229 n.31
Maxamuud Cabdi Nuur, 107
Maxamuud Xaaji Axmed Cali, 110
Maydh, 51
Mazinetti (Italian playwright), 61
Mazrui, Ali, 161
Mecca, 73
Meillet, Antoine, 9
Menelik II, 58, 59, 72-73, 75
Mentuhotep III (Egyptian king), 45
M. Jaamac Maxamad "Afballaar," 110

Moore, Barrington, Jr., 6, 132
Moreno, Martino, 88-89
Moresby (captain in Indian navy), 70
Muhammad ibn Salih, 73
Muhammad (the Prophet), 45, 46, 50
Muhammad 'Alī, 46, 48, 70
Muqdisho, 45-46, 127; demonstrations in, 63; education in, 65; language situation in, 88, 91, 93, 96
Murale, 165
Muslim League, 100
Muslims, 8. *See also* Arab; Egypt; Islam; *wadaad*
Mussolini, Benito, 61-63
Muuse Bashiir, 120
Muuse X. I. Galaal: as political actor, to influence script decision, 92, 104, 108-11, 116, 238 n.76; on Somali culture, 37, 41, 51-52, 125; as writer in the Somali language, 86, 88

Naipaul, V. S., 16
Nasser, Gamal Abdul, 48-50
Needham, Rodney, 227 n.31
Ngala, Ronald, 107
Northeastern Province (Kenya). *See* Kenya, Somali cultural areas in
Northern Frontier District (Kenya). *See* Kenya, Somali cultural areas in
Nuovi Ovuzzonti (Muqdisho), 127-28
Nutting, Anthony, 161

Obiya, 59, 98
Ogaadeen, 23, 28, 38, 40, 72, 165. *See also* Ethiopia, Somali cultural areas in
Okelo-Odongo, Tom, 166
Oman, 46
Orwell, George, 160
Osgood, Charles, 207
Ottoman Empire, 70
Outram, Colonel James, 34, 71

Pelloux, Luigi, 60
Perham, Margery, 75, 76
Peters, R. S., 226 n.10
Piaget, Jean, 155, 168
Pitkin, Hanna, 157-59
Political culture, 4, 14-17, 132-36, 162, 223-24
Political participation, 3-4, 12
Political thought, 4. *See also* Political culture
Pratt, R. Cranford, 160-61
Punt, Kingdom of, 45

Qumaan Bulxan, 40, 42
Qur'an, 53-54, 85, 91, 94, 187
Qur'anic schools, 53-55, 79, 118, 130, 192-93

Rabemananjara, 15
Radio Muqdisho, 25, 31, 42, 115, 187
Radwan Pasha (Egyptian governor), 47-48
Rag waa raggii horay; hadalna waa waxay yireen, 41-42, 171-72, 214-16
Rahanwiin, 23, 26, 131. *See also* af-Rahanwiin
Ras Xaafuun, 45, 47, 71
Rayne, Major H., 75
Red Sea coast, 45-46, 57, 59, 70-71
Reece, Alys, 76
Reece, Gerald, 77
reer (clan), 25
regional disparities, 12-14
Révoil, George, 58
Richards, M., 207
Rodd, J. R., 73
Rose el-Youssief (Cairo), 49
Royal Geographical Society, 71
Rubattino, Raffaele, 57-58
Russia, 71, 75

Saalixiya (Sufi order), 53, 73, 95
Sab, 23, 29-30
Sabri, Husain Zalficar, 49
Saciid Yuusuf Samantar, 113
Samaale, 23, 30
Salaan Carrabey, 38-40, 42, 80-81
Sadler, J. H., 78
Salisbury (British secretary of state for foreign affairs), 69
Sapeto (Lazarist missionary), 58
Sapir, Edward, 139-41
Saudi Arabia, 55
Scarfoglio, Eduardo, 58
Scott, Donald, 55
Scotton, Carol, 10-11, 149
Seif I, 46
Seylac, 45, 47-48, 54, 70, 78
Shafi'ite, 26, 53
sheekh, 195. *See also* Islam; *wadaad*
Sheekh (Somali secondary school), 80, 128
Sheekh Axmed Gabyow, 123
Sheekh Cabduraxmaan Sheekh Nuur, 86-87
Sheekh Daarood. *See* Daarood Jabarti bin Isma'il
Sheekh Maxamad Cabdi Makaahiil, 86
Sheekh Maxamad Cumar Cabdi, 102
Sheekh Uways ibn Maxamad al-Baraawi, 86
Sheekh Yuusuf bin Axmed al-Kawneyn, 85
shir (Somali assembly), 130
Shire Jaamac Axmed, 92, 102-5, 109, 116, 120-21
Shī'ite, 52
Siddiqi, A. R., 124
Siegel, Sidney, 183

Simons, Robert T., 59-60
Siyaad, General. *See* Maxamad Siyaad Barre
social mobilization, 12, 13, 128
social stratification, 8-11. *See also* Somali people, social structure of
Somalia (geographical entity): colonial policies in, 44, 48, 60, 221; language situation in, 4-5; prospects for economic growth in, 21-22, 58; regionalism in, 7, 127-32. *See also* Italian Somalia
Somaliland (British). *See* British Somaliland
Somaliland National League, 81
Somali language: as basis for national identity, 23, 129; as medium of instruction, 134; as official language, 19, 102-3, 224; pride in, among Somalis, 31-33; related to other languages, 25, 162; remains unwritten, 85; role in Somali politics, 163
Somali News (Muqdisho), 107, 113
Somali people, 29-37; Arab influence assessed, 56; authority roles among, 29; caste groups among, 29; clan cleavages among, 23; cultural factors of, 20-21, 136; democratic traditions of, 35-36, 131; diplomacy among, 39-41, 210-13; genealogical origins of, 45, 50-51; language of, 37-42; nationalism of, 27-29; nobility of, 30; nomadic cycle of, 21; poetry of, 25, 37-41; political history of, 27; political institutions of, 25-26; religion of, 37, 53-54, resistance to authority by, 36; resistance to colonialism by, 34-35; school attendance among, 66; social structure of, 7, 29, 123-26, 130, 194-95, 222; view of Italians by, 68-69; xenophobia of, 33-34
Somali Republic (now Somali Democratic Republic): citizenship law of, 42; clan influence in, 81-82; external trade by, 135-36; independence of, 28, 81, 88; investment strategy of, 126; language policy of, 7, 110-11; Linguistic Commission (1971) appointed by, 115-19; Ministry of Education, 55-56, 106, 117, 124-25, 128, 133; National Assembly, 104-6, 114, 123; need for personnel skilled in English, 123; school enrollment in, 123-24; Supreme Revolutionary Council, 114-15, 117-18, 120-21, 129. *See also* British Somaliland; Italian Somalia
Somali Youth League: emergence of, 50, 77, 80; language policy of, 86, 90, 95, 98-100, 112; politics in, 63, 81, 83, 107-108
Speke, John, 71
Stace (British administrator), 72
Stalin, Joseph, 9
Strelcyn, S., 108
Stroyan (British lieutenant), 71
Sudan, 48, 52, 55, 71, 73
Suez, 48, 57, 70
Sunni, 52-53
Swahili, 4, 10-11, 15-16, 25, 86, 165-66

Tadjoura, 47, 70-71
Taleex, 74
Tawfiqi (Egyptian Khedive), 48
Thant, U, 111
Thucydides, 160
Tittoni (Italian foreign minister), 61
Tocqueville, Alexis de, 3, 226 n.10
Touval, Saadia, 80
Travis, William, 21-22, 69
Trimingham, J. Spencer, 51
Tubiana, J., 108
Tunisia, 59
Turiello, Pasquale, 58
Turkey, 70-71, 78

Ucciali, Treaty of, 59
Uganda, 48, 73
Umberto (Italian king), 60
UNESCO: funds literacy campaigns, 124; Language Commission Report (1966), 87, 89, 93-94, 108-14; Report on Education (1962), 55, 106
United Arab Republic. *See* Egypt
United Nations, 63, 75, 79
United States, 80, 136
University Institute (Muqdisho), 66

Vatican, 58-59
Verba, Sidney, 17, 132
Voice of Kenya, 191
Vygotsky, Lev, 155

Waajeer, 31, 42, 77, 165-67, 169, 187
Wadaad, 26, 131; role of, in language controversy, 85, 88, 93, 101, 118; role of, in Somali society, 41, 83, 195
Wahhabis, 47
Walwal, 62
waq (Somali god), 54
waraanle, 26, 83, 131
Wardheer, 102
Wargeyska Somaliyed (Muqdisho), 92
Warsangeli, 23, 72
Waryaa, 42
Weltanschauung, 17, 145
Whiteley, Wilfred, 206
Whorf, Benjamin Lee, 141-47, 150, 152-54, 162, 241 n.18
Wittgenstein, Ludwig, 152-54, 156-57

Xaaji Cabduraxmaan Garyare, 95
Xaaji Diiriye, 95, 108
Xaaji group, 95, 100, 108
Xaaji Maxamad Xuseen, 50, 98-100

Xaaji Sharma'arke, 70
Xaaji Yuusuf Cigaal, 95
xabash, 29, 65
Xamar (*reer*), 98, 236 n.44
xeer, 25
Xersi Magan Ciise, 90, 111-12, 116
Xiddigta Oktobar (Muqdisho), 120, 122
Xuseen Adam, 91, 93, 96
Xuseen Sheekh Axmed Kaddare, 87, 104-105, 116
Xuseen Sheekh Maxmuud, 107

Yaasiin Cismaan Yuusuf Keenadiid, 89, 98-101, 104, 116
Yuusuf Cali, 59-60, 62
Yuusuf Ismaaciil Samatar, 106
Yuusuf Jaamac Cali Dhuxul, 31, 186
Yuusuf Maxamuud, 26

Zaid ibn'Alī ibn al-Husain. 46
Zanzibar, 59-60